Student's Dictionary of Composers

Student's Dictionary of Composers

Harold Dexter

First published 1984 by
International Music Publications
60-70 Roden Street, Ilford, Essex IG1 2AQ

ISBN 0 86359 120 5

International Music Publications is a partnership of
Chappell Music Ltd. and EMI Music Publishing Ltd.

Production Services by Book Production Consultants, Cambridge.

Typeset by Witwell Ltd, Liverpool.

Printed and bound in Great Britain by The University Press, Oxford.

HAROLD DEXTER has been involved in many aspects of music since he was a Cambridge organ scholar and music teacher in Lincolnshire grammer school. He has been active as an amateur conductor and WEA lecturer in the Midlands where he was a frequent broadcaster as an organ recitalist and choirmaster. In 1956 he became Master of the Music at Southwark Cathedral and a professor at the Guildhall School of Music and Drama. Since 1968 he has been in charge of the Graduate Course and Head of the General Musicianship Department for many years.

During recent years he has been active in music education as an examiner, adjudicator and lecturer; and as music editor, adviser and author in varius publishing enterprises. He holds the degrees of MA and Mus.B., the diplomas of FRCO and ARCM in piano performance, and the Archbishops' Diploma in Church Music.

STUDENT'S DICTIONARY OF COMPOSERS is designed for both students and amateur music-lovers. It combines short essays on all major composers with factual precis on the significant names of both musical history and the present-day musical scene. Although in the first instance a reference work, the text is light enough for casual reading. Highly-technical descriptions have been avoided, and replaced with a style which is more straightforward, without any loss of clarity of meaning. Often the author has added his own personal viewpoint, and this, it is hoped, will add a further interest perhaps less often found in other works of this kind.

A

ABEL, Karl Friedrich (1723–1787)
A pupil of J.S. Bach in Leipzig and one of the last viola de gamba players of the 18th century. He associated with J.C. Bach in London and is remembered for his symphonies. His opera *Love in a Village* (1760) has received occasional performances in this century, as have some of his harpsichord sonatas and concertos. There are two portraits of him by Gainsborough.

ADAM, Adolphe Charles (1803–1856)
Parisian composer of Opéra Comique, remembered for the music of the ballet 'Giselle' (1841). His opera *Le Postillon de Longjumeau* is still popular in France.

ADAM DE LA HALLE (c. 1231–c. 1287)
Famous Trouvère of Northern France. Sometimes considered to have written the first 'opera' in *Robin and Marion*, a single-line musical dialogue.

ADDINSELL, Richard (1904–1977)
English composer of film and incidental music, who became famous for the *Warsaw Concerto* from the film *Dangerous Moonlight*.

AGRICOLA, Alexander (1446–1506)
Burgundian composer of masses and motets.

ALAIN, Jean Delphin (1911–1940)
French composer of organ music. His most famous piece is *Litanies*.

ALBENIZ, Isaac Manuel Francesco (1860–1909)
Famous Spanish composer and pianist. After an astonishing childhood — he improvised publicly at four in Barcelona and became a vagabond at 10, supporting himself by 'trick pianism' — he tried to discipline his gifts as a pupil successively of Pedrell, Liszt, d'Indy and Dukas.
Most of his music stems from his improvising at the piano. He found inspiration in early salon music and in the Spanish guitar, trying to reproduce its effects in very difficult piano pieces — especially the 12 pieces that make up *Iberia*. He was associated with Fauré in Paris where he lived from 1893. His most popular composition is the well-known *Tango in D*.

ALBERT, The Prince Consort (1819–1861)
As the husband of Queen Victoria, he introduced German Romantic music to the Court, especially that of Mendelssohn. He was himself a well-trained minor composer.

ALBERT, Eugen d' (1864–1932)
Scottish pianist and composer of operas who settled abroad after studying under Liszt. The best known of his sixteen operas is *Tiefland* (Prague, 1903) which received several American performances in English; he also played his 2nd Piano Concerto with the Boston Symphony Orchestra in 1905.

ALBERTI, Domenica (c. 1710–1740)
Italian composer remembered for the 'Alberti Bass', an accompaniment based on broken chords.

ALBINONI, Tomaso Giovanni (1671–1751)
Italian composer who as a child took violin and singing lessons. In 1694 he achieved his first compositional success: the opera *Zenobia Regina De' Palmireni*, and the same year his twelve Trio Sonatas, Opus 1, were published. Over his 47 years' career as

a composer his two main areas of activity were instrumental ensemble music — sonatas and concertos — and secular vocal music — operas and solo cantatas.
Little survives of Albinoni's vast operatic output, although his cantatas demonstrate his melodic skill and harmonic invention. The spurious *Adagio in G minor* which brought the composer's name to the fore in recent times was in fact written by the Italian musicologist and critic Giazotto Remo (b. 1910).

ALBRECHTSBERGER, Johann Georg (1736–1809)
The teacher of Beethoven and writer of a famous textbook of composition. His own compositions are now forgotten.

ALCOCK, John (1715–1806)
Organist of Lichfield Cathedral whose organ pieces are still performed. He also wrote several harpsichord suites.

ALCOCK, Walter Galpin (1861–1947)
Distinguished organist of Salisbury Cathedral who played at three coronations. His organ and church music is still performed and his Organ Tutor still used.

ALDRICH, Henry (1647–1710)
Distinguished classical scholar and theologian of Christ Church College, Oxford, and writer of some effective church music, such as the service in G, which, like his numerous *catches*, is still occasionally heard.

ALISON, Richard (fl. c. 1600)
English composer of madrigals and editor of a famous collection of metrical psalm tunes.

ALKAN (Originally MORHANGE), Charles Henri Valentin (1813–1888)
French virtuoso pianist whose piano music is usually very demanding and enjoys increasing popularity. After experience as a child-prodigy and a short visit to London in 1833, his life was spent in almost monastic seclusion as a piano teacher in Paris, though he occasionally played at fashionable soirées and was sought out by such celebrities as Liszt; he was also friendly with Chopin and writers such as Victor Hugo.
His music is a strange mixture of surface brilliance and the macabre, while his piano-studies far exceed their original technical purpose. His piano transcriptions rival those of Liszt.

ALLEGRI, Gregorio (1582–1652)
Remembered mainly for the polychoral setting of the *Miserere*, which was reserved for the exclusive use of the Sistine Chapel, until Mozart wrote it out after hearing it performed there.
His introduction to the Chapel was a tenor singer (he was already an ordained priest). Most of his works are still in manuscript in various Italian libraries though two volumes of polychoral *Concertini* were printed in 1618 and 1619 and many smaller works are known.

ALWYN, William (b. 1905)
English composer of music in many genres, especially for films. He first attracted attention with his piano concerto of 1930. His work includes music for over fifty films, largely written during the 2nd World War, such as *Desert Victory* (1943). More recently he has had three symphonies performed.

AMBROSE, Saint (fl. c. 400)
Bishop of Milan and important musically for the *Ambrosian* style of plainsong associated with N. Italy. He is thought to have composed most of the standard Long Metre Office Hymns, and his collection of plainsong melodies was the first in Christian History. Two hundred years later it was extended and modified by Pope Gregory.

ANERIO, Felice (c. 1560–1614)
Succeeded Palestrina as a composer of the Sistine Chapel and remembered for his motets.

ANGLEBERT, Jean Baptiste Henri d' (1628–1691)
Court harpsichordist to Louis XIV; his keyboard music is still performed. Succeeded at the French Court by his son, Jean Henri (1661–1747), and then by Couperin.

ANTHEIL, George (1900–1959)
American composer, considered as one of the leaders of the avant-garde especially for his use of unusual sources of sound in descriptive scores for film and ballet. He wrote six symphonies, several concertos, three string quartets, three violin sonatas and piano music.

ARBEAU, Thoinet (pen-name for JEHAN TABOUROT) (1519–1595)
French collector of dance tunes. *Orchésographie* has been used by modern composers such as Peter Warlock (*Capriol Suite*).

ARCADELT, Jacob (c. 1510–c. 1567)
Flemish composer of madrigals and church music who was attached to St. Peter's and the Sistine Chapel in Rome.

ARDITI, Luigi (1882–1903)
Italian operatic conductor and composer remembered for a vocal waltz, *Il Bacio* ('The Kiss').

ARENSKY, Anthony (1861–1906)
Russian composer of operas, piano and chamber music. Like Tchaikovsky, he was influenced by the Romantic German school of Brahms as well as the stricter Nationalism of 'The Five'. Most of his life was spent as a practical musician in Moscow, though in England he is remembered largely for his *Piano Trio* and shorter piano pieces.

ARIOSTI, Ahilio (1666–1740)
Colleague of Handel in his London operatic ventures and himself the composer of Italian operas for the courts of South Germany and Austria.

ARMSTRONG, Thomas Henry Wait (b. 1898)
Organist of Christ Church College, Oxford, and Principal of the RAM well known for his choral compositions.

ARNE, Thomas Augustine (1710–1778)
Composer of *Rule Britannia* and such Shakespearian settings as *Where the bee sucks*. Known in his day as a leading London composer of oratorio (*Artaxerxes* and *Judith*), opera (*Thomas and Sally*), church music for the Roman Catholic rite and keyboard pieces which are still widely played.
His son Michael (1740–1786) is remembered for the song *The Lass with the Delicate Air*.

ARNELL, Richard (b. 1917)
English composer of ballets, film music and three operas. His intrumental works include five symphonies and several concertos.

ARNOLD, Samuel (1740–1802)
Organist of the Chapel Royal and Westminster Abbey whose church music is still performed. Prominent in his lifetime as an operatic composer and as the editor of Handel's music in 36 volumes. He also added a supplement to Boyce's *Cathedral Music*.

ARNOLD, Malcolm Henry (b. 1921)
Prolific English composer of symphonies and concertos where his orchestral experience as a trumpeter shows in his professional expertise. He has been particularly successful in his sonatas for piano and solo instruments and in his entertaining ensemble pieces.

ARUNDELL, Dennis Drew (b. 1898)
Associated with a wide variety of dramatic and musical activities in Cambridge and London. Composer of incidental music and active as an operatic translator.

ATTERBERG, Kurt (1887-1974)
Swedish composer and critic. His opera *Fanal* is considered to be an excellent example of Swedish Nationalism and in addition to four other operas, he also wrote nine symphonies and five concertos.

ATTEY, John (fl. 1622)
One of the last of the English Lutenist composers.

ATTWOOD, Thomas (1765-1838)
Composer of music for theatre and the organist of St. Paul's Cathedral. A pupil of Mozart and friend of Mendelssohn. His anthems *Teach Me O Lord* and *Come Holy Ghost* are still performed.

AUBER, Daniel Francois Esprit (1782-1871)
Important composer of about 40 operas mainly for the Paris Opéra Comique, including *Masaniello* (1828) and *Fra Diavolo* (1830). Later head of the Paris Conservatoire and musical director to Napoleon III.

AUBERT, Jaques (1689-1753)
Famous French composer of music for the violin and for the stage. Among his works are five books of violin sonatas with bass, 12 *Suites de concert de symphonie* and 10 concertos for four violins and bass.

AURIC, Georges (b. 1899)
Pupil of d'Indy and one of 'Les Six' — a loose association of young French composers with similar aims around 1920. A successful composer for films and ballet as well as a writer of piano and orchestral works. He has been associated with Diaghilev in *Les Matelots* (1924) and Cocteau in very many films between 1930 and 1950 including the famous *Moulin Rouge*. More recently he has used serial and other contemporary techniques in his highly professional ballet score *Phèdre* (1949). He has also been prominent as a critic.

AVISON, Charles (1710-1770)
Organist of Newcastle-upon-Tyne Parish Church and remembered for his numerous concertos, mainly for his own instrument.

B

BABBITT, Milton (b. 1916)
American composer of electronic music who has been much influenced by his mathematical studies. He explored total serialism (of rhythm, dynamics and attack as well as of pitch) in the 1950's.

BACH (Family)
Over 50 musicians of this name are recorded between 1650 and 1800 as German composers and musicians, all dominated by Johann Sebastian and, to a lesser extent, his sons.

Johann Christian (1735–1782)
Johann Sebastian Bach's youngest son, who became organist at Milan Cathedral and then for 25 years a leading operatic composer in London, during which time he was in the service of George III. (Hence the two nicknames — the 'Italian' Bach and the 'English' Bach.) His symphonies are still played and his London orchestral activities were closely associated with Abel and the Hanover Square Rooms.

Johann Christoph (1642–1703)
A cousin of Johann Sebastian's father remembered mainly for the motet *I Wrestle and Pray* and some keyboard pieces.

Johann Christoph Friedrich (1732–1795)
The ninth son of Johann Sebastian Bach, whose music is still occasionally performed.

Johann Sebastian (1685–1750)
Together with Handel, J.S. Bach brings the Baroque musical style to its highest point. His whole life was passed in North Germany and, apart from his period at Cöthen (1717–22) when he wrote mainly instrumental music for the court, the rest of his life was occupied as a church musician in the Lutheran Church. He was twice married, his second wife Anna Magdalena being especially remembered for 'her' book of keyboard pieces; amongst his 20 children were several famous musicians and composers. (See below.) After leaving Cöthen, his last 28 years were spent at Leipzig as Cantor of St. Thomas' School and Church; his sight began to fail in 1749 and he died completely blind the next year.

ORGAN WORKS
His musical training was largely 'picked up' from his family as a boy soprano and later as a violinist, at Lüneberg and Weimar. He was soon appointed, however, as an organist at Arnstadt and his reputation during his lifetime was largely based on his virtuosity on this instrument. His organ works cover his whole life but many of his major works belong to his stays at Arnstadt, Muhlhausen and Weimar successively up to 1717. A large proportion of these works are Preludes based on the Lutheran chorales (chorale-preludes) e.g. the collection of preludes for the Church's Year known as the 'Little Organ Book' (*Orgelbüchlein*). Amongst the longer works are the Preludes (Toccatas, Fantasias) and Fugues, six Trio Sonatas and the *Passacaglia*. From the Leipzig period came two printed collections of chorale-preludes and a final manuscript revision known as 'The 18'.

CHURCH CANTATAS
The largest part of his output for the church is to be found in the Church Cantatas, nearly 200 of which have survived. Most of these are again based on the Lutheran chorales but include, besides large scale choral movements with orchestral accompaniments, simple

chorale settings, solos and duets, often with important 'obligato' instrumental parts; e.g. *Wachet Auf* or the six Christmas cantatas together known as the *Christmas Oratorio*. The climax of his church music dates from the Leipzig period: the two enormous settings of the Passion According to St. John and St. Matthew, the *Mass in B minor* and the *Magnificat*.
INSTRUMENTAL WORKS
During his life Bach wrote major works and often sets of works for most instruments of the period. The following are extant:
1. Sets of unaccompanied and accompanied sonatas for the violin, cello, flute, gamba; works for oboe, lute and various trio combinations.
2. Three sets of suites (French, English and Partitas) for the harpsichord, the monumental collection of 48 Preludes and Fugues (two in each of the 12 major and minor keys) known as the *Well-tempered Clavier*, many miscellaneous works and smaller pieces such as the two and three-part *Inventions*.
3. Four orchestral suites, concertos for the harpsichord and violin and a considerably larger number of concerti grossi (far more than for solo instruments) notably those for two violins, two and three harpsichords and the great series of six *Brandenburg Concertos* for different solo groupings.

Karl (Carl) Philipp Emanuel (1714–1788)
Johann Sebastian Bach's third son who was in the service of Frederick the Great for 28 years and then for 21 years director of music in the five churches in Hamburg. His importance as a composer depends firstly on his position as a transition-figure between the Baroque style of his father and the new 'Viennese' style of Haydn, who was much influenced by his music. Secondly, he was the prime example of the rather intimate style of expression associated with the philosophy of 'Affeckt' in his keyboard pieces.

Wilhelm Friedemann (1710–1784)
Johann Sebastian Bach's eldest son, who is still celebrated for his harpsichord music. His outstanding gifts were unfortunately not paralleled by psychological balance, and his brilliant early promise was never realised.

BAIRSTOW, Edward Cuthbert (1874–1946)
Organist of York Minster from 1913 to his death, who composed church music such as *Save Us O Lord* and *Jesu, the very Thought of Thee*. *Let All Mortal Flesh* and *Though I Speak with the Tongues of Angels* are performed in most English cathedrals. Bairstow was also prominent as a teacher and as Professor of Music at Durham University.

BALAKIREV, Mily (1837–1910)
One of the group of Russian composers known as 'The Five' and, as a result of meeting Glinka, a prominent Russian 'Nationalist'. He was very successful as a pianist and is remembered particularly for *Islamey*, a piano fantasy and *Russia*, an orchestral symphonic poem. He had considerable influence on Moussorgsky, Rimsky-Korsakov and Borodin and when Glinka died took over responsibility for furthering the composer's nationalist compositions.

BALFE, Michael William (1808–1870)
Irish composer of *The Bohemian Girl* (1843) after a successful earlier career as an orchestral violinist and singer, largely abroad in France, Germany and Russia. Several other operas were produced at Drury Lane — sometimes with recitative, sometimes with spoken dialogue — but no other opera has stayed in the repertoire.

BANISTER, John (1630–1679)
Leader of Charles II's band and composer for the first public concerts in London.

BANTOCK, Granville (1868–1946)
Successful composer of orchestral music in a folk-song idiom; e.g. *Hebridean Symphony*, and generally stimulated by exotic ideas as in the Persian *Omar Khayyam*. He was active as a musical educator first as Principal of the Birmingham School of Music and later as Professor of the University there.

BARBER, Samuel (1910–1981)
American composer in a late Romantic style. A movement from the *Seranade* Op. 1 (1930) has reached a wide public as the *Adagio for Strings.* He was both student and professor at the Curtis Institute and closely associated with Menotti, who provided him with the libretto for two of his operas. He is best known for his two symphonies, three concertos (for violin, 'cello, and piano respectively) and his songs.

BARNBY, Sir Joseph (1838–1896)
Prominent English composer of hymn tunes and church music in the Victorian period. He is perhaps best known for the part song *Sweet and Low* but was active in his life as a choral conductor of Bach and for introducing Dvòrak's and Wagner's music to English audiences. After a distinguished career as an organist — he was Precentor of Eton (1875–1892) — he became Principal of the GSM.

BARRAQUÉ, Jean (b. 1928)
A pupil of Messiaen, prominently associated with the French avant-garde movement of the 1960's.

BARRAUD, Henri (b. 1900)
French composer of 'incidental' and chamber music, who was influenced by Dukas and Aubert. He organised the music for the *Paris International Exposition* of 1937 and became for a short period Director of Music for the Paris Radio in 1945.

BARTÓK, Béla (1881–1945)
A major composer particularly involved with Hungarian folk music and 20th century musical language. Born on the borders of modern Hungary, Yugoslavia and Rumania, he had a boyhood marked by physical illness and economic hardship but made a public appearance as composer/pianist when he was 10. In his early teens he was much influenced by Richard Strauss and his early *Kossuth* Symphony struck a patriotic note in its sympathy with the Hungarian separatist movement from the Austro-Hungarian Empire. This was first heard in a Hallé concert in 1904.

Bartók had already formed his life-long friendship with Kodály and in 1905 the two started their scientific exploration and recording of the genuine folk music around them — not just in the Hungarian districts but as far afield as Turkey (1913) and North Africa (1936).

Apart from the objective examination of folk-music, Bartok was concerned with being able to compose naturally in his national idiom and from the 1st String Quartet of 1908 the Hungarian 'style' was always present in his music. Strauss's influence was superseded by that of Debussy and the modern austerities of Neo-Classical composers such as Stravinsky and later Prokofiev. His teaching at the Budapest Academy from 1907 to 1934 tended to emphasize some of these influences as did also the Great War and the political unrest of the region. *The Miraculous Mandarin* and *Bluebeard's Castle* from this period are still heard in the opera house. From the same period is the highly dissonant 2nd Quartet.

Bartók was prominent in the programmes of the International Society for Contemporary Music with performances of Violin Sonatas in 1922 and 1923. He also became an international figure as a composer/pianist and the 3rd Quartet was heard in America in 1928.

Although the 1930's were marked by such vintage works as the 4th and 5th Quartets, the *Music for Strings, Percussion and Celesta* and the *Sonata for Two Pianos and Percussion*, this was also the period when Bartok's Aryanism was investigated by the Nazis and the composer finally left Europe for America.
The 'American' period is marked by a certain stylistic mellowing and the personal sadness of his last 10 years. These characteristics are evident in the 6th Quartet (1939). He experienced economic hardship again — only ameliorated by American commissions which led to such works as the 3rd Piano Concerto and the *Concerto for Orchestra* (1943).
The six books of *Microcosmos* form a genuinely 20th century introduction to pianism and the main aspects of Bartók's style, and he wrote similar *miniatures* for the violin. The violence of his *Allegro Barbaro* moods is only one aspect of a great musician, man and teacher.
He was married twice, each time to pupils younger than himself and lived long enough to find American popularity, but the strain on his health did not allow him to enjoy his success.

BATESON, Thomas (c. 1570–1630)
Organist of Chester Cathedral and later Christchurch Cathedral, Dublin. Composer of many fine madrigals.

BATTEN, Adrian (c. 1588–1637)
Active church music composer and organist of St. Paul's Cathedral, London. Several 'short' and 'verse' anthems and service settings by him are still in the cathedral repertoire.

BATTISHILL, Jonathan (1738–1801)
London organist, theatre musician and composer. Best known work is the anthem *O Lord, Look Down from Heaven*.

BAX, Arnold Edward Trevor (1883–1953)
Master of the King's Musick from 1942, he was trained at the RAM and was a prolific composer of chamber, piano, choral and orchestral music including seven symphonies and concertos for various instruments. He was very much interested in folk-lore and legend (particularly Celtic) and many of his works e.g. *The Garden of Fand* and *Tintagel* reflect this.

BEDFORD, David (b. 1937)
English composer who studied under Lennox Berkeley at the RAM and in Venice with Nono. His best known work has been the large-scale cantata *Star Clusters, Nebulae and Places in Devon* (1972) which is typical of the composer's use of aleatoric and improvisatory techniques. He has often worked with children and pop groups and tends to use innovatory notation, though his music is generally thematically based on slow-moving chordal clusters and repeated melodic motifs.

BEETHOVEN, Ludwig van (1770–1827)
Born in Bonn of Flemish ancestry, Beethoven spent his working life in Vienna. His monumental greatness as a composer is enhanced by his historical position at the end of the Classical period of Mozart and Haydn and as the starting point of Romantic music.
His upbringing was economically deprived as a result of family alcoholism but coming as he did from a family of musicians, he was surrounded by music of all kinds: he was introduced to Bach's '48', he was employed as an organist in the Court Chapel and as a viola-player in the Opera House where the repertoire included Mozart, Gluck, Cimarosa and Grétry. He was soon much in demand as a pianist and teacher in Vienna and had some lessons in composition from both Mozart and Haydn.
The conventional division of his work into

three periods has some value — up to 1802, 1802–12 and 1812–27:

1. The first period includes the first two symphonies, the first three piano concertos, the first six string quartets of Op. 18, several piano trios and violin sonatas (including the *Spring Sonata*) and 11 piano sonatas (including the *Sonata Pathétique* and 'Funeral March' Sonata.)

2. The middle period is marked by mature and sustained emotional intensity, a general concern with such non-musical ideas as the ideals of the French Revolution and 'the heroic', and large-scale breadth of melodic and structural concepts. From this period come six symphonies including the *Eroica* (No.3), the 5th (with its recurring 'Fate' motif) and the *Pastoral* (No. 6), the piano concertos in G and E flat/b (*The Emperor*), the violin concerto, the three *Rasumovsky* string-quartets, the *Archduke* piano trio, the *Kreutzer* violin sonata, several piano sonatas including the *Waldstein* and *Appassionata*, and his only opera, *Fidelio*, which in its various versions occupied most of this period.

3. The last period is associated particularly with such piano sonatas as the *Hammerklavier* and Op. 109–111, the last six string quartets from Op. 127 onwards, the 9th Symphony, the last movement of which includes choral variations in a setting of Schiller's *Ode to Joy*, and the enormous *Missa Solemnis*.

Beethoven's deafness was evident as early as the *Eroica* but became progressively worse throughout his life; he was consequently driven more and more from ordinary society and never married. This withdrawal from the world resulted in slow movements of sustained mysticism, elemental contrasts and structural intensity (e.g. *Die Grosse Fuge*) as opposed to the human intensity of his earlier style.

Beethoven's influence on his successors was so enormous that even 50 years later such a strong musical character as Brahms waited long before writing his 1st symphony, and made no secret of his awareness of the influence of Beethoven's 9th.

BELLINI, Vincenzo (1801–1835)

Born in Sicily, musically active in North Italy but died near Paris at the age of 34. Composer of many fine operas at a period when the *bel canto* style of singing was at its highest. Chopin was both a friend and great admirer of the composer's gifts.

La Sonnambula (1831), *Norma* (1831) and *I Puritani* (1835) are 'classical' singers' operas and make enormous dramatic demands especially on the prima donna.

BENEDICT, Sir Julius (1804–1885)

A pupil of Weber and successful operatic composer and conductor, who also wrote oratorios and cantatas. Although German by birth, he lived the last 50 years of his life in England and was knighted in 1871. *The Lily of Killarney* is still performed occasionally.

BENJAMIN, Arthur L. (1893–1960)

Australian pianist and composer who studied and later settled permanently in London, teaching piano at the RCM. Composed in various forms including symphonic works, film music and four operas. His most popular piece is *Jamaican Rumba*.

BENNET (BENET), John (fl.c. 1600)

Madrigal composer — little is known about the composer's life. *All Creatures Now* was his contribution to *The Triumphes of Oriana* and this has remained his most popular piece.

BENNETT, William Sterndale (1816–1875)

Composer of exceptional promise in early years. Studied at the RAM and invited by Mendelssohn to Germany when still in his teens, he was introduced to Schumann who gave him much encouragement. Although in later life he did not fulfil early promise, he achieved academic distinction as Principal of the RCM and Professor of Music at Cambridge. The overture *The Naiads* (1836), the oratorio *The Woman of Samaria* (1867) and the anthem *God is a Spirit* are his best known works.

BENNETT, Richard Rodney (b. 1936)
Studied at the RCM and under Boulez. Composer in many forms including opera and symphony; also successful in film-music and active in cabaret and light music. The opera *The Mines of Sulphur* (1965) and the piano concerto (1968) have been especially successful.

BERG, Alban (1885–1935)
Ardent disciple of Schönberg and a leading composer of the 'Second Viennese School'. His opera *Wozzeck* (Berlin 1925) attracted great public attention. A second opera *Lulu* was left unfinished but has been recently completed. His *Violin Concerto* (1935) written shortly before his death was commissioned by the violinist Louis Krasner, the form being inspired by the sudden death of Manon Gropius, the 18-year-old daughter of Alma Mahler (by her second marriage). Although most of his work after 1925 uses the Twelve Note technique, Berg often compromises with earlier formal, harmonic and melodic styles in his generally rich Romantic characterisation and involvement.

BERIO, Luciano (b. 1925)
Italian avant-garde composer, a pupil of Dallapiccola, who made his reputation with *Nones*, a setting of W.H. Auden and *Mutazioni* for chamber orchestra. His recent works have been almost entirely electronic. The series of pieces *Sequenza I — VII* are all for the solo voice or other solo instruments and involve imaginative interpretation of, or improvisation on, non-musical symbols.

BERIOT, Charles Auguste de (1802–1870)
Celebrated violin virtuoso and composer of seven violin concertos and a *Violin School* which is still used in violin teaching. The husband of the famous contralto, Malibran.

BERKELEY, Sir Lennox Randel Francis (b. 1903)
Former pupil of Nadia Boulanger. He has written two operas (of which the *Dinner Engagement* has been especially successful), some graceful piano music, a flute concerto and church music — including a *Missa Brevis*, *Magnificat* and *Stabat Mater*. His chamber music includes two string quartets, an oboe quartet and a violin sonata.

BERKELEY, Michael (b. 1948)
The son and pupil of Sir Lennox. After training at Westminster Cathedral, studying at the RAM and under Richard Rodney Bennet, he attracted attention with *Meditations* for string orchestra (1977). This was followed by the *Oboe Concerto* (1977), *Fantasia Concertante* (1978) and *Uprising* (1980), a one-movement symphony. His major chamber works have been the *Violin Sonata* (1979) and the *Chamber Symphony* (1980), and there have been several successful shorter vocal and choral works.

BERLIN, Irving (b. 1888)
A prolific composer of popular songs. *White Christmas* from the film *Holiday Inn* is unquestionably one of the most well-known songs ever written.

BERLIOZ, Louis Hector (1803–1869)
The most important French Romantic composer, he is especially remembered for his genius in writing powerful and colourful descriptive music often for very large orchestral forces.
He arrived in Paris in 1821 as a medical student but soon became a music student

at the Conservatoire whose director, Cherubini, found him unco-operative — the first of many musical relationships. Amongst his student compositions was a Mass written for an orchestra of 150 and he eventually won the *Prix de Rome* at the Conservatoire in 1830. By this time several important early compositions had been performed, including the *Waverley Overture* (based on Scott) and *Eight Scenes from Faust* (based on Goethe). This enthusiasm for Romantic writers was paralleled by his passion for Shakespeare (he had a stormy affair with an English actress, Harriet Smithson whom he later married), and a life-long admiration for Gluck and Beethoven.

He developed the technique of the *idée fixe*, later adapted by Liszt and Wagner as the leitmotif — a theme persisting throughout the movements of a work but modified and coloured so as to recall non-musical ideas in different contexts.

Berlioz was particularly attracted to the scenic, the macabre and the psychological pressures of obsession. His most popular work, the early *Symphonie Fantastique* (1829), for instance, was an autobiographical and often nightmarish account of the affair with Harriet Smithson, the subtitle, *Episode in the Life of an Artist* being based on De Quincey's *Confessions of an Opium-Eater*. Similarly, *Harold in Italy* was based on Byron's *Childe Harold* with a solo viola representing the hero. His large-scale works included the enormous *Requiem* (1837), *La Damnation de Faust* (1846), an 'opéra de concert', and *L'Enfance du Christ* (1854), his only oratorio.

The attractions of the opera house resulted in the successful *Benvenuto Cellini* (1838) and *Béatrice et Bénédict* (1862), both of which contain fine music together with many less inspired moments. His final opera (or rather operatic cycle), *Les Troyens* (based on Virgil) has proved successful in the modern operatic repertoire but was never heard complete by the composer; Part II was performed in 1863 but the first part had to wait until 1890 for its premiere.

Berlioz was also very important as a 'travelling' orchestral conductor and as a writer of memoirs and a textbook on orchestration. His influence on his successors has been as mixed as his own life-style and often depended on the involvement of a particular conductor such as Weingartner or Hamilton Harty. France's lack of interest has to some extent been counter-balanced by his influence on Nationalist composers such as the Russian 'Five', Janácek, Nielsen and Richard Strauss.

BERNERS, Lord Gerald Hugh Tyrwhitt-Wilson (1883–1950)

An artist, writer and composer who, before succeeding to his title in 1918, composed under the name of Gerald Tyrwhitt. His compositions include the one-act opera *Le Carrosse du Saint Sacrement* and a number of ballets.

BERNSTEIN, Leonard (b. 1918)

Brilliant American musician, equally distinguished as a conductor, pianist, lecturer, writer and composer.

This division of his energies extends to the two genres of 'light' and 'serious' composition. In the first category is *Fancy Free* (1944) and *West Side Story* (1957) besides film scores such as *On the Waterfront* (1954). Best known of his serious works is *Chichester Psalms* (1965) but he has also written three symphonies subtitled *Jeremiah* (1942), *The Age of Anxiety* (1949) and *Kaddish* (1963) besides an opera *Trouble in Tahiti* (1952).

BERTINI, Henri Jerome (1798–1876)

A prolific composer for the piano repertoire who is best known for his piano studies which are still widely used.

BERWALD, Franz Adolf (1796–1868)
Born in Stockholm he wrote six symphonies, two operas and numerous other works. The 4th symphony, *Singulière* (1845), is still in the modern symphonic repertoire.

BEST, William Thomas (1826–1897)
Acclaimed as the greatest concert organist of his day, he arranged, composed and edited music for his instrument. He was organist at the St. George's Hall, Liverpool.

BEVIN, Elway (fl. 1600)
A composer of church music and author of a noted book on theory. He was organist of Bristol Cathedral. The service in the Dorian mode is still performed in cathedrals.

BIBER, Heinrich Ignaz Franz von (1644–1704)
A great violinist and a considerable violin composer, remembered particularly for his use of *scordatura* (altered tuning of open strings). Most of his life was spent in Salzburg where he became Kapellmeister in 1684. Besides operas, he also wrote 16 'biblical' sonatas based on the life of Mary.

BILLINGS, William (1746–1800)
An American self-taught musician who wrote hymn tunes which have recently been revived as *National* music in the USA.

BINCHOIS, Gilles (c. 1400–1460)
He was first a soldier but became a musician and eventually chaplain to Philip the Good, composing church music and chansons.

BIRTWISTLE, Harrison (b. 1934)
Prolific English composer who absorbed early such influences as those of Stravinsky, Varese and Webern and was associated with composers such as Peter Maxwell Davies and Alexander Goehr in avant-garde performances.
He was trained as a clarinettist at the RMCM and RAM and the texture of clarinets, solo voices and percussion is characteristic of much of his work. Birtwistle has worked his way from miniatures, often owing something to mediaeval techniques as in the early *Refrains and Choruses* (1957), to longer structures frequently based on earlier 'component parts' like *The Triumph of Time* (1972). He has established himself as one of the most striking of the experimentalists of his generation.

BISHOP, Henry Rowley (1786–1855)
A well-known London opera conductor and composer who was Professor of Music at Edinburgh and Oxford Universities. He is universally known for the song *Home, Sweet Home*, which originally appeared in a ballad-opera. *Lo Here the Gentle Lark*, a coloratura aria with flute obligato, is also still performed.

BIZET, Georges (1838–1875)
Remembered primarily for the opera *Carmen* (1875) and, since its rediscovery in 1935, the wonderful *Symphony in C* which dates from his 17th year. He spent all his life in Paris where he studied at the Conservatoire under Gounod and Halévy. In spite of this early brilliance, few of his operas were successful, though the piano duet/orchestral suite *Jeux d'Enfants* and the orchestral selection from *L'Arlésienne* have retained their popularity in the concert repertoire.

BLACHER, Boris (1903–1975)
Composer of operas, ballets, orchestral and piano music and director of the Berlin Hochschule. His style is neo-classical and often satirical and ironic; its rhythmic vitality and clarity of colour and texture owe something to Stravinsky.

BLISS, Arthur (1891–1975)
Studied at Cambridge and at the RCM under Stanford and Vaughan Williams. He was for a time Professor of Music at the University of California and also Musical Director of the BBC. In 1953 he was appointed Master of the Queen's Musick. His compositions include large-scale choral and orchestral works, film scores and ballet music, of which the cantata *Pastoral* (1928), *A Colour Symphony* (1922), *Music for Strings* (1935), *Piano Concerto* (1938) and the Ballet *Checkmate* (1937) are important.

BLITHEMAN, William (d. 1591)
Organist of the Chapel Royal composing church music and virginal music. He was the teacher of Bull.

BLOCH, Ernest (1880–1959)
Studied in Switzerland, Belgium, Germany and France receiving recognition in 1910 with a performance in Paris of his opera *Macbeth*. He spent some time in Switzerland as a conductor before moving to the USA where he conducted and held various educational positions.
His music makes considerable use of Hebrew melodies as in the *Sacred Service* (1933) and *Schelemo* for cello and orchestra (1916). His *Violin Concerto* (1938) is still a repertoire work, together with his *Viola Suite* (1919) and his five published string quartets.

BLOMDAHL, Karl-Birger (1916–1968)
A Swedish composer whose works include symphonies, concertos, chamber music and an opera *Aniara* (1959). His early music seems to be influenced by Nielsen and Hindemith but in *Amagra* he uses electronic and other contemporary techniques.

BLOW, John (1649–1708)
One of the 'first generation' choirboys at the Chapel Royal when it was reformed on the accession of Charles II in 1660. He was appointed organist at Westminster Abbey but resigned the post in favour of Purcell, whom he may have taught. His church music includes 'full' anthems such as *Salvator Mundi* and 'verse' compositions with string orchestra such as *I Beheld and Lo*. His masque *Venus and Adonis* is one of the few to have survived from the period and has regular modern stage performances.

BOCCHERINI, Luigi (1743–1805)
Distinguished cellist who did much to regularise the instrument's fingering and wrote many sonatas for it. Remembered especially for his many string quintets (all containing a fifth part for a 'tenor violin' an octave below the normal instrument together with a regular string quartet) but he also wrote extensively for other media — string trios, string quartets, symphonies and vocal works.

BOËLLMANN, Leon (1862–1897)
French organist, whose music includes the *Symphonic Variations* for cello and orchestra and attractive organ pieces such as the popular *Suite Gothique*.

BOELY, Alexandre Pierre Francois (1785–1858)
Celebrated French organist whose music (mainly for his own instrument) set new standards of scholarship; he also influenced such composers as César Franck with his playing of Bach.

BÖHM, Georg (1661–1733)
A north-German composer who wrote suites, passions, preludes and fugues, chorale preludes etc.

BOÏELDIEU, François Adrien (1775–1834)
Remembered as the composer of *The Caliph of Bagdad* (1800), he spent his life in

Paris except for a period as director of the Royal Conservatoire at St. Petersburg. His first opera was produced when he was 18, and he had lessons from Cherubini three years later. He was particularly successful in comic operas such as *La Dame Blanche* (1825) but nowadays only his scintillating overtures are normally played.

BOITO, Arrigo (Enrico) (1842–1918)
The Italian librettist of Verdi's *Otello* and *Falstaff* who was also the successful composer of *Mefistofele* (1868). He was an active supporter as a journalist of the then new Austro-German symphonic school and opposed the traditional Italian opera *bel canto* style. Verdi's later style owed much to him.

BORODIN, Alexander (1833–1887)
One of the Russian Nationalist composers, 'The Five', after he met Balakirev in 1862. Throughout his adult life in St. Petersburg (Leningrad) he was a professional chemist, and besides his scientific research, he was also a Professor of the Academy of Physicians. His compositions are therefore relatively few in number but outstanding in quality; they range in style from the early influence of Mendelssohn and Schumann to the brilliant originality of harmony, oriental rhythms and orchestral colours of the *Polovtsian Dances*. His larger works include the opera, *Prince Igor* (1878), two string quartets and two symphonies, besides works completed by Rimsky-Korsakov and Glazunov after his death.

BOTTESINI, Giovanni (1821–1889)
The greatest double-bass virtuoso and composer in musical history who also wrote operas and oratorios for his native Italy. The double-bass concertos are still performed.

BOUGHTON, Rutland (1878–1960)
Remembered as the composer of *The Immortal Hour* (1914) and *Bethlehem* (1915). He was a pupil of Stanford at the RCM and taught at the Birmingham School of Music under Bantock, with whom he shared an enthusiasm for Celtic legend and folk music. Much of his creative life was spent at Glastonbury where he planned Wagnerian-type festivals based on the Arthurian sagas.

BOULANGER, Lili (1893–1918)
Promising French composer, who in spite of ill-health, left important works such as the symphonic poems *D'un Soir Triste* and *D'un Matin de Printemps* and the cantatas *Hymne au Soleil* and *Les Sirènes* besides some chamber works.

BOULANGER, Nadia (b. 1887)
The sister of Lili and perhaps the most important teacher of composition in this century. Her own compositions include an opera and songs. She has also been active as a critic, lecturer, conductor and organist.

BOULEZ, Pierre (b. 1925)
One of the distinguished students of Messiaen at the Paris Conservatoire who became himself a leader of avant-garde trends in such works as *Le Marteau sans Maître* (1955) and, with such composers as John Cage and Stockhausen, a prominent figure at the Darnstadt festivals in the 1950's. He was a highly original and successful orchestral conductor of the BBC Symphony Orchestra but has now given up this activity to become director of a French electronic research station. In 1976 he conducted the centenary cycle of Wagner's *Ring* at Bayreuth.

BOWEN, York (1884–1961)
English composer and pianist, educated at the RAM. Besides three piano concertos, a violin concerto and viola concerto, he is remembered for some shorter piano pieces designed for teaching.

BOYCE, William (1710–1779)
A choirboy of St. Paul's Cathedral whose church music such as *I Have Surely Built Thee a House* and the two settings of the canticles in C and A are still in the Cathedral repertoire; he also completed Maurice Green's collection of *Cathedral Music.*
Although he suffered from partial deafness, he became Composer to the Chapel Royal and Master of the King's Musick. In addition he was the successful composer of *The Chaplet* (1749), a two-act entertainment which was played 129 times at Drury Lane up to 1773. His eight symphonies (really three-movement overtures) were rediscovered in the 1930's and are now extensively performed.

BRAHAM, John (1774–1856)
A London singer remembered for his song *The Death of Nelson* from his opera *The Americans* (1811).

BRAHMS, Johannes (1833–1897)
The most important German symphonic composer of the second half of the 19th century. He was born in Hamburg in a musical but humble environment and almost became a child virtuoso pianist; after a fairly good 'grammar school' education until he was 15, he earned his living playing in taverns and making musical arrangements for publishers.
In 1853 he toured as accompanist with a Hungarian violinist and met Schumann who, though already ailing, wrote an enthusiastic article on Brahms and his music, referring to him as 'he who should come'. After Schumann's breakdown the following year he became very close to Clara and her family, and this romantic attachment lasted throughout their lives though Brahms never married.
Professionally, Brahms was a prominent though never flamboyant pianist right up to his later years and occupied several important posts as conductor. As a composer, there is little sign of technical development in his music; he was always a perfectionist in his revisions and self-criticism but seems to have had an intuitive sense of style, spontaneous flow and a natural grasp of formal structure. His sympathies lay with the direct musical expression of the earlier Viennese style of Beethoven rather than with the 'new programme' style of Berlioz, Liszt and Wagner and he was often pilloried by the latter's devotees as a 'die-hard reactionary'. In fact, however, his music was as profoundly Romantic as it is classically based and was always permeated by the simple melodic shapes of German folk-tunes.
The *German Requiem* (1868) was the first generally recognised major success although modern performances of the first piano concerto (1859), the early piano music, songs and chamber music are heard as frequently as his later works. The orchestral works are relatively late: the 1st Symphony was completed after 20 years of revisions in 1876 and the 2nd followed closely, together with the *Violin Concerto* (for his lifelong and scholarly friend, Joachim) and the *Academic Festival* and *Tragic* overtures. The 2nd Piano Concerto (1881), 3rd Symphony (1883) and 4th Symphony (1884) owe something to the excellent orchestra at Meiningen under Bülow just as his later works for the clarinet such as the *Quintet* (1891) were inspired by the orchestra's clarinettist, Mühlfeld. Brahms wrote in all forms except opera and his emotional maturity is especially evident in his last work, *Four Serious Songs* (1896) with biblical text, the youthful ardour having been transmuted to a philosophic and sometimes bitter resignation.

BREWER, Alfred Herbert (1865–1928)
An active minor composer associated with Gloucester Cathedral as chorister and organist.

BRIDGE, Frank (1879–1941)
A pupil of Stanford at the RCM who became an excellent viola player, conductor and teacher (of Britten amongst others). His songs, piano miniatures and chamber music are still often performed.

BRIDGE, Frederick (1844–1924)
A composer of oratorios, cantatas and anthems and involved in musical research. He was Professor of Music at London University and organist at Westminster Abbey for over 40 years.

BRITTEN, (Edward) Benjamin (1913–1976)
The most important British composer of the second half of the 20th century. An unusually prolific composer as a schoolboy, he had early piano lessons with Harold Samuels and composition teaching from Frank Bridge. He was less successful under Arthur Benjamin and John Ireland at the RCM but his early compositions — the *Sinfonietta*, the *Phantasy Quartet* and the choral variations *A Boy was Born* — led to five years' work as a film composer including a collaboration with the poet W.H. Auden on *Night Mail. Variations on a Theme of Frank Bridge* and an appearance at a prom as soloist in the *Piano Concerto* followed in 1937. He went to America with Auden and Isherwood at the outbreak of war in 1939 where his life-long partnership with the singer Peter Pears began and resulted in the song-cycles *Les Illuminations* and *Seven Sonnets of Michelangelo*. Auden provided the libretto for *Hymn to St. Cecilia* and from 1940 came the *Violin Concerto* and *Sinfonia de Requiem*.
He returned to England in 1942 when the two cantatas *A Ceremony of Carols* and *Rejoice in the Lamb* heralded his long involvement with the opera house; Sadler's Wells opened after the war with the very successful *Peter Grimes* and his first chamber-opera *The Rape of Lucretia* appeared at Glyndebourne. *Albert Herring* was closely associated with Snape and Aldburgh in Suffolk and the first Aldburgh Festival was held in 1948.
Commissions followed fast: *The Young Person's Guide to the Orchestra* (1946) was a film-score. *Let's Make an Opera* made the 1949 Aldburgh Festival memorable, *Billy Budd* was written for the Festival of Britain (1951), *Gloriana* for the Coronation celebrations (1953) and the *War Requiem* for the rededication of Coventry Cathedral (1961). *Noye's Fludde* appeared at the 1958 Aldburgh Festival and from 1964 to 1968 the Church Parables were yet another genre — the quasi-liturgical unconducted chamber-opera.
Visits to Russia led to the *Symphony for Cello and Orchestra* (1963) written for Rostropovich and by this time such works as the *Spring Symphony* (1949) and *A Midsummer Night's Dream* (1960) were being widely performed. His health became poor in 1973.
Britten had an uncanny knack of setting words and a wonderful flare for the 'occasional' piece where his instinctive sense of effect had full play. His directness and simplicity attracted a wide audience especially where he was writing for children as in the *Missa Brevis*, *Let's Make an Opera* and *Noye's Fludde*.

BRUCH, Max (1838–1920)
Important German Romantic composer, remembered mainly for his Violin Concerto No.1 in G minor (1866) and *Kol Nidrei* for cello and orchestra (1880). During his lifetime he seemed to be more important as a choral and operatic conductor and as a successful conductor. From 1880 to 1883 he was director of the Liverpool Philharmonic Society and received many honorary awards, including those from Cambridge and the French Académie des Beaux-Arts. Otherwise, his professional life was spent mainly in Germany. He made considerable use of

folk-music in his compositions; besides his natural German and Hebrew melodies, there were important works such as the Scottish songs, the *Scottish Fantasy* for orchestra and important collections of Swedish dances, Russian songs and an *Adagio on Celtic Melodies*. His gift for flowing melody, Romantic orchestral colour and solo string technique was unfortunately insufficient to keep his three symphonies and several operas in the 20th century repertoire though the 2nd and 3rd Violin Concertos are still performed.

BRUCKNER, Anton (1824–1896)
Major 19th century Austrian symphonist. Although showing musical gifts as a child, Bruckner was a very late developer; his schoolmaster father died when Bruckner was 23 and, although he received basic training at the nearby monastery of St. Florian where he was later to become organist (1851–56) and was eventually buried, his early work was as a teacher at St. Florian. At the age of 26 he attended a Teachers' College at Linz but by this time he was increasingly involved as an organist thanks to his unusual technique and flair as an improviser. It was only on his appointment as cathedral organist at Linz (1856–68) that he gave up general teaching. As a result of this unusual background he lacked self-confidence throughout his life. As a composer he was largely self-taught but continued to have lessons, often with younger men, until after he left Linz for Vienna at 44. By this time he had produced most of his liturgical masses including the often performed works in E minor (No. 2 with wind instrument accompaniment) and in F minor (No. 3 and considered one of his greatest works); these are large-scale concert-masses, deriving from Beethoven and Schubert in their Austrian warmth and melody. He had also been present at the 1865 première of *Tristan und Isolde* and Wagner's musical and personal influence remained with him throughout his life. After his 1st Symphony in Linz in 1868, he devoted himself almost entirely to symphonic writing in Vienna and was childlike in his gratitude for the honours that were later given him. But public reception of his symphonies was slow; after the 3rd Symphony was dedicated to Wagner in 1877, he was consistently persecuted by the Brahmsian party under the critic Hanslick and only partly 'rescued' by the young conductor, Hans Richter, with his performance of the 4th Symphony (the *Romantic*) and the *Te Deum* in 1881.
Bruckner's own insecurity was exaggerated by these experiences and he spent much of his later life continually revising his works — often as a result of questionable advice from younger men whose own orchestral style was more akin to Wagner's than the 'block-colouring' of the earlier Viennese style that was Bruckner's starting-point; it is only during recent years that Bruckner's earlier versions have been again preferred and performed. His symphonic style seems to spring from Beethoven's 5th with its drama of inner conflict in the first movement, the song of faith in his adagios, the bucolic dance of his scherzos and the soul's eventual triumph in the finale. But the enormous paragraphs of devout Catholic belief are Bruckner's own although Wagner's shadow appears again in the 7th Symphony (1885). Bruckner never heard his 5th Symphony and only two movements of the gigantic 6th, but the equally monumental 8th (1892) together with the unfinished 9th have been heard often by devoted Brucknerians together with most of the earlier works in their entirety.

BULL, John (c. 1562–1628)
'The Liszt of the Virginals'. After training as a boy at the Chapel Royal and a spell as organist at Hereford Cathedral, Bull returned to the Chapel Royal and became the most famous of all virginal executants

and composers. His famour *Walsingham Variations* in the Fitzwilliam Virginal Book is virtuoso music of the highest order. His output is extensive but uneven and his vocal compositions are few. He left the service of Prince Henry (James I's eldest son) in 1612 to take up a similar post in Brussels and later at Antwerp Cathedral where his style was to influence Sweelinck and later Baroque composers.

BUONONCINI, Giovanni Battista (1670–1747)
He enjoyed success as a composer in Italy, London and Vienna. While in London he proved to be an operatic rival to Handel and the two composers were both pilloried by Pope in *The Dunciad* as 'Tweedledum and Tweedledee'.

BURGON, Geoffrey (b. 1941)
Trained as a trumpeter and composer at the GSM and has since achieved prominence both as a successful composer of incidental music in television serials and in a series of major works from *Alleluia Nativitas* (1970) to *Veni Spiritus* (1979) which includes the *Requiem* (1976) and *Fall of Lucifer* (1977).

BURMÜLLER, Norbert (1810–1836)
A composer of great promise who was greatly admired by Schumann but died before reaching maturity. Still important for some excellent and tuneful piano studies.

BUSH, Alan Dudley (b. 1900)
Studied at the RAM where he became the Professor of Composition. He is a composer of choral, piano and chamber music and his political views influence his writing.

BUSH, Geoffrey (b. 1920)
Studied at Oxford and composes stage, orchestral, choral and chamber music.

BUSONI, Ferrucio Benvenuto (1866–1924)
Famous pianist of half German and half Italian parentage who became a cosmopolitan teacher and composer with particular sympathy for Bach and the Viennese composers. His compositions parallel his numerous arrangements for piano and are very forward-looking in a neo-classical style. His opera, *Doktor Faust*, was completed after his death by his pupil, Jarnach, and is occasionally performed, together with his *Piano Concerto* and *Fantasia Contrapuntistica*.

BUTTERWORTH, George Sainton Kaye (1885–1916)
Remembered as the composer of *The Shropshire Lad* song cycle and orchestral rhapsody, Butterworth was an important member of the English folksong revival and a friend of Vaughan Williams and Cecil Sharp. He was killed in action after being awarded the Military Cross for Gallantry.

BUXTEHUDE, Dietrich (1637–1707)
The greatest composer of the Middle Baroque period who established an important north-German tradition by his *Abendmusiken* services in 1673. Bach is said to have walked 200 miles to hear him and clearly knew his organ compositions. Some of these compositions are almost pictorial treatments of the German chorales in fantasias and preludes; Buxtehude further developed the multi-sectional toccata and kindred forms which included brilliant pedal solos, preludial movements, chromatic chordal passages, fugues and chaconnes, later integrated in Bach's own organ works. Some church cantatas and arias together with harpsichord suites are being increasingly performed.

BYRD, William (1542 or 1543–1623)
The greatest and most prolific of the Tudor composers. Byrd 'was bred up to

musick under Thomas Tallis', was organist of Lincoln Cathedral when he was about 20 and from 1570 was a Gentleman of the Chapel Royal. Although he was a Catholic recusant and wrote largely for the unreformed church, he remained in royal favour until his death. Together with Tallis he was granted a monopoly of music printing and *Cantiones Sacrae* appeared under their joint names in 1575 and included 17 motets from each of them. His important works for the English Church including two complete sets of canticles — the *Great* and *Short* services, the 2nd and 3rd *Evening Services* — besides important full anthems such as *Sing Joyfully* and verse anthems like *Christ is Risen* (the latter with string accompaniment) seem to date largely from his earlier years.

Succeeding series of *Cantiones Sacrae* in 1589 and 1591 and the *Gradualia* in 1605 and 1607 cover an immense range of Latin motets including a complete set for the liturgical year; *Haec Dies*, *Ave Verum Corpus*, *Justorum Animae* and many more like them belong to many cathedral and choral repertoires. Other publications include madrigals: *Psalmes, Sonets, and Songs of Sadness and Pietie* (1588), *Songs of Sundrie Natures, Some of Gravitie and Others of Mirth* (1589) and the final *Psalms, Songs and Sonnets* (1611) — the last containing two string fantasias. Of unknown date are the three Latin masses (to three, four and five voices) and the nearly 150 virginal and string pieces. This immense range is of a uniformly high technical and artistic standard. The virginal pieces are well up Bull's standard of inspiration. The string *Fancies* and *In Nomines* led to a whole school of 17th century consort compositions. The spirituality of the Latin Church music was continued in the seriousness of the madrigals and the songs for solo voice and strings, such as the famous *Lullaby*, are worthy of Dowland himself. Apart from Shakespeare, no Renaissance Englishman had such a range and stature.

C

CAGE, John (b. 1912)
American avant-garde composer and pianist, who was attracted to percussion and multi-media music as early as 1938. He was the first to write for the *prepared piano* (about 1938) in which the strings of the piano are modified by the insertion of extraneous objects, so producing a variety of different percussive effects. His later emphasis on the continuous 'noise' of the environment is exemplified by his 'silent' piece, *4′ 33″* (1952) which also stressed the importance of duration as opposed to rhythm in music. He had earlier introduced the 'chance' (aleatoric) in *Music of Changes* (1951). Later works have used tapes and electronic techniques. Cage's importance has been much enhanced by his writing and lecturing for important American Universities.

CAIX D'HERVELOIS, Louis de (c. 1670–1760)
Parisian-born performer on the viola da gamba and composer for the same instrument for which he wrote five books of solo pieces and books of duets. He also wrote three books of flute sonatas.

CALDARA, Antonio (1670–1738)
Composer of over 70 operas and 30 oratorios, (as well as motets, masses and string sonatas) who held various musical appointments in Italy, Spain and Austria.

CALKIN, Jean Baptiste (1827–1905)
Organist in Ireland and later in London who became a distinguished teacher and composer, writing services, anthems, glees, solo songs, piano and organ music etc.

CALLCOTT, John Wall (1766–1821)
A prominent London musician of his day, famous as a composer of glees and catches.

CAMIDGE, Matthew (1758–1844)
The most important of a distinguished family of Yorkshire organists who published organ, harpsichord and teaching pieces. His father John (1735–1803), the composer himself, his son John (1790–1859), and his grandson Thomas (1828–1912) were successively organists at York Minster.

CAMILLERI, Charles (b. 1931)
Maltese composer resident in England since 1951. He has been mainly self-taught and much influenced by Maltese folk music. More recently this ethnomusicological influence has tended to come from Africa and the Orient, and out of this material he has forged his own personal style, which seems to be largely concerned with the mystical aspect of space. His many works in various mediums include *Missa Mundi*, *Cosmic Visions* and *Noospheres*.

CAMPION (Campian), Thomas (1567–1620)
English composer, poet (he wrote the words for all his own songs), and physician who was among the most prolific of the English lute-song writers. He studied for the legal profession from 1581 to 1584, and received his MD at the University of Caen in France, in 1605. He wrote a treatise on metre — *Observations in the Art of English Poesie* (1602) — and later a musical treatise — *A New Way of Making Fowre Parts in Counter-point* (c.1614).
Campion's works are all for voices, and his music is attractive, melodic, and often marked by sectional repetition and occasionally sequence. In his early masque *Lord Hayes* (1607) the first signs of opera can be detected, but later works of this type show no further developments in this style.

CARDEW, Cornelius (1936–1981)
English composer and pianist who worked with Stockhausen in the electronic studios at Cologne during 1958–60. He was active in avant-garde music and toured widely with his own compositions. These include piano music *Octet 1959* and the orchestral *Autumn '60.*

CAREY, Henry (1690–1743)
Remembered as the composer of *Sally in our Alley* although his words for this song were later reset by other hands in a more obvious form. Important theatrical composer and playwright, especially of ballad operas (after 1729 in the style of *The Beggar's Opera*).

CARLTON, Richard (c. 1558–1638)
A Norfolk vicar and composer of madrigals.

CARROLL, Walter (1869–1955)
Manchester musical educationist remembered for his short descriptive piano pieces. These together form a graded progression from the elementary *Scenes on a Farm*, to more advanced collections such as *Woodland Fantasies.*

CARTER, Elliot (b. 1908)
Successful American composer who left his post-graduate work at Harvard to study in Paris under Nadia Boulanger 1932–35. Since then he has been involved mainly in academic work at Yale. From the first his compositions have won many awards.
His early works seem to be in the neo-classical tradition while the 1st Symphony (1942) and *Holiday Overture* (1944) recall Copland. After the war his music became more complex resulting in the *Piano Sonata* (1946) and the *Wind Quintet* (1948). In the two *String Quartets* (1951 and 1959) the principle of metrical modulation, which uses modified tempos in a way analogous to key-change, becomes a formal principle. Later works have added to Carter's reputation, especially the *Piano Concerto* (1967) and the *Concerto for Orchestra* (1970).

CARULLI, Ferdinando (1770–1841)
Neapolitan guitarist and composer for his instrument. He had great success in Paris in 1808 and wrote over 300 guitar pieces.

CASELLA, Alfredo (1883–1947)
Studied under Fauré at the Paris Conservatoire before becoming an international pianist and conductor. As a composer he could be classed as an anti-romantic. His works for the theatre vary from 'choreographic comedies' to opera and 'lay oratorio'. Among his many instrumental works are three symphonies and several concertos as well as chamber and piano works.

CASTELNUOVO-TEDESCO, Mario (1895–1968)
A pupil of Pizzetti and composer of songs, choral and piano music and operas. His reputation was for tuneful refinement.

CAUSTUN, Thomas (d. 1569)
Mentioned in 1552 as a member of the Chapel Royal, and remembered for his settings of the canticles in the 1549 and 1552 Books of Common Prayer; also for his contributions to John Day's *Certaine Notes* (1560).

CAVALIERI, Emilio di (c. 1550–1602)
Italian organist who became a member of the *Camerata*, the group of amateur noblemen who tried to recapture the spirit of Ancient Greek drama in *stile rappresentativo* which led to the birth of opera. His most famous work is the 'dramatic oratorio' *La rappresentazione di Anima, e di Corpo* (1600), but he also wrote in the earlier dramatic *intermedii* style and was responsible for detailed instructions on

ornamentation and continuo-playing.

CAVALLI, Pietro Francesco (1602–1676)
Venetian singer, organist, and eventual successor to Monteverdi at St. Mark's. Apart from a few church works in the polychoral tradition, his reputation depends on his 28 extant operas (14 more have only survived in libretto), of which *La Calisto* (1651) is the best known. Most of the scores are incomplete, but it has recently become clear that Cavalli is the natural representative of the Venetian operatic generation following Monteverdi's *L'Incoronazione di Poppea* (1642).

CESTI, Marc Antonio (1623–1669)
A Franciscan monk and pupil of Carissimi who composed operas, solo cantatas etc. He was in turn musical director of the Medici Court at Florence, a chorister of the papal choir in Rome, and assistant musical director of the Imperial Court in Vienna.
In the tradition of Cavalli, he is remembered especially as the composer of operas such as *Il Pomo d'Oro* (Vienna 1667).

CHABRIER, Emmanuel (1841–1894)
In his early career he was employed in the civil service and respected as a brilliant pianist by the Franck group of musicians, the Impressionist painters, and the Symbolist poets with whom he associated. On gaining recognition as an opera composer, he resigned his government post becoming assistant conductor to Lamoureux, assisting him in the early Wagner performances in Paris. His orchestration and harmonies could be regarded as predecessors to those of Debussy and Ravel. His opera *Gwendoline* (1886) and the orchestral *Rhapsody España* (1883) are still performed.

CHAMBONNIÈRES, Jacques Champion de (1602–1672)
Harpsichordist to Louis XIV and composer for his instrument. His compositions are still in print.

CHAMINADE, Cécile (1857–1944)
Remembered as a concert pianist and composer of tuneful and graceful short piano pieces. She also wrote orchestral music, ballets and songs.

CHARPENTIER, Gustave (1896–1956)
French operatic composer remembered almost entirely for *Louise* (1900) which perhaps owes its continued popularity to the sentimental realism of the story (featuring the working girls of Paris), rather than to any refinement of musical technique. He spent much of his later life on popular education in music and drama.

CHARPENTIER, Marc Antoine (1634–1704)
French contemporary of Lully who cooperated with Molière in *Le Malade Imaginaire* (1673) and with Corneille in *Médée* (1693) besides leaving 17 other operas. He left much church music mainly for Louis XIV's Chapel at Versailles or the Sainte Chapelle in Paris. Much of the music is on the grand scale and owes something to his teacher Carissimi, although he also wrote extensively for three-part choirs in convents.

CHAUSSON, Ernest (1855–1899)
A pupil of César Franck who is remembered for his *Poème* for violin and orchestra (1897). His *Symphony* followed in 1898. Both works are indebted to Franck and Wagner but also marked by Chausson's own characteristic delicate melancholy and fastidiousness of detail.

CHERUBINI, Maria Luigi Carlo (1760–1842)
A Florentine composer, who after being

brought up in the old Italian contrapuntal tradition and writing comic Neapolitan operas, made his home in Paris and led the grand opera tradition of the Napoleonic period with *Médée* (1797) and *Les Deux Journées* (1800). (Beethoven acknowledged his influence on *Fidelio.*) His later years were largely devoted to the Paris Conservatoire where he was director from 1822 onwards, and for which he wrote his famous *Cours de Contrepoint et de la Fugue* (1835).

CHILD, William (1606–1697)
English composer of church music whose long life extends from his period as organist at St. George's Chapel, Windsor, from 1632 until its closure in the Civil War from 1643. At the Restoration in 1660 he became a Gentleman of the Chapel Royal and was present at Charles II's coronation in 1661. He wrote 20 *Psalms* for two trebles and bass (published in 1639) and (in manuscript) at least 40 anthems and 20 services, only a few of which are still performed.

CHISHOLM, Erik (1904–1965)
Studied at Edinburgh University (D. Mus) and held posts in Nova Scotia, Singapore and Cape Town. Compositions include piano concertos and ballets; he conducted various opera and ballet companies in Britain and promoted contemporary music in Glasgow.

CHOPIN, Frederic François (1810–1849)
Great Romantic Polish pianist and composer whose life was spent mainly in Paris. His originality was apparent in early childhood in spite of disciplined teaching. As a pianist, he was largely self taught, resulting in a highly individual approach to piano technique with unconventional fingerings and pedallings and the then unfashionable relaxed wrist. Polish national style made an early impact on him. (His first published compositions were Polonaises dating from his seventh year.)
In 1828 he met the virtuoso Hummel in Warsaw. After two infatuations with Polish girls and realising that he was unhappy in the role of brilliant extrovert, he left Warsaw for the wider European stage. By this time he had already written the two piano concertos and several nocturnes. The salon style of the nocturnes owes something to Bellini's delicate melodic style and he certainly had absorbed the influence of John Field's *Nocturnes*; but he was led inevitably to the French delicate subtlety of expression and by 1835 had established himself with the Rothschild family in Paris both as a teacher and player in the aristocratic soirées. The Polish mazurkas and the polonaises continued to flow from his pen together with more studies, nocturnes and valses while the first *Ballade* dates from 1835.
Chopin's affaire with the novelist, Georges Sand, started in 1837 and continued for 10 years. They spent the winter of 1838 in Majorca where his health soon declined and he only finished the 24 Preludes with difficulty. Dramatic and tragic pieces such as the C sharp minor *Scherzo*, the C minor *Polonaise* and B flat minor *Sonata* (with the funeral march) date from this period.
His later works include the *Barcarolle*, the B minor *Sonata* and the last two *Ballades* besides the posthumous pieces in various genres. Finally, in spite of devoted care from a Scottish pupil, Jane Sterling, and an enthusiastic English welcome, he found composition impossible. He died of consumption.
Almost all Chopin's music is for the piano and is stylistically unique; it is marked by extreme sensitivity, power and pathos, and is almost always on a miniature scale. In 1832 he had considered having piano lessons from the virtuoso Kalkbrenner and from about 1840 he used textbooks like that of Cherubini's to fill out his own intuitive approach. This keen self-criticism

prevented him from ever being facile; all his compositions are wrought with infinite care for detail.

CIMAROSA, Domenico (1749–1801)
Neapolitan operatic composer who was described as 'the Italian Mozart'. He is remembered mainly for the comic opera, *The Secret Marriage* (1792) but also wrote nearly 40 other operas which were performed in London, Paris, Vienna, Dresden, and St. Petersburg — as well as Italy. He also wrote several oratorios, cantatas, and a mass.

CLARKE, Jeremiah (c. 1670–1707)
A composer of songs, harpsichord music, theatre music and church music and one time organist of St. Paul's Cathedral. Remembered especially for his keyboard *Trumpet Voluntary*.

CLARKE-WHITFIELD, John (1770–1836)
A composer of church music which was widely sung. During his life he held various posts as organist in Irish and English cathedrals, and in two Cambridge colleges.

CLEMENS NON PAPA (c. 1510–c. 1556)
A composer of masses and motets belonging to the Flemish School.

CLEMENTI, Muzio (1752–1832)
A child virtuoso in Rome as organist, pianist and composer, but he completed his education from 1766 in England where he spent the rest of his life. He is especially remembered for his piano sonatinas and the studies in *Gradus ad Parnassum*. He was active in London as an operatic conductor but also travelled as a pianist in Europe. He established the three-movement Viennese sonatas with his three sonatas of 1773 and can be called the 'father of modern piano-playing'. Amongst his pupils were J.B. Cramer, John Field, Moscheles and Meyerbeer, and he founded a successful piano and publishing firm.

CLÉRAMBAULT, Louis Nicholas (1676–1749)
French organist of St. Sulpice, Paris. His *Premier Livre d'Orgue* (the second never materialised) is still regularly played.

COFFEY, Charles (d. 1745)
Composer of the ballad opera *The Devil to Pay* (1731) which was much performed in Britain, the North American Colonies, and in Germany, where it sparked off a vogue for Singspiel.

COLERIDGE-TAYLOR, Samuel (1875–1912)
British composer whose father was a Sierra Leonean doctor and whose mother was English. He was brought up in South London and admitted to the RAM in 1890 as a violinist. While he was still a student his *Clarinet Quintet* was performed in Berlin by the Joachim Quartet (1897). *Hiawatha's Wedding Feast* (1898) was written under Stanford's tutelage at the RAM and the trilogy was completed by 1900 with *The Death of Minnehaha* and *Hiawatha's Departure*. Successive works such as the *Violin Concerto* (1911) and *A Tale of Old Japan* (1911) were less successful. His early death broke off a busy and fruitful professional life.

COOKE, Arnold Atkinson (b. 1906)
English pupil of Hindemith whose three symphonies and chamber music represent an individual trait in English music.

COOKE, Benjamin (1734–1793)
Organist of Westminster Abbey remembered for his *Evening Service* in G. Besides his many church compositions, he also wrote many secular cantatas such as the setting of Collins' *Ode on the Passions*.

COOKE, Henry (c. 1616–1672)
A choirboy at the Chapel Royal and later an officer in the Royalist Army during the Civil War — hence 'Captain Cooke'. At the Restoration he reformed the choir of the Chapel Royal and judging by Pepys' description was one of the greatest choirmasters in its history. Amongst his choirboys were Turner, Wise, Blow, Tudway, Humfrey and Purcell. A few of his many church compositions are still performed. He also collaborated with Davenant in *The Siege of Rhodes*.

COPERARIO, John (c. 1570–1627)
English composer (Cooper) in the service of James I as lutenist and violist. His principal works were for court masques, but he is also important for his chamber music which is divided between the older *Fantasies for Viols*, and the new music for 'violins'; manuscript organ continuo parts also exist for many of these pieces.

COPLAND, Aaron (b. 1900)
American composer who has been active in encouraging a genuine national style based partly on jazz with a jauntiness characteristic of American speech, and partly on international 20th century idioms and different folk styles. Works such as *El Salon Mexico* (1936) seem reminiscent of *Les Six*, while *The Quiet City* (1939) is in the Vaughan Williams' tradition. *In the Beginning* (1947) is an unaccompanied choral setting from Genesis with unmistakeable Jewish overtones. His ballets such as *Billy the Kid* (1938) and *Rodeo* (1942), together with some excellent music to such films as *Of Mice and Men* (1939), are often performed. He has also composed a piano concerto and three symphonies.

CORELLI, Arcangelo (1653–1713)
Famous violinist whose compositions form the climax of the Italian baroque style. His childhood was spent near and in Bologna but from 1675 he lived in Rome — from 1689 under the patronage of the Pope's nephew, Cardinal Ottoboni. His Monday concerts were famous throughout Italy and attracted pupils even from England. His four books of trio sonatas (1681–94) established his reputation as a composer while the first set of six solo violin sonatas (1700) popularised the polyphonic style of violin playing and certainly influenced J.S. Bach's unaccompanied violin works. The sheer technical difficulty of this set perhaps led him to the simpler 'suite' style of the second set; it certainly appears that Corelli's own technique as a player was surpassed by his younger contemporaries such as Locatelli, and Geminiani. Even Handel on his Italian visit is said to have seized Corelli's violin to demonstrate his musical intentions.
He was buried at the Pantheon at the height of his prosperity, leaving the *Concerti Grossi* (Op. 6) to be published posthumously; these in their turn were to some extent the model for Handel's *Concerti Grossi* and even Bach's *Brandenburg Concertos*. Corelli's best known work is the *'Christmas' Concerto* from the same set.

CORNELIUS, Peter (1824–1874)
Composer of poetical songs and part-songs who was a friend of Wagner. His opera, *The Barber of Bagdad* (1858) was very popular as is his famous carol setting, *Three Kings*.

CORNYSHE, William (c. 1465–1523)
Court composer at the English court of Henry VII and Henry VIII and famous for his music for pageants, banquets and plays, especially at the 'Field of the Cloth of Gold' (1520). He was for a time Master of the Singing Boys of Westminster Abbey (1480–91) and six extensive liturgical works survive of which the *Magnificat Regale* is the best known. He also wrote several satirical settings of the 'swash-buckling' poet, John Skelton.

COSTA, Michael Andrew Angus (1806–1884)
Spent most of his life in England where he was a renowned opera, oratorio and orchestral conductor. His compositions include two oratorios: *Naaman* and *Eli*.

COUPERIN, François (1668–1733)
Nicknamed 'le Grand' and the nephew of Louis, he was the supreme composer for the clavecin, although his reputation depends on relatively small-scale descriptive pieces, arranged in 26 suites of between 3 and 12 pieces (*Ordres*) and published in four books from 1713 to 1730.
Couperin was first of all a famous organist, and held the post at Saint-Gervais from 1685 to 1723. He became *Organiste du Roi* in 1693 at Sainte Chappelle and was an active musician at Versailles. Here he provided church music of which the most famous is *Leçons de Ténèbres* (c. 1714) — a setting of Jeremiah for soloists and continuo.
He is also important in bringing together the French and Italian traditions of the trio sonata especially in *Quatre Concerts Royaux* (1722) and in the two famous *Apothéoses*, *de Lulli* and *de Corelli* (1725). His famous texbook *L'Art de Toucher le Clavecin* (1716) gives instructions on fingering, ornaments and style; it was known to Bach and is still an important source of French Baroque practice.

COUPERIN, Louis (c. 1626–1661)
The eldest of three brothers, all of whom were distinguished violinists, organists and composers taught by Chambonnières. He is remembered for his forward-looking clavecin pieces.

COWARD, Sir Noel (1899–1973)
English playwright, actor and composer of musical comedies and operettas. Perhaps his most famous work is *Bitter Sweet* (1929) of which he was both composer and librettist.

COWEN, Frederick Hymen (1852–1935)
English pianist, conductor and composer who studied at the Leipzig Conservatory after appearances as a child prodigy both as pianist and composer. His works include six symphonies, five operas and many choral works.

CRAMER, Johann Baptist (1771–1858)
A piano pupil of Clementi who won a high reputation as a pianist. He wrote many sonatas and concertos and his piano studies are still in use. He lived most of his life in London founding the publishing firm of Cramer & Co.

CRESTON, Paul (b. 1906)
An organist and teacher in New York and almost entirely self-taught as a composer. Works include five symphonies, 12 concertos, chamber and choral music etc.

CREYGHTON, Robert (c. 1639–1734)
Remembered for his Services in E flat and B flat and his harmonic mannerism, the *Creyghtonian cadence*. He was professor of Greek at Cambridge and Precentor of Wells Cathedral.

CROCE, Giovanni dalla (c. 1558–1609)
A priest and composer of madrigals and motets. His church music was intended for St. Mark's, Venice with its multi-voiced polychoral tradition and many of the madrigals are in the form of dramatic comedies often in Venetian dialect.

CROFT, William (1678–1727)
English organist and composer who was a pupil of Blow. He was a member of the Chapel Royal from 1700 and organist of Westminster Abbey from 1708. He is remembered as the composer of the *Burial Service* and of the tune *St. Anne* to O *God*

our Help besides much other church music, harpsichord and organ pieces. He also wrote chamber music for violin and recorders and incidental music to plays by Steele and Farquhar.

CROTCH, William (1775–1847)
Norwich child prodigy who was organist at Christ Church, Oxford at 15 after playing to the Royal princesses at three years old. In 1797 he became Professor of Music at Cambridge and organist of St. John's College, and in 1822 became the first Principal of the RAM. His compositions date from early childhood and besides much church music include oratorio *Palestine* (1812).

CUI, César (1835–1918)
A precocious child musician of mixed descent who was associated with Russian nationalism as one of 'The Five'. He was a professional military engineer whose musical allegiance was slanted more towards the German Romantics and Chopin than towards the mature style of Mussorgsky or Balakirev. He was a prolific composer as well as being a critic, and produced 11 operas and many choral and piano works.

CZERNY, Carl (1791–1857)
Austrian child prodigy and later pupil and friend of Beethoven. He later gave up public performance to devote himself to piano teaching, composition and arrangement. Much of the latter remained in manuscript. His works number over a thousand, and include 24 masses, many symphonies and chamber works; but it is by his many piano studies that he is remembered — especially the various *Écoles de la Vélocité*. In these he established the modern system of equal fingering in piano technique.

D

DALE, Benjamin (1885–1943)
English composer, trained at the RAM and remembered mainly for his polished chamber music, especially the works inspired by Lionel Tertis (*Suite for Viola and Piano* — also orchestrated — 1906) and the *Phantasy* in D (1911, for the same combination). His choral and orchestral works have been less successful though his shorter piano pieces are still played.

DALLAPICCOLA, Luigi (1904–1975)
Italian pianist and avant-garde composer. From 1930 he was actively involved with the ISCM. Although he was acquainted with Berg and to a lesser extent, Webern and Schonberg, serialism takes its place with Busoni's neo-classicism in his music. He has been particularly successful in opera (*Il Prigioniero*, 1950) and choral works, while his early orchestral *Partita* (1930) is still performed.

DANDRIEU, Jean Francois (1682–1738)
Parisian organist and harpsichordist whose three books of harpsichord pieces and organ book (1724–34) are still performed. He was organist of the French Chapel Royal from 1721. The *Noëls* (c. 1720) were written by his uncle, Pierre.

DANIEL, John (c. 1565–1630)
English lutenist and composer of several sets of Ayres (1606) 'for the lute, viol and voice'. Some of the later songs for four voices with treble and bass lutes are often highly chromatic.

DANKWORTH, John Philip William (b. 1927)
British jazz musician and symphonic composer, trained at the RAM. Most of his earlier compositions were for combined jazz and symphonic musicians: *Improvisations* (1959), *Escapade* (1976), the *String Quartet* (1971) and *Piano Concerto* (1972). More recently he has been active in film and incidental music. His wife is the distinguished singer Cleo Laine. The series of commissions from major orchestras has continued with *Grace Abounding* (1980) and *The Diamond and the Goose* (1981). His many honours have included the CBE and several degrees.

DAQUIN, Louis Claude (1693–1772)
French organist and composer who played before Louis XIV at the age of six and followed Dandrieu as organist of Sainte Chapelle in 1739. His *Noëls* are still played and the famous *Coucou* was published in his first book of harpsichord pieces (1735).

DARKE, Harold (1888–1976)
English organist and composer of church music, his *Communion Service in F* being one of the best of its generation. He was probably the most distinguished player and teacher of his period and his concerts at St. Michael's Church, Cornhill did much to popularize the music of Parry and Vaughan Williams.

DAVIES, Peter Maxwell (b. 1934)
English composer, conductor and teacher. His early orchestral work *Prolation* (1959) was a prize-winning entry for the ISCM Festival, but it was as a result of his teaching at Cirencester Grammar School that *O Magnum Mysterium* (1960) reached a wider public. He is an active conductor of avant-garde music such as his *Eight Songs for a Mad King* (1969). Much of his music, however modern stylistically, owes a great deal to the medieval paraphrase techniques, as in the opera *Taverner* (1972) and the two Fantasias on *In Nomines* of

John Taverner (1962 and 1964). He now lives in the Orkneys and has been recently active in the Kirkwall Festival.

DAVIES, Walford (1869–1941)
Prolific English composer who is now remembered mainly for his educational work as Professor of Music at the University of Wales and even more for his BBC musical talks from 1924 until the outbreak of the 2nd World War. Most of his earlier work grew from his post of organist at the Temple Church (1898–1923). Later he was organist of St. George's Chapel, Windsor (1927–32). The most famous of his compositions is *Solemn Melody* (1908) though the cantata *Everyman* (1904) is still occasionally performed.

DAVIS, Carl (b. 1936)
American composer of television and film scores now living in England. He has been especially successful in light music genres and has also written two ballets, three operas and more recently the symphony *Lines on London* (1980).

DAVY, John (1763–1824)
The composer of *The Bay of Biscay*, several comic operas and much incidental music.

DAVY, Richard (fl. 1500)
The composer of a four-part passion according to St. Matthew — the earliest English harmonised version of the crowd's part *(turba)*, though still using the plainsong Gospel tone of the narrative.

DEBUSSY, Claude Achille (1862–1918)
French Impressionist composer. His background was not particularly musical but he was admitted to the Paris Conservatoire at ten as a pianist, where he ultimately won the famous *Prix de Rome* (1884). He was early connected with the poetry of Verlaine, and later with that of Mallarmé and Baudelaire. In 1880 he was employed by Tchaikovsky's patroness as tutor to her children. To this awareness of Russian composers such as Borodin and Rimsky-Korsakov was added his experience of Wagner in 1888 and Javanese music at a Parisian exhibition in 1889, while earlier in Italy he had marvelled at Liszt's pedalling — and at his suggestion heard music by Lassus and Palestrina; later in 1891 he met the Café pianist Erik Satie. All these influences helped to produce Debussy's mature style evident in the *String Quartet* (1893) and the *Prélude à L'Après Midi d'un Faune* (1894). The opera *Pelléas et Mélisande* was produced in 1902 and also belongs to this period, as do the orchestral *Nocturnes*. *La Mer* (1905) and *L'Images pour Orchestre* (1911) followed, and again to this same period belong the great piano works which culminated in the first book of *Preludes* (1910) and the second book in 1915. Debussy's songs cover most of his life and are largely sensuous and penetrating settings of his favourite symbolist poets such as the *Trois Poèmes de Stéphane Mallarmé* (1913).
In spite of all the literary and non-musical associations, Debussy's music is 'pure' in the way that all ideas are transmuted into, and used as, self-sufficient sound just as the impressionist painters used light as a source of precise colour. Much of his harmony is traditional in using tonality and 19th century chords in new juxtapositions; on the other hand, he found new inspiration in the harmonic series and the 'vagueness' of the whole tone scale.
At the end of his life Debusy seemed to look ahead to neo-classicism in the three sonatas of 1915–17. He always despised academic rules of harmonic progression and savoured sound for its own sake, usually preferring understatement to direct expression.
Following his first marriage to Lily Texier he married the cultured Mme. Emma

Bardac. From 1914 he suffered increasingly from cancer.

DEERING, Richard (d. 1630)
Popular English composer of Latin motets who spent much of his life (1612-25) abroad. Most of his motets were published between 1617 and 1619 in Antwerp — the majority with a basso continuo part. He was a Roman Catholic convert, and was appointed organist to Henrietta Maria on her marriage to Charles I. Cromwell is said to have been 'much taken' by the composer's motets.

DELIBES, Léo (1836-1891)
Celebrated Parisian ballet composer. He entered the Conservatoire at 10 and earned his living at first as singer, organist and operatic accompanist. He wrote several operettas for the Théâtre Lyrique before his collaboration in a ballet score in 1866. His most famous ballet *Coppélia* was written in 1870 and *Sylvia* in 1876. His opera *Lakmé* (1883) was almost as successful. Tchaikovsky praised Delibes at the expense of Brahms, and Stravinsky included him in a list of great melodists (while excluding Beethoven).

DELIUS, Frederick (1862-1934)
Born the son a Bradford industrialist, Delius awakened to music when he heard the close harmony of negro spirituals in Florida, where he was trying to establish himself as an orange grower. Although he later attended the Leipzig Conservatoire, he considered himself in the main self-taught. The musical influences on him were largely limited to Grieg, Wagner and Victorian and Negro hymnody, but he was always a musician of nature and readily responsive to such writers as Walt Whitman and Nietsche.
His major works include the opera *A Village Romeo and Juliet* (1901), *A Mass of Life* (1905) and *Requiem* (1916), the last two based on Nietsche; but it is the shorter orchestral tone poems (sometimes with voices) as in *Sea-Drift* (Whitman — 1903), *Brigg Fair* (1907), *On Hearing the First Cuckoo in Spring* (1912) or the Prelude to *Irmelin* (1932) which have proved most popular.
Delius owed much to the inspired conducting of Sir Thomas Beecham after 1907. From the early 1920's, although increasingly paralysed and blind, he managed to dictate several works to Eric Fenby, his musical amanuensis. After his marriage to a painter in 1897 he lived near Fontainebleu. Delius has been described as a 'Romantic Impressionist' but it has been his misfortune that his highly personal style has been used in a commercial context from the 1930's onwards.

DIABELLI, Antonio (1781-1858)
Popular Austrian composer and publisher now remembered only for the Waltz on which Beethoven based his greatest set of variations (Op. 120).

DIBDIN, Charles (1745-1814)
Celebrated English composer of sea songs including *Tom Bowling*. After experience as a chorister at Winchester Cathedral, he was successively organist, actor-singer and finally a prolific composer of stage works (often to his own libretto). He also wrote several novels.

DIEREN, Bernard van (1884-1936)
Dutch composer who became an 'English' composer and critic, and whose many interests included science, literature and drawing. His 'unemotional' and often polyphonic style was hailed by such critics as Cecil Gray as 'the music of the future' but this judgement has not been confirmed since his death.

d'INDY, Vincent (1851-1931)
Although he showed early signs of precocity, d'Indy decided on a musical career relatively late and spent many years

in musical explorations before becoming the major French educational force, and the apparent rival of Debussy as a composer. The major influences on him were César Franck (whose hagiographer he became), Berlioz, German music (especially Bach and Wagner) and the orchestration of Rimsky-Korsakov.

After hearing *Parsifal* in 1882, he made a conscious effort to revive the French folk lore of the Cevennes and the symphonic variations, *Istar* (1896) is probably the first of his mature works.

His position in French music was confirmed by his directorship of the Société Nationale de Musique and his work at the Schola Cantorum; his large-scale works of the next decade were generally welcomed e.g. *Jour d'été à la montagne* (1905) while his operas *Fervaal* (1897) and *L'Étranger* (1903) were contrasted with *Pelléas et Mélisande* (1902). Practically all d'Indy's work is based on contrasted religious or political ideas, and his last opera *La Légende de Saint Christophe* was the scandal of 1920 with its anti-semitism and fanatical Catholicism. Little has been done during the last sixty years to assess d'Indy's importance. Can he be seen as a French Wagner or as a fastidious heir to Berlioz? The 20th century seems largely to have ignored him.

DITTERSDORF, Karl Ditters von (1739–1799)

German violinist and composer, who after a varied earlier career lived in Vienna from 1774 to 1790. His numerous compositions were enormously popular: 10 volumes of 'Haydnesque' symphonies, many concertos (especially for violin), quartets and masses as well as over 20 operas in Singspiel style.

DOHNÁNYI, Ernst (1877–1960)

After leaving the Budapest Royal Academy, Dohnányi was a successful concert pianist though his repertoire did not extend beyond the Viennese classics. Later he taught at the Berlin Hochschule and then from 1919 he returned to Hungary as Director of the Budapest Academy and subsequently became conductor of the Budapest Philharmonic and Hungarian Broadcasting Service. He eventually settled in the USA.

Some of his early chamber music was praised by Brahms but apart from piano music such as the four Rhapsodies (Op. 11), only the *Variations on a Nursery Song* (Op. 25) is still generally performed.

DONIZETTI, Gaetano (1797–1848)

Italian composer of more than 70 operas of which no less than 10 are acknowledged essentials of the operatic repertoire. His famous comic opera *L'Elisir d'Amore* (1832) shows another facet of his genius. The great 'prima donna' operas — *Lucrezia Borgia* (1833), *Maria Stuarda* (1834) and *Lucia di Lammermoor* (1835) — represent a stylistic movement away from Rossini which prepared the way for the vintage Verdi works. Although the comic opera *La fille du Régiment* (1840) was written for the Paris Opéra Comique it was more successful in its Italian translation. *Don Pasquale* (1843) is the last of these repertoire works but it is certain that there will be many future attempts to revive others.

The popularity of his works in recent decades has proved that Donizetti's melodic sweetness is allied to dramatic intensity so that he can no longer be written off as merely a comic-patter composer; even the incredible speed with which he wrote could still result in musico-dramatic masterpieces — as in the last act of *La Favorite* (1840) which was composed in under four hours.

DOWLAND, John (1562–1626)

English lutenist, composer and greatest contributor to the *Ayre*. He was a convert to Roman Catholicism and spent much

time abroad — both early in his life (1580) in Paris, in the 1590's in Italy and from 1598 to 1606 as lutenist to Christian IV of Denmark. From 1612 he was in the Royal Service in London and played under Orlando Gibbons at the funeral of James I (1625).
Little of his lute music was published in his lifetime and much still awaits transcription, though such a popular piece as *Lachrimae* was arranged by many distinguished composers for virginals/organ. Dowland's songs were published in four books from 1597 to 1612 (by which time five editions of the first volume had appeared). Each volume contained 21 songs with melody and lute tablature on one page and parts for ATB on the opposite page. These books contained such masterpieces as *Fine Knacks for Ladies*, *Weep You No More* and *Come Away Sweet Love*. Dowland's reputation as a song composer can be compared with that of Schubert and Wolf.

DRAGONETTI, Domenico (1763–1846)
Famous Italian double-bass player and composer. He lived in England during Haydn's visit (1794) and met Beethoven in Vienna (1808–09), thereafter being in demand for the recitative passage in the last movement of the 9th Symphony. Besides his incredible technique and sight-reading, he was valued for the musicality of his playing and for 52 years played at the first cello desk in Royal Philharmonic concerts, with Lindley — accompanied by his dog Carlo!
His compositions are mainly concertos for his own instrument but also include many arrangements such as the pedal parts of some of Bach's organ works.

DUFAY, Gulielmus (c. 1400–1474)
Flemish composer who was a member of the Papal choir 1428–37 and afterwards held canonries at Cambrai and Mons. He left over seven masses and 87 motets together with 59 French and seven Italian Chansons, and is considered the first great Burgundian polyphonic composer.
Although his early music (the Italian *Chansons*) are composed in medieval style in that the third voice was later added to a two-part composition, his mature music is often for four voices; it uses canonic techniques and often implies tonal cadences.

DUKAS, Paul (1865–1935)
Parisian composer and teacher whose reputation rests almost exclusively on *L'Apprenti Sorcier* (1897), an orchestral programmatic scherzo based on Goethe's poem. The year before, his *Symphony in C* had appeared and this, together with the opera *Ariane et Barbe-Bleue* (1907), which was almost a rival of Debussy's *Pelléas et Mélisande*, is still performed and valued for its Gallic delicacy and orchestral colour. Towards the end of his life Dukas destroyed a large number of unpublished compositions. His teaching was at both the Conservatoire and at the École Normale. He was also prominent as a musical administrator on behalf of the French Government.

DUNHILL, Thomas (1877–1946)
English composer and teacher. He was a pupil of Stanford at the RCM and made his name with several chamber music works. Later he wrote light operas and a symphony, but is now remembered for such songs as *Cloth of Heaven* (Yeats) and various educational pieces.

DUNSTABLE, John (c. 1385–1453)
Leading English composer of the first half of the 15th century. Little is known of his life except that he was involved with astrology and travelled widely; most of his works are found in Italian libraries and certainly influenced Dufay and his school. The best known of his works is the

isorhythmic four-part motet *Veni Creator* and the famous three-part chanson *O Rosa Bella.*

DUPARC, Henri (1848–1933)
Famous Parisian song writer who was one of the earliest of César Franck's pupils. Several instrumental pieces were performed and published but much was later destroyed in self-criticism. From 1885 he suffered from a mental breakdown and lost all interest in music, living in retirement in Switzerland.
His 14 songs (*or mélodies*) are mainly settings of symbolist poets and were all composed between 1868 and 1884. By any standard they are highly original and as historically important as those of Fauré.

DUPORT, Jean Louis (1749–1819)
Composed for the cello and was an even greater cellist and composer than his brother Jean Pierre, for whom Beethoven wrote two cello sonatas.

DUPRÉ, Marcel (1886–1971)
Famous French organist and composer. His record as an executant from the Paris Conservatoire onwards was unequalled and the improvisations in his world-wide recital tours were unique. Although his earlier compositions include an oratorio and chamber music, he is important now mainly for his organ works, such as the *Three Preludes and Fugues* (Op. 7) and *Variations sur un Noël* (Op. 20).

DUPUIS, Thomas (1733–1796)
English organist and composer whose *Voluntaries* are still played.

DURANTE, Francesco (1684–1755)
Italian composer of church music and keyboard sonatas. He was a pupil of Alessandro Scarlatti and counted amongst his own pupils Pergolesi and Paisiello. Among his compositions are about 14 masses, 50 *Motets a Capella* and eight *Quartetti Concertanti* for two violins, violas and figured bass.

DUREY, Louis (1888–1979)
Prominent Parisian composer associated with Milhaud, Honegger, Satie and Cocteau at the end of the First World War, and then, in 1920, one of 'Les Six'. He retired to the south of France almost immediately. Only a few of his works are still performed, the best known probably being *Le Bestiaire* and his *Sonatina* for the flute.

DURUFLÉ, Maurice (b. 1902)
French organist and composer, a pupil of Guilmant, Vierne and Dukas. He is best known for his *Requiem* (1947) and for the *Organ Suite* (1930). The influences on his music include plainsong, and Fauré, Debussy and Ravel. He has always composed with difficulty (and very self-critically) so that his whole reputation rests on only nine works.

DUSSEK, Jan Ladislav (1760–1812)
Bohemian pianist and composer. He had some lessons from C.P.E. Bach and ended an exciting career under the patronage of Talleyrand in Paris. He was one of the first of the virtuoso pianists and among his 77 opus numbers are many piano pieces which have been adopted educationally.

DVOŘÁK, Antonin (1841–1904)
Great Czech Romantic composer. Although showing early promise, Dvorák was not widely recognised until Brahms and the distinguished critic, Hanslick, awarded his E flat Symphony (published posthumously) an Austrian State Prize in 1874. The musical influences on him initially were mainly Schubert and Beethoven, but these were soon outweighed by his natural attraction to Bohemian folk music and, less fruitfully, to the influence of Wagner.
His many excellent arrangements of folk

music proved consistently popular e.g. the *Slavonic Dances* (1878 and 1886); while his choral works — *Stabat Mater* (1877), *The Spectre's Bride* (1884), the *Requiem* (1890) and the *Te Deum* (1892) — soon made him a welcome visitor to England.

His orchestral works have always been popular but it was not until his visit to America (1893–96) that *From the New World* brought these works into the normal orchestral repertoire, and since then Symphonies No.4 in G and No. 2 in D minor (the numbering is confused) have remained firm favourites. His late *Cello Concerto* (1895) is one of the finest in this genre and his chamber music makes use of the Bohemian contrast between the slow Dumka and the abandoned Furiant in many of the string quartets and piano trios (once again America was responsible for the best-known of these, the so-called *American Quartet* in F.)

The famous *Humoresque* is typical of many tuneful and well-wrought piano pieces, just as the *Biblical Songs* can be taken as representative of the 100 or so songs. Only the nine operas have stayed rooted in Prague and unknown outside Bohemia though *Rusalka* (1900) is said to be full of poetic feeling and charming melodies. Dvorák followed Smetana in making Czech national music an essential part of the European cultural heritage. His work as a teacher and administrator was the official reason for his visit to America; his successors were his pupils Suk and Novák. To posterity, however, his heritage seems to be his melodic and harmonic charm and the natural and occasionally naive way he expands these spontaneous inspirations.

DYKES, John Bacchus (1823–1876)

English cleric and composer of many famous hymn tunes (such as *Dominus Regit Me* to *The King of Love* and *Melita* to *Eternal Father*) besides many services and anthems.

DYSON, George (1883–1964)

English composer and educator, remembered as the Director of the RCM 1937–52 and as the composer of the *Canterbury Pilgrims* (1931) and *St. Paul's Voyage to Melita* (1933). *The New Music* (1924) was one of the earliest attempts to write entertainingly about 20th century music.

DZERZHINSKY, Ivan (1909–1978)

Russian pianist and composer whose first opera *Quiet Flows the Don* (1935) was chosen by the Soviet authorities at the time of the Great Purge as the prototype of simple proletariat culture as opposed to Shostakovich's *Lady Macbeth of Mzensk* which was described as 'modernist' and 'formal'. Few of his works have been performed outside the USSR but he has produced over 10 other operas in his easy folk song style in recent years.

E

ECÇARD, Johannes (1553–1611)
German composer of church music. He was a pupil of Lassus and is particularly important for his versions of German chorales (mostly in five parts and described as *Geistliche Lieder*) published between 1574 and 1597. Best known is an adaptation to English words, *When to the Temple Mary Went.*

ECCLES, John (c. 1650–1735)
Master of the King's Band from 1700. Besides Birthday and New Year's Odes for the court, he wrote theatre music for many famous London productions, including *Don Quixote* (with Purcell 1694), *Love for Love* (1695) and Congreve's *Way of the World* (1700).
He was the eldest son of an eccentric Quaker musician, Solomon (1618–83), who accompanied the puritan Fox to the West Indies but died in London; he published several 'ground-basses with divisions'.
Henry Eccles, Solomon's second son, was also a member of the King's Band and after 1710 held a similar post at the French Court; he published in Paris in 1720 and 1723 12 solos for the violin and two books of sonatas for viol (viola), the last of which are still often performed.

EDWARDS, Richard (c. 1523–1566)
Master of the children of the Chapel Royal from 1561. He produced one of the earliest 'musical dramas', acted and sung by the children in 1565 at Lincoln's Inn. He is remembered now for his madrigal *In Going to my Naked Bed*, the words of which are also his.

EINEM, Gottfried von (b. 1918)
Austrian operatic composer who studied in England, France and Italy and after a short imprisonment under the Nazis, with Boris Blacher. Most of his professional life has been spent as repetiteur at various German opera houses but, after visiting America in 1953, he returned to Vienna as a member of the board of directors of the State Opera. The best known of his operas is *Dantons Tod* (1947) but in this, as in his orchestral, chamber and vocal music, his style remains as unintegrated tonal, if dissonant, 19th century language. His operas and ballets are, however, admired for their passion and eloquence.

ELGAR, Sir Edward (1857–1934)
Great English composer of the late Romantic period.
Elgar was self-taught as a composer but had the stimulus of a lively provincial musical society at Worcester. He made himself into a good violinist and competent keyboard player like his father and was at an early age involved in local music-making, including playing in the orchestra at the yearly Three Choirs Festival. His father's music shop provided the opportunity of discovering other orchestral instruments, while the Cathedral and Festival performances deepened his knowledge of the 19th century English repertoire although, by modern standards, he lacked systematic experience of music before 1700, of folk music and most importantly, of opera. He acquired considerable experience in conducting locally, first as bandmaster, then with the Worcester Amateur Instrumental Society and as successor to his father as organist at the Roman Catholic church; for all of these he wrote copiously though still on a small scale.
After his marriage in 1889 his horizons broadened and two years in London led to a further move to Malvern; by this time the

Froissart Overture had been performed at the Worcester Festival of 1890. Then began the series of larger-scale choral works which met both the social needs of the period and also Elgar's own need for encouraging stimulus. Most of these are based on such Romantic characters as *King Olaf* (1896) and *Caractacus* (1898) — the latter being operatic in its ambitions.
This choral phase culminated in the *Dream of Gerontius* (1900), an acknowledged masterpiece and the result of years of pondering on Newman's poem.
Elgar's success in matching the catholic spirituality of the text however proved as far ahead of Protestant taste as his advance in musical style which bewildered choral societies, and it achieved its present popularity relatively slowly. The two later oratorios *The Apostles* (1903) and *The Kingdom* (1906) have not received the same universal acceptance, and the projected third work of the trilogy never appeared.
By this time such mature instrumental works as the *Enigma Variations* (1899), the earlier *Serenade for Strings* (1892, performed 1905) and the *Introduction and Allegro* (1905) had prepared the way for his large-scale 1st Symphony, the *Violin Concerto* (1910) and 2nd Symphony (1911). The last was dedicated to and in memory of King Edward VII and together with such 'patriotic' music as the *Pomp and Circumstance* Marches was largely responsible for the civic honours conferred on him — he was made Master of the King's Musick in 1924 and became a baronet in 1931 (he was knighted in 1904).
The Great War resulted in an increase of this patriotic output, but also led to the 'sunset' quality of the *Piano Quintet* and the *Cello Concerto* in 1919. After Lady Elgar's death in 1920 he 'went off the boil' as he himself put it and no further major works appeared.
Elgar worked his way to large-scale instrumental compositions and the background influence of Wagner suggests a parallel with Bruckner. By this late period he had forged his own elegiac harmonic language and without use of folk song, had produced the English term 'Elgarian'.

ELLINGTON, 'Duke' (1899–1974)
Black American composer and pianist who was one of the leading 'big-band' jazz musicians in the twenties, and who continued to be prominent in this style for over 30 years.

EMMETT, Daniel (1815–1904)
American musical entertainer who composed *Dixie* which became a national song in the Southern States during the American Civil War.

ENESCO, Georges (1881–1955)
Rumanian violinist and composer who, at 13, was a pupil of Fauré at the Paris Conservatoire, and whose *Rumanian Poem* was performed three years later. His compositions include an opera, three symphonies and a fair amount of chamber music which finally established him as a representative Rumanian nationalist composer.
Other activities involved conducting and teaching — he is especially remembered as having taught Yehudi Menuhin.

ESTE (Est or East), Thomas (d. 1609)
Early music publisher and composer, especially remembered for his editions of Morley and other madrigal composers and for *The Whole Books of Psalmes* (1592) which included a varied collection of tunes such as *Winchester Old* to *While Shepherds Watched.*
His son Michael (c. 1580–1648) was organist of Lichfield Cathedral and published six books of madrigals and anthems. He contributed to *The Triumphes of Oriana* in 1601.

F

FALLA, Manuel de (1876–1946)
Leading Spanish Nationalist composer born in Cadiz, and particularly associated with the colourful and passionate folk music of Andalusia which contrasted with his own quiet and withdrawn personality. An early Spanish opera was performed in 1902 but it was not until Falla moved to Paris that the advocacy and friendship of Debussy, Dukas, Ravel and Stravinsky led to a performance of *La Vida Breve* in 1913. He returned to Madrid at the outbreak of the 1st World War and he wrote *Nights in the Garden of Spain* for piano and orchestra (1915). *Love the Magician*, a ballet which included the famous *Ritual Fire Dance* and the *The Three-Cornered Hat*, and which in its final repertoire ballet form of 1919 involved Massine and Picasso, was one of the most successful of Diaghilev's productions. His *Harpsichord Concerto* (1926) was written for Wanda Landowska. He died in South America where he emigrated in poor health at the end of the Spanish Civil War, leaving unfinished a setting of an epic Catalan poem on Atlantis.

FARMER, John (fl.c. 1600)
English (or perhaps Irish) composer whose book of madrigals was published in 1599 and who contributed to the *The Triumphes of Oriana* (1601). He is best remembered for *Fair Phyllis I Saw Sitting All Alone* and some of his psalm-tune contributions to East's collection of 1592.

FARNABY, Giles (c. 1560–1640)
English virginal and madrigal composer. His *Canzonets to Fowre Voyces* (1598) includes almost the only eight-part English madrigal. The *Fitzwilliam Virginal Book* contains more than 50 of his keyboard pieces together with four pieces by his son Richard.

FARRANT, John (fl. c. 1600)
Organist of Salisbury Cathedral and composer of the *Evening Canticles* in D minor which are still sung.

FARRANT, Richard (c. 1530–1581)
English organist and church composer remembered for his Service in A minor and the two short anthems *Call to Remembrance* and *Hide Not Thou Thy Face*. He was master of the choristers and organist at St George's Chapel, Windsor, and was therefore responsible for yearly productions by the choirboy actors there, though only two of his stage songs are known.

FAURÉ, Gabriel (1845–1924)
French composer, organist, and administrator. His background was humble but he was accepted as a non-playing student boarder at the then new *École Niedermeyer*, an institution designed to produce all-round church musicians. Here he was strongly influenced by the young Saint-Saëns. He spent many years as assistant to both Widor at St. Sulpice and Saint-Saëns at the Madeleine and he eventually succeeded the latter there in 1896, the same year in which he was appointed to the Conservatoire as Professor of Composition. In 1905 he was appointed Director of the Conservatoire where his leadership proved fruitful both in widening the curriculum and in developing such students as Ravel and Nadia Boulanger.
His refined songs and chamber music made an immediate impression of freshness and his style was enriched by Wagnerian harmony and the modality of earlier music. His pianistic style remained in the salon tradition of Chopin's Nocturnes and he was quite unaffected by the grand Romantic gestures of his contemporaries. By 1890 he had matched his sense of subtle understatement to the

symbolism of Verlaine's verse in such songs as *Clair de Lune*.
Fauré had little enthusiasm for large-scale orchestral textures and even his incidental music for *Pelléas et Mélisande* was scored by his pupil Charles Koechlin. His hauntingly beautiful *Requiem* (1888) similarly is marked by reticence and a sensitive classical transparency which became more and more characteristic of his final 'Grecian' phase, during which his emotional isolation was accentuated by the onset of deafness.

FAYRFA, Robert (1464–1521)
Leading English composer under Henry VII who was a Gentleman of the Chapel Royal and organist of St. Albans. At the end of his life he was in charge of the royal musicians at the 'Field of the Cloth of Gold'. Amongst his 33 extant works are six large-scale masses and two magnificats besides motets and secular three-part songs. The Church Music is normally scored for five voices (probably doubled by instruments) though the long sections are often of widely varying textures such as the treble and bass duo at the beginning of the Gloria of the *Magnificat Regale*.

FELTON, William (1715–1769)
English cleric, organist, harpsichordist and composer who was attached for much of his life to the musical establishment of Hereford Cathedral. His opus numbers include 32 concertos for organ/harpsichord and strings and 16 suites of *Easy Lessons for the Harpsichord* published between 1744 and 1759.

FERGUSON, Howard (b. 1908)
English composer, trained at the RAM, whose compositions are in the mainstream of the British diatonic tradition, and marked by a distinctive craftsmanship and originality. They include chamber music, works for orchestra, a piano concerto, piano pieces such as the popular *Five Bagatelles* (1944) and some songs.

FERRABOSCO, (Family)
A distinguished family of musicians of Italian origin, the first of whom (Domenico Maria, 1513–74) published 45 four-part madrigals in Venice in 1542. His eldest son Alfonso (1543–88) was in the service of Queen Elizabeth I of England both as a musician and as a secret agent (as shown by numerous letters to the Earl of Leicester and Sir William Cecil). He was responsible for a masque in 1572 given before Elizabeth and the French Ambassador and 20 of his madrigals were included in *Musica Transalpina* (1588 and later).
Alfonso's son of the same name (1575–1628) was, on the accession of James I (1602), in his service as a violinist. He is remembered partly for the masques in which he collaborated with Ben Jonson between 1605 and 1611. Later, in the service of Prince Charles (King Charles I from 1625), he became Composer in Ordinary and his most important works were fantasias and pavans for viols. He fills an important place in English musical history between the string fancies of Byrd, and those of Purcell.

FESTA, Constanzo (1490–1545)
Italian composer of many graceful madrigals published in Rome in 1537. Some of his church music is to be found in the Vatican library where he was *Maestro di cappella*.

FESTING, Michael Christian (d. 1752)
English violinist and composer. Besides several positions in London (he was a member of the King's private band and director of the Italian Opera) he was the founding secretary of the Society of Musicians.
His compositions include violin sonatas and concertos, symphonies for strings and wind, and settings of Milton and Addison.

FIELD, John (1782-1837)
Famous as the 'inventor' of the *Nocturne*, Field was born in Dublin into a rather undistinguished musical family who made serious attempts to launch him as a child prodigy. He was eventually apprenticed to Clementi in London where his duties included demonstrating as well as selling pianos and, in 1802, accompanying Clementi to various European musical capitals. Field was particularly successful in Paris and St. Petersburg and remained there on Clementi's departure the next year as a kind of commercial representative. He made his first appearance in Moscow in 1806 and apart from a concert tour (1832-35), remained in Russia for the rest of his life. Besides his concert performances he had a lucrative teaching connection (his pupils included Glinka), although his irregular and dissolute lifestyle did not make for financial stability. Although now remembered exclusively for his 20 nocturnes (several of these not originally so called), Field also wrote seven very popular piano concertos and four piano sonatas. His style of playing, as described by Liszt, was marked by relaxed smoothness and 'inexhaustible embellishments'. Chopin was profoundly influenced by Field's nocturnes both in feeling and in technical details, although unlike Field, Chopin wrote out the subtle ornamentation.

FINNISSY, Michael (b. 1946)
English avant-garde composer, trained at the RCM and in Italy. He has been active at the London School of Contemporary Dance and received many commissions from abroad. His work for the music theatre has ranged from the *Eight Mysteries* (1972-79) — each of which lasts from 14 to 30 minutes and requires two or more singers, usually actors and a group of virtuoso instrumentalists — to the large-scale chamber opera *Medea* (1976) and *Mr. Punch* (1977) written for *The Fires of London*. He has also written extensively for voices and instruments in such works as *Sir Tristram* (1978), for the Nash Ensemble, and for solo piano and similar ensembles in the two piano concertos, No. 3 (1978) and No. 5 (1980). His many *Songs* however are usually for single instrumentalists.

FINZI, Gerald (1901-1956)
Distinguished English composer of songs and several longer orchestral works including concertos for cello and clarinet. He was particularly attracted to the 17th century metaphysical poets and *Dies Natalis* (1940) for high voice and string orchestra is a most sensitive realisation of Traherne's mysticism. His 'post-Elgarian' diatonic style came to him from his teacher Bairstow at York.

FIOCCO, (Family)
An 18th century family of musicians of Venetian extraction who held important posts in Brussels. Two of them at least are remembered as composers:
Pietro Antonio (1650-1714) the leader of the court band in Brussels and the composer of *Sacri concerti* (1691) and several masses and motets.
Joseph Hector (1703-1741) a distinguished harpsichordist whose *Pièces de Clavecin* are still played.

FISCHER, Johann Caspar Ferdinand (c. 1665-1738)
Important Bohemian composer of keyboard music that anticipates Bach's stylistic practices. His Op.2 *Les Pièces de Clavessin* (1696) consists of eight short suites in the French style: Prelude and *ad lib* dances such as gavottes, minuets, bourrees and even aria with variations, rather than the usual allemande, courante and sarabanda of Froberger.
More important was *Ariadne musica neo-organoedum* (1702) which introduces preludes and fugues in 20 different keys —

only the absence of C and F majors, and G, B flat and E flat minors separates the work from the pattern of *The 48*. It is clear that these short pieces, together with his organ chorale-preludes, were both well-known to Bach and often served as starting points to Bach's longer essays in the same style, e.g. the E major fugue in Book II of *The 48* is identical with Fischer's subject in the same key.

FLOTOW, Friedrich von (1812–1883)
Remembered as the aristocratic German composer of *Martha* which appeared as a ballet in Paris in 1844 and then as an opera in Vienna three years later. It is based on an English story of Richmond Fair in Queen Anne's reign and included the Irish folk-song *The Last Rose of Summer*. It has been a favourite item in the operatic repertoire ever since but its composer never again approached its success in his 17 other operas.

FRANÇAIX, Jean (b. 1912)
Prolific French composer of orchestral works and ballets. He was a pupil of Nadia Boulanger and favoured clear neo-classical textures; his use of pungent dissonance led to a near-riot at the first performance in Paris of his 1st Symphony in 1932. From the same year dates his popular *Piano Concertino*, which well represents his crisp and witty style.

FRANCK, César (1822–1890)
Major Romantic composer of Flemish extraction who appeared as an infant prodigy on the piano together with his brother as violinist. The family moved to Paris and he entered the Paris Conservatoire in 1837 where his feats of contrapuntal improvisation became legendary. He continued his virtuoso touring career with his brother (1842–43) at his father's insistence and his four piano trios (Op. 1) brought him to the notice of Liszt, Chopin, Meyerbeer and Donizetti. After his marriage in 1848 however, he earned his living in Paris as an organist and teacher. The unceasing round of hard work which followed was rarely relieved by worldly success during the rest of his life. He eventually became Professor of the Organ at the Conservatoire in 1872 but his Wagnerian sympathies, though attracting distinguished pupils such as D'Indy and Chausson, repelled his colleagues just as his devotion to chamber music was poles removed from the popular opéra comique. The Parisian public knew him as the undemanding organist of St. Clotilde.
Following his early 'concert-pianist' style, Franck's works were mainly for the organ or the church, although he was a slow developer in his chosen style. The first works which are still generally played appeared around his 40th year in the *Six Pieces* for organ, though the oratorios and symphonic poems were curiously uneven. After the *Three Pieces* for organ in 1878, there followed the series of successful major works by which he is remembered: the *Piano Quintet* (1879), *Prelude, Chorale and Fugue* for piano (1884), the *Variations Symphoniques* for orchestra and piano (1885), the *Violin Sonata* (1886), the *Symphony* (1986–88) and the *Three Chorals* for organ (1890).
Franck used a chromatic style deriving from his organ playing, and developed an individual approach to Liszt's cyclic form and Wagner's leitmotif construction. His works, like Bruckner's, tend to move from probing questions to perhaps rather facilely triumphant answers; it is clear from D'Indy's adulatory biography that this simplistic trait is a perfect musical equivalent of the beloved composer's saintly personality.

FRANKEL, Benjamin (1906–1973)
English composer of film music, educated in Germany, who first earned his living as a café pianist and violinist in London. Besides over 100 film scores, he also wrote

seven symphonies and four string quartets. His unfinished opera *Marching Song* has recently been completed by Buxton Orr.

FRANZ, Robert (1815–1892)

Important lieder composer who was immediately recognised by Schuman in *Neue Zeitschrift* on the evidence of his first set of 12 songs written in 1843. His career as an organist/conductor was threatened by deafness from 1841 and Liszt and Joachim eventually raised £5000 by concerts in 1872 on his behalf.

Besides his 257 songs, Franz spent much time in editing Baroque composers such as Bach although his added accompaniments in lieu of a continuo part are now unlikely to be heard.

FRESCOBALDI, Girolamo (1583–1643)

Great Italian organist and composer born in Ferrara where he studied with Luzzaschi, the cathedral organist. He was in Antwerp in 1608 where he published his first book of five-part madrigals and presumably heard the playing of Sweelinck. His *Fantasias à 4* were published the same year in Milan and on November 1st he became organist of St. Peter's, Rome where he remained for the rest of his life, except for a spell as organist to the Grand Duke of Tuscany in Florence (1628–34). His reinstatement at St. Peter's and the reported audience of 30,000 at his performance there, besides his reputation as a singer and lutenist, give a clear idea of his reputation.

Frescobaldi's keyboard compositions include *Ricercare e canzoni francesi* (1615), *Toccatas* (1614–37), *Fiori musicali* (1635), a liturgical collection, and *Capricci sopra diversi soggetti* (1624), the last of which contains an illuminating preface dealing with the performing practices of the period: the rhythmic and tempo variations and the permissible omissions.

FRICKER, Peter Racine (b. 1920)

English composer whose early works won important prizes and received performances at such festivals as Darmstadt and Cheltenham. Since 1953 he has been an active teacher at Morley College, the RCO and University of California. His wide range of compositions include four symphonies, several concertos and chamber music works, choral music, songs and incidental music.

FROBERGER, Johann Jacob (1616–1667)

German pupil of Frescobaldi who was appointed court organist at Vienna in 1637. He left the court in 1657 and by 1662 was in London as organ-blower to Christopher Gibbons at Westminster Abbey. He played the harpsichord before Charles II. His printed works include *Toccatas, Canzonas and Ricercars*, and *Suites de Clavecin* (all published posthumously); there are 222 sheets of similar pieces in the Vienna State Library. He died in France.

G

GABRIELI, Andrea (c. 1510–1586)
Venetian composer of madrigals and church music. A pupil of Willaert at St. Mark's, Venice, later becoming organist there himself. Some of his pieces used antiphonal groups of choirs and he seems to have encouraged the use of instruments with voices. His pupils included his nephew Giovanni, and Leo Hassler.

GABRIELI, Giovanni (1557–1612)
Remembered as the greatest of the early Baroque polychoral composers. Like his uncle he became organist at St. Mark's, Venice, and although his reputation was international (his pupils included Schutz and Praetorius) he never seems to have left Venice. His *Sacrae symphoniae* of 1597 and 1615 contain motets of up to 19 voices and instruments. In his most famous instrumental piece *Sonata pian e forte* for two 'choirs' of sackbuts (trombones) headed by a cornetto (a wooden instrument with a brass mouthpiece) and violin respectively, he exploits dynamic and echo effects. The well known motet *In ecclesiis* is scored for three groups:
1. Four solo singers with instruments.
2. Four-part choir with instruments.
3. Six-part brass group.

With each of the groups in a separate gallery in St. Mark's, his massive and often chromatic style must have sounded overwhelming to his contemporaries.

GADE, Niels Vilhelm (1817–1890)
Danish Romantic composer who was friendly with and influenced by Mendelssohn and Schumann. His works include eight symphonies, chamber music, lieder and some choral works (two of which he introduced at the Birmingham Festival in 1876). Most of his life was spent in Copenhagen as an organist and conductor.

GAGLIANO, Marco da (1575–1642)
Florentine cleric and composer of *Dafne* (1607), one of the earliest operas, which was published the following year together with a wide-ranging preface by the composer on performance and staging. He also wrote madrigals and church music.

GALILEI, Vincenzo (c. 1520–1591)
The father of Galilio the astronomer. Galilei published two books of madrigals in 1574 nd 1587 and was a distinguished lutenist. He is also important for his philosophical writings which led to the operatic movement of the *Camerata*, and for his own early attempt in the monodic style. This was a setting of Dante for single voice and simple lute chords based on what was *thought* to be the declamatory practice of Ancient Greek Tragedy.

GALUPPI, Baldassare (1706–1785)
Venetian operatic composer largely remembered for some tuneful string pieces. He was famous for his comic operas with their concerted finales and travelled as far afield as Russia.

GARDINER, Henry Balfour (1877–1950)
English composer whose works achieved much success between 1900 and 1920. Among these are a symphony, orchestral pieces such as *Shepherd Fennel's Dance* (1911), chamber music and some popular choral pieces.

GARDNER, John (b. 1917)
English composer who after study in Oxford and service in the RAF has been engaged in both teaching and practical music-making.
He has written extensively for choirs, including cantatas for Christmas (1966) and

for Easter (1970), and for orchestra and chamber music combinations. Works include a symphony (1951), piano concerto (1957), oboe sonata (1953), and a chamber concerto for organ and eleven instruments (1969). His opera, *The Moon and Sixpence* (1957), was commissioned by Sadler's Wells Opera.

GARRETT, George Mursell (1834–1897)
Organist of St. John's College, Cambridge from 1857 and remembered for his various settings for the Anglican service, especially perhaps *Garrett in F* though this now seems rather undistinguished.

GAUL, Alfred Robert (1837–1913)
The composer of the still-popular oratorio *The Holy City* (1882) and much church music. His musical style is very characteristic of English music of the period.

GAUNTLETT, Henry John (1815–1876)
Still remembered as the composer of such hymn tunes as *Once in Royal David's City*, *Jesus Lives*! and *Ye choirs of New Jerusalem*.
He was important in his lifetime for his work (as an amateur) in organ design and in the revival of plainsong. In 1846 he was chosen by Mendelssohn to play the organ part in the first performance of *Elijah* in Birmingham.

GEMINIANI, Francesco (c.1680–1762)
A pupil of Corelli and considered on his arrival in England in 1714 as the foremost representative of his style of playing. Besides his *Art of playing the Violin*, (Op. 9) he published 36 sonatas and 30 concertos for the violin. Apart from a few years in Paris and Dublin, he lived in London and was a prominent member of the musical scene there for most of his life.

GERHARD, Roberto (1896–1970)
Spanish composer who emigrated to England in 1939 after the Spanish Civil War. His Catalonian musical nationalism started from the teaching of Felipe Pedrell but his later works, which include four symphonies, owe rather more to Schönberg.

GERMAN, Edward (1862–1936)
Famous English composer of light operas and incidental music. At an early age he learnt to arrange for a band he formed in his home town of Whitchurch (Shropshire) and later entered the RAM as an organist and violinist.
His music for *Henry VIII* (1892) at the Lyceum included the popular *Shepherd's Dance* and by this time his 1st Symphony had been performed at the Crystal Palace. But it was after the successful completion of Sullivan's unfinished last opera that *Merrie England* appeared in 1902. *Tom Jones* did not quite reach the same high level in 1907 and it was perhaps inevitable that the visions of a second Gilbert and Sullivan era should fade after the 1st World War. German's gifts were melodic charm and harmonic sophistication rather than dramatic intensity.

GERSHWIN, George (1898–1937)
American composer of Russian-Jewish extraction who was attracted to the popular music of Jerome Kern and Irving Berlin besides the new jazz idiom of 1914. After some training as a pianist and work with a publisher in Tin Pan Alley, he became involved in musicals with some successful songs. *Rhapsody in Blue* (1924) for piano and orchestra owed its origin to Paul Whiteman (it was orchestrated by his arranger) and led naturally to the *Piano Concerto* (1925) which Gershwin scored himself.
Besides such shows as *Lady Be Good* with the Astaires, and many famous songs with his brother Ira as lyricist, Gershwin had bigger musical ambitions and even

approached Ravel as a possible teacher. He completed some excellent film scores in the Hollywood of the 1930's and finally produced *Porgy and Bess*, an ambitious folk-opera, in 1935. His musical importance lies in his bringing together the two strands of popular and art music by his sophisticated treatment of the jazz idiom in such pieces as the *Three Preludes* for piano. He died rather suddenly of a brain tumour in 1937.

GESUALDO, Carlo (1560–1613)
Prince of Venice and most daring harmonic innovator among the later madrigalists. He was famous as a lutenist and notorious as the murderer of his unfaithful wife and her lover. His first four books of madrigals (1594–96) were all successful enough in the traditional style to be reprinted several times. The last two (1611) sound modern by any standards and exploit big chordal and short exclamatory effects using pivot notes to link completely alien tonalities in direct and powerful expressive strokes.

GIBBONS (Family)
Christopher (1615–1676)
Second son of Orlando who became organist of Winchester Cathedral in 1638, organist to Charles II, and of Westminster Abbey in 1660. He wrote a very large number of string fantasies and some anthems besides collaborating with Matthew Locke in the music for Shirley's masque *Cupid and Death* (1653).

Edward (c. 1568–1650)
Eldest brother of Orlando. He was working as a priest-vicar at Exeter in 1609. Some church music is extant.

Ellis (1573–1603)
Second brother of Orlando. Little is known of his life but Morley included two of his madrigals in *The Triumphes of Oriana.*

Orlando (1583–1625)
Great English Jacobean composer. He left King's College, Cambridge to become organist of the Chapel Royal in 1605; his royal duties included playing the virginals from 1619 and he was also organist at Westminster Abbey from 1623. Two months after the accession of Charles I he died of apoplexy while at Canterbury with the Chapel Royal, awaiting the arrival of the Queen from France. His output was large, though little was published in his lifetime other than *Madrigals and Mottets of five parts: apt for Viols and Voyces* (1612). He is best known for such large-scale 'full' (i.e. without solos) anthems as *Hosanna* and *O Clap Your Hands* and the melodious 'short' service. Historically, he is more important for the 25 'verse' (i.e. with solos) anthems such as *This is the Record of John* and *See, See the Word is Incarnate* (both with string accompaniments) and the larger second (verse) *Service*. This newer style had few precedents and many noble successors. His madrigals are marked by a serious approach as in the famous *Silver Swan* and *What is Our Life*?
Gibbons followed Byrd in his treatment of the *String Fantasias* — twenty four à three and four more à six; all explore the new fugal possibilities. His keyboard works (40–50 pieces) are found in such collections as the *Fitzwilliam Virginal Book* and include fantasias, variations and dances, and range from the charm of *The Hunt's Up* to the magnificence of the *Organ Fantasy* à four.

GIBBS, Cecil Armstrong (1889–1960)
English composer whose songs and part-songs are still performed. He also had some success with incidental music and comic operas in the early 1920's.

GILES, Nathaniel (c. 1560–1633)
Organist of Worcester Cathedral, St. George's Chapel, Windsor, and finally of

the Chapel Royal. A composer of church music.

GIORDANO, Umberto (1867–1948)
Italian composer of *Andrea Chenier* (1896) based on the life of the French poet who was first a liberal supporter of the French Revolution and finally its victim. This opera was performed throughout Europe and certainly influenced Puccini in *Tosca*; it has perhaps held its place in the operatic repertoire because of its dramatic tenor role. *Fedora* (1898) had less success outside Italy.

GLAZUNOV, Alexander (1865–1936)
Russian composer, born into the musical circle of Balakirev, and the favourite pupil of Rimsky-Korsakov. His 1st Symphony was performed when he was 16 and later conducted by Liszt at Weimar. In 1899 he became a professor at, and in 1905 the Director of, the St. Petersburg Conservatory where he remained, a musical conservative under the Soviet regime until 1928, when he emigrated to Paris. In the early years of the century he travelled widely and his compositions were very successful; it is rare nowadays, however, to hear performances of any of the eight symphonies, two piano sonatas, three string quartets or concertos, From 'the little Glinka', he developed into 'the Russian Mendelssohn'.

GLIÈRE, Reinhold (1875–1956)
Russian composer whose music was popularised by the Bournemouth Symphony Orchestra under Sir Dan Godfrey. His early work includes three symphonies, several tone poems and chamber music, but after the Russian Revolution he was more active in ballet and opera.

GLINKA, Michael (1804–1857)
The 'father of Russian music' by virtue of the Russian stories, atmosphere, and musical character of the two operas *A Life for the Tzar* (1836) and *Russlan and Ludmilla* (1842). Russian music at that time, except for folk music and that of the Orthodox Church, was almost completely dominated by Italy and Germany and Glinka's background shared these influences. As a man, he was a weak character, 'a talented Russian gentleman of his time, prettily proud, little developed, full of vanity and self-adoration' (Tchaikovsky). Glinka's vocal writing owes much to Italy but the patriotic story, orchestral and often exotic colouring, and the occasional 'supernatural' harmonies were exactly what 'The Five' needed as a starting point. It is rare now for any of his music to be performed outside Russia other than the overtures of these two operas. *Russlan and Ludmilla* was never popular even in Russia, but of the historical and musical influence of the earlier work there can be no question; Borodin, Rimsky-Korsakov, Moussorgsky and Tchaikovsky were all lavish in their enthusiasm.

GLUCK, Christoph Willibald von (1714–1787)
German Bohemian opera composer and reformer. Of humble origins, he earned his living in Prague (1732–36) by teaching and playing keyboard and string instruments. He then moved to Vienna taking a position as chamber musician in the Lobkowitz household. He went to Milan the following year where he studied under Sammartini and from 1741 produced his first operas. He heard Rameau's operas in Paris with Prince Lobkowitz in 1745, and later in London met Handel and Arne. He published six trio sonatas besides producing an Italian pasticcio and performing on the glass harmonica.
By the time he was 40 he had had much experience as a travelling operatic conductor and had written about 20 (Italian) operas, usually with resounding

success. The movement towards 'reform' centred on Vienna and was led by such aristocrats and intellectuals as Calzabigi and Winckelmann; the former claimed to have 'chosen' Gluck to lead the movement against the excesses of Italian opera, in particular the domination of the solo-singer and the lack of dramatic integration. The result was the epoch-making *Orfeo ed Euridice* (1762) to a libretto by Calzabigi. Although Gluck continued to write in the more traditional Italian style, *Alceste* (1767) included a preface that identified the composer with the aims of the reformers. After *Paride ed Elena* (1770) his last two 'reform' operas were produced in Paris: *Iphigenie en Aulide* (1774) and *Iphigenie en Tauride* (1779). The new principles provoked a Parisian furore between Gluck's supporters and those of Piccini who represented the traditional Italian opposition.

Apart from the professional expertise that Gluck brought to all his work, his operatic reforms had little effect on his immediate successors. Mozart, for instance, in spite of their mutual admiration, ignored Gluck's precedent in his final opera seria, *La Clemenza di Tito*. On the other hand Gluck's example was an inspiration to the 19th century especially to Cherubini, Berlioz and Wagner. To the 20th century his statuesque musical style is moving in its *bel canto*, and powerful in its absence of distracting detail from the choral and orchestral ensembles. All the 'reform' operas have received memorable productions in recent years, even if few of them are regular members of the operatic repertoire.

GOEDICKE, Alexander Fedorvich (1877–1957)

Russian composer and pianist. His works include patriotic works such as *Glory to the Soviet Pilots*, a cantata to meet the requirements of the USSR, besides three symphonies and earlier music in the Arensky tradition.

GOEHR, Alexander (b. 1932)

Son of Walter (below) who trained at the RMCM and the Paris Conservatoire. A composer of orchestral, chamber and vocal music, he uses serial techniques in polyphonic style.

Walter (1903–1960)

German pupil of Schönberg who, after holding various German theatrical and radio appointments, became a staff conductor of the BBC (1946–49) and a well-known composer of broadcast incidental music.

GOETZ, Hermann (1840–1876)

Remembered as the composer of *The Taming of the Shrew* (1874) and a fastidious *Symphony in F*. Although his music was published and highly valued in England, his life was spent in Germany and after 1867 in Switzerland.

GOMBERT, Nicolas (c. 1500–1556)

Flemish pupil of Josquin des Pres who was choir master to the Emperor Charles V and from 1537 at the Imperial Chapel in Madrid. His 250 extant compositions include unusually expressive motets, psalms and chansons.

GOSS, John (1800–1880)

English organist and composer. He was organist of St. Paul's Cathedral (1838–72) and Composer to the Chapel Royal from 1856. The anthems such as *If We Believe* (for the funeral of the Duke of Wellington) and O *Saviour of the World*, are still widely performed, and the hymn tune to *Praise my Soul the King of Heaven* still retains its freshness.

GOSSEC, Francois Joseph (1734–1829)

Belgian symphonic and operatic composer, who with the help of Rameau became the conductor of a private band in Paris in

1751. For this group he wrote his 1st Symphony and published his first quartets in 1754 — the year before Haydn's first quartet and five years before Haydn's first symphony. He is later credited with introducing horns and clarinets into the opera orchestra. Little is ever heard now of his symphonies (over 30), chamber and church music or operas, but he is remembered as one of the favoured composers of the Revolution and as one of the three founders of the Conservatoire.

GOUDIMEL, Claude (c. 1514–1572)
French Huguenot composer who, after writing a book of chansons in 1549 and several masses, produced *Psalms in the Form of Motets*. His complete set of harmonised tunes for the 150 metrical psalms included the *Old Hundredth* and other Genevan tunes used in the 'Old' metrical psalms of Sternhold and Hopkins (1562).

GOULD, Morton (b. 1913)
American composer who after appearances as an infant prodigy has become a distinguished composer for the theatre and films. He makes extensive use of American themes and besides three symphonies and several concertos, has produced other works such as *American Symphonettes*, *Concertette*, *Concerto for Tap Dancer and Orchestra*, etc.

GOUNOD, Charles Francois (1818–1893)
Successful and influential French composer of operas and church music. After a brilliant childhood, he lived in Rome for several years (after winning the *Prix de Rome* at the Paris Conservatoire), where he heard and imitated performances of Palestrina at the Sistine Chapel. This involvement with liturgical style resulted in an unaccompanied mass which was performed in Vienna in 1840. In Germany he met Mendelssohn and Schumann, returning to Paris as a church musician (he almost became a priest). The famous *Messe Solennelle* of this period had its first performance in London.
Gounod's connection with the opera house seems to have been inspired by the singing of his future mother-in-law, but success eluded him until *Faust* in 1859 which is still an essential part of the operatic repertoire. *Romeo and Juliet* (1867) was almost as successful in France. He lived for several years in England after the Franco-Prussian War of 1870 and *La Rédemption* (1881) was performed by most of the English choral societies. (He founded the Albert Hall Choral Society which was later renamed the 'Royal Choral Society'.)
His later 'oratorio' style of simple recitative (even on a monotone) with chromatic chordal accompaniment had a 'dubious effect' on Victorian musical taste, but he handed on to Bizet and Massenet a tradition that he had received from Berlioz. The combination of mysticism and sensuality in his music was paralleled by an emotional instability which clouded the final years of his life.

GOUSSENS, Eugene (1893–1962)
Son and grandson of distinguished operatic conductors and the brother of several famous orchestral players, he himself combined conducting with composition. His works include orchestral, piano and chamber music of neo-classical leanings, the one-act opera *Judith* (1929) and the oratorio *Apocalypse* (1951).

GRAINGER, Percy Aldridge (1882–1961)
An Australian pianist and composer, educated in Germany and a naturalised American. Grieg introduced him to an interest in folk music and most of his compositions showed this influence (e.g. the arrangements of Irish reels in the early *Molly on the Shore* for string quartet, and the famous *Country Gardens*).

GRANADOS, Enrique (1867–1916)
Spanish pianist and composer of the (early) *Spanish Dances* and (later) *Goyescas*. After private study in Paris he returned to Barcelona where he founded his own piano school. His operatic compositions are in the Zarzuela tradition but have not become international repertoire pieces. Granados was inspired by the Spanish traditions of the 18th century especially the works of Domenico Scarlatti and the world of the painter Goya. His musical style, however, has German overtones of the 19th century.

GRAUN, Carl Heinrich (1704–1759)
German singer and composer of successful operas and church music, especially *Der Tod Jesus* a Passion-Cantata which is still regularly performed in Germany. Graun was for 20 years in charge of the music at Potsdam under Frederick the Great.

GRAY, Alan (1855–1935)
English organist and church music composer who succeeded Stanford as organist of Trinity College, Cambridge (1892–1930). His cantatas, organ and chamber music were widely performed in their day.

GREAVES, Thomas (fl. 1600)
Lutenist and composer of 15 songs 'to be sung to the Lute and Base Viol' and *Songs of Sadnesse for the Viols and Voyces* (1604).

GREENE, Maurice (1695–1755)
Organist of St. Paul's Cathedral in 1718, Composer to the Chapel Royal in 1727 and Professor of Music at Cambridge in 1730. His reputation as a composer depends on his *Forty Select Anthems* (1743). These include the well-known *Lord Let Me Know Mine End*. Towards the end of his life Greene started the collection that was to become Boyce's *Cathedral Music*.

GREGORY I 'The Great' (540–604)
Pope from 590, he is credited with the collection of the main corpus of Roman liturgical plainsong melodies (599) which included the recension of the earlier Ambrosian collection and perhaps the composition of certain texts. He was also responsible for the founding of the *Schola Cantorum* which trained liturgical singers and which provided musicians to accompany St. Augustine to England (597) where a similar school was founded at Canterbury.

GRETCHANINOV, Alexander (1864–1956)
Russian composer of operas and church music. He was a pupil of Rimsky-Korsakov and emigrated first to Paris and then in 1941 to New York where he wrote some children's operas. His musical style follows naturally from traditional 19th century harmony and neither counterpoint nor modernism attracted him. The *Domestic Liturgy* is a careful transcription of the Russian Orthodox service.

GRÉTRY, Andre Ernest Modeste (1741–1813)
Belgian operatic composer who trained as a church musician in Rome and eventually established himself in Paris from 1768 as the 'French Pergolesi'. His tragedies were less successful although *Richard Coeur-de-Lion* (1784) is said to be his best opera. After 1791 he wrote seven operas for Republican taste.

GRIEG, Edvard Hagerup (1843–1907)
Norwegian composer of Scottish extraction, well-known for his *Piano Concerto* (1879) and the incidental music to Ibsen's *Peer Gynt*. Grieg was trained at Leipzig and Copenhagen in the Mendelssohn tradition; it was not until 1866 that he became aware of Scandinavian folk music. He saw much of Liszt in Rome in 1870, his popularity in England beginning with his visit to a Philharmonic Concert in

1888. He was accompanied by his wife and both gave the first of many joint song recitals introducing his songs to a wide public. In spite of the success of the concerto and several sonatas, most of Greig's work reveals the taste of the miniaturist and depends on the unique way he combines 'Norwegian style' melodies (with their falling A-G sharp-E motif) with German romantic harmony. His music is, however, strongly individual, although its influence seems to have been confined to Delius and Percy Grainger.

GRIGNY, Nicolas de (1672–1703)
Organist of Rheims Cathedral and remembered for his *Pièces d'Orgue* (posthumously published in 1711) which were copied out by J.S. Bach in his youth; these pieces are still regularly played, being among the most attractive of the French classical period.

GROVLEZ, Gabriel (1879–1944)
French pianist, singing teacher and conductor of opera houses in Lisbon, Chicago and Paris. He is remembered for his symphonic poems, songs and such sophisticated piano music as *L'Almanach aux Images* (1911) based on poems by Klingsor.

GRUENBERG, Louis (1884–1964)
American composer of Russian extraction who trained as a pianist in Vienna and later under Busoni. His opera *Emperor Jones* (1933) uses some jazz idioms.

GUILMANT, Felix Alexandre (1837–1911)
Famous French organist and organ composer. He was active as an editor of old French music and as a teacher; his pupils included Dupré and Bonnet. Only isolated pieces from among his large output of eight sonatas and numerous liturgical pieces are still performed.

GURLITT, Cornelius (1820–1901)
Well-known as the composer of numerous piano pieces of limited technical standard used in musical examinations, but prominent in his lifetime as a German organist and operatic composer.

GURNEY, Ivor (1890–1937)
Distinguished English song writer. He was a pupil of Stanford and Vaughan Williams and showed early lyrical promise but never fully recovered from being wounded, gassed, and shell-shocked in the 1st World War. From 1922 he was a permanent inmate at Dartford Mental Hospital.

GYROWETZ, Adalbert (1763–1850)
Facile Bohemian composer of 30 operas, 40 ballets, 19 masses, 60 symphonies, 60 string quartets, 40 violin sonatas and many smaller pieces. In Paris several of his symphonies were taken to be by Haydn, and had to be claimed adamantly by Gyrowetz. He himself was friendly with both Mozart and Haydn but outlived the popularity of his works.

H

HABA, Alois (1893–1972)
Czech composer remembered for his use of quarter-tones in operas, choral, symphonic and chamber works. Besides several text-books on this subject, he designed new instruments especially to play his works and wrote for 8-tone and 12-tone systems. He also wrote diatonic and serial music — especially on 'social themes' after the 2nd World War.

HADLEY, Patrick (1899–1973)
English composer of vocal and choral music who was Professor of Music at Cambridge (1946–62). *The Trees So High* (1932) for baritone, chorus and large orchestra and *My Beloved Spake* (1936) for chorus and orchestra are still performed.

HAHN, Reynaldo (1875–1947)
A composer born in Venezuela but living in Paris from the age of three and a pupil of Massenet. After some precocious sonatas and symphonies, he was involved as composer and conductor of opera, operetta, ballet and incidental music. He is now remembered for his many charming songs.

HALÉVY, Jacques Francois (1799–1862)
French-Jewish composer of *La Juive* (1835) and about 20 other less successful operas. He was a pupil of Cherubini at the Paris Conservatoire and he himself taught Gounod and Bizet there.

HAMILTON, Iain (b. 1922)
Scottish composer and pianist resident first in London and then in the United States. He was trained at the RAM under William Alwyn and first attracted attention with his *Clarinet Quintet* (1949). His orchestral works include two symphonies, two piano concertos and several other concertos for various instruments, but he has written most readily for chamber combinations such as the 2nd String Quartet (1965).

HANDEL, George Frederick (1685–1759)
One of the two supreme Baroque composers, Handel showed outstanding musical gifts as a child in Saxony and student in law up to his 18th year. He was an organist at the cathedral at Halle, his home town, from 1702 until he left for Hamburg in the following year. In Hamburg he was employed as an (extra) violinist and then harpsichordist at the opera house under Keiser, and during this period four of his Italian operas were produced. The setting of the St. John Passion with German text also dates from this period.
In 1706 Handel left Hamburg for Italy where he studied the works of Carissimi, Alessandro Scarlati and Corelli. *Dixit Dominus*, one of three Latin Psalms appeared in Rome the following year, his opera *Rodrigo* (1707) was performed in Florence, the early serenata, *Acis and Galatea* (1708), in Naples and another successful opera *Agrippina* (1709) in Venice.
In early 1710 Handel was appointed Kapellmeister to the future King George I of England, who was then Elector of Hanover. George allowed him to visit London the same year and then again in 1712; from that date onwards England was his home. At that time in London, Italian opera had supplanted the older Purcellian tradition and Handel's earlier years there up to 1733 are remembered mainly for a series of operatic ventures, *Rinaldo* (1711) and *Giulio Cesare* (1724) being two of the better known of the 30 masterpieces of this period. At first these operas brought Handel triumphs and money (including a

Civil List pension of £600 p.a.) but his ventures were later threatened, first by rival enterprises under Bononcini and Ariosto, and then by the gradual change of taste epitomised by the satirical and racy *Beggar's Opera* (1728) arranged by Gay and Dr. Pepusch. Although the series of 46 Italian operas did not end until the year of *Messiah* (1741), Handel's finances remained unsettled between 1728 and 1738.
His other London activities, however, included court music: the *Utrecht Te Deum* (1713); the *Water Music* (c. 1716); the *Coronation Anthems* (1727) including *Zadok the Priest*; music for the Duke of Chandos (11 anthems 1717–19); and the pastoral cantata *Acis and Galatea* (1720). Most of the instrumental works, such as the 16 organ concertos and the 12 *Concerti Grossi* were published rather later, but the *Suites de Pièces* (1720) for harpsichord, and much of the chamber music belongs to this period.
Handel had already written his first English oratorio in 1720 (the first version of *Esther*) but it was not until 12 years later that the form became an important part of his professional life: *Deborah* (1733), *Alexander's Feast* (1736), *Israel in Egypt* (1737) led to the immortal *Messiah* (1742). Other similar works included *Samson* (1743), *Judas Maccabaeus* (1746), *Solomon* (1748), and *Jephtha* (1751). Long before this Handel had become the Protestant institution that was to dominate English music for a century and a half by its dramatic power, grandiose simplicity and moral dignity. With few exceptions, Handel's musical style remained firmly based on the *bel canto* tradition of Italy and the string idiom of Corelli, but he also summed up the religious aspirations of the English period. His emotional directness is largely due to the focus of the single 'affection' of each movement; it is quite different from the implied 'half-meaning' of the music of the next two centuries. Handel is still, perhaps, the most underrated of the world's musical geniuses.

HANDL, Jacob (Gallus) (1550–1591)
Austrian composer of the Venetian school of church music. He was a Cistercian monk and choirmaster in one of the churches in Prague from 1585. His motets were often in 8 and 12 parts and occasionally very chromatic.

HARRIS, Roy (b. 1898–1979)
American composer who has succeeded in intergrating a tonal and often polyphonic technique with recognisable elements of the American 20th century scene. He has written 11 symphonies, several concertos and chamber music works, besides many occasional orchestral and choral pieces.

HARRIS, William Henry (1883–1973)
Organist successively of New College and Christ Church Cathedral, Oxford and from 1933 to 1961 of St. George's Chapel, Windsor. Although his compositions included such major works as the *Hound of Heaven* (1919), he is now remembered for such fine anthems as *Faire is the Heavens* and for his liturgical music.

HARRISON, Julius (1885–1963)
English operatic and concert conductor who, after 1940, devoted himself exclusively to composing large-scale works, the best known of which is the *Mass in C* (1948).

HARTY, Hamilton (1879–1941)
Irish pianist, conductor and composer. He was already an organist at eight, and after moving to London in 1900, became a distinguished piano accompanist. His best known work is *The Mystic Trumpeter* (1913) a setting of Whitman for voices and orchestra.

HARWOOD, Basil (1859-1949)
English organist and composer. At Ely Cathedral and Christ Church, Oxford, he wrote Anglican church music which has survived, notably *O How Glorious is the Kingdom* and the *Service in A Flat*. The fine *Organ Sonata* in C sharp minor Op. 5 is still a regular repertoire piece.

HASSE, Johann Adolph (1699-1783)
German composer of over 100 Italian operas in the *bel canto* tradition, as well as many masses, oratorios, concertos and sonatas. He is now remembered for one or two arias in anthologies, especially the two arias from *Artaserse* (1730) which were sung each night for 10 years by the castrato Farinelli, to Philip V of Spain to ease his melancholia.

HASSLER, Hans Leo (1564-1612)
Nuremberg organist and composer of church music in the Venetian style. Much of his 'Italian' work is for as many as 12 voices, but he is now remembered mainly for the four-part settings of well-known chorale melodies (1607 and 1608). The Passion chorale *O Sacred Head Sore Wounded* was adapted from one of his compositions.

HATTON, John Liptrot (1809-1886)
English theatrical composer remembered for his song, *To Anthea*. He also wrote church music, oratorios and many partsongs. Two of his operas were produced in Vienna and at Covent Garden.

HAUER, Josef Mattias (1883-1959)
Austrian theorist and composer of atonal music though he remained quite uninfluenced by Schönberg. He derived his atonality from the harmonic series and some of the Tropes of 12 notes are treated like the melos in Greek music. His own compositions, often sounding like Scriabin or Satie, include two operas, two masses and varied chamber and orchestral works.

HAYDN, Joseph (1732-1809)
Great Austrian (or Croatian) composer of the Classical period. Haydn spent his childhood in the choir school of St. Stephen's, Vienna, where he also studied the keyboard and violin although he seems to have been largely self-taught as a composer. After his dismissal at 16 from St. Stephen's over a silly joke, he continued his musical self-education in straitened circumstances — 'I certainly had the gift, and by hard work I managed to get on'. The hard work included study of Fux's *Gradus* and C.P.E. Bach's first six clavier sonatas and his first (comic) opera (1752). Haydn's circle of friends widened and he became a member of his first aristocatic musical establishment where he applied the example of Emmanuel Bach to the wider field of the household string and wind group. This led to his appointment in 1761 to the musical establishment of Prince Esterházy where he was to remain for 30 years.
Prince Esterházy's musical establishment was soon considerably enlarged when his brother, Prince Paul Anton, and enthusiastic and enlightened music-lover, succeeded to power. In 1766 Haydn became sole conductor and moved with the court to the magnificent new palace at Esterház where the geographical isolation forced him 'to become original'.
Although Haydn was not the first to write quartets and symphonies, a regular supply of those new works was required and it is in these two media that his historical reputation was made. Although he had already written 18 so-called string quartets, they were rather in the nature of divertimenti, most being in five movements with two minuets (they were probably often performed with doubled strings and wind). By 1769 Haydn had produced nearly 50 symphonies, mostly in the 'stile galant' but, as his manuscripts testify, fashioned with consummate technique and infinite care. From this date his music becomes

more emotionally charged, his quartets more contrapuntal and his range of keys wider. In 1771 he showed himself aware of C.P.E. Bach's new *Sturm und Drang* movement with the six Op. 33 *Russian* quartets, written 'in an entirely new and special manner'. The same stylistic progress is to be found in his keyboard sonatas and church music, e.g. the *Stabat Mater* (1771). During Haydn's last decade at Esterház the flow of mature masterpieces continued. Besides such works as the *Seven Words from the Cross* (1785 — the so-called 'passion') and the *Oxford Symphony*, he provided for the Prince four more sets of quartets, many concertos — over 175 for him to play on the *baryton* (his favourite instrument) — and 13 operas for the Court theatre. By this time his reputation had spread throughout Europe, Mozart had dedicated his six quartets to Haydn and the older composer began to be influenced by the younger.

When Prince Esterházy died in 1790 Haydn moved to Vienna, and almost immediately agreed to visit London at the invitation of the violinist-impresario, Salomon. The six London Symphonies written for the 1791 visit together with a second set for the 1794 visit represent his supreme achievement in instrumental music. While he was in England he was inspired by one of the Handel commemoration festivals to continue his series of choral works; the immediate result was *The Creation* (1798) and the last six masses (including the *Nelson Mass*) of the same year.

Haydn is traditionally the senior of the group of great Viennese composers which included Mozart, Beethoven, and Schubert, and there can be little doubt of the direct influence of Haydn on the young Beethoven, although Haydn probably received as much from Mozart as he gave. The enormous range of his compositions has still not been appreciated by the 20th century in its entirety — his works are still being recovered and heard again by a new public. The *London Symphonies*, *Creation* and the *Emperor Quartet* retain their honoured place in the repertoire, although much of his magnificent output is only now receiving attention by recording companies.

HAYDN, Michael (1737-1806)

The younger brother of Joseph who followed him as soloist at St. Stephen's and became organist and conductor at the Salzburg court. Both Leopold and Wolfgang Mozart had high opinions of his compositions and the latter copied out some of his church music for performance in Vienna. Michael was inevitably overshadowed by his brother and at one point almost became an alcoholic, but his compositions — especially for the church — were always highly valued. Problems of authenticity led to the famous *Toy Symphony* being ascribed to Joseph.

HEAD, Michael (1900-1976)

English song composer, singer and pianist. At public events he often accompanied himself. He was active as an adjudicator at competitive festivals where his songs are still frequently heard.

HEDGES, Anthony (b. 1931)

English composer, active as pianist, conductor, critic and academic (since 1963 at Hull University). His large output covers many types of music including music for children and amateurs, light music, as well as film and incidental music. His recent works have included a symphony (1975), the oratorio *The Temple of Solomon* (1979), the opera *Shadows in the Sun* (1976) and a piano trio (1977).

HELLER, Stephen (1813-1888)

Hungarian pianist and composer who was friendly with Liszt and Chopin and was much admired both as teacher and performer. Of his 157 opus numbers of piano pieces only his easier 'teaching' pieces are still generally played.

HENRY VIII of England (1491–1547)
An able and enthusiastic musician who is credited with five four-part and 12 three-part songs, 14 pieces for three viols and two non-extant masses. The three-part ballad *Passetyme with Good Cumpanye* is his best known piece.

HENSCHEL, Sir George (1850–1934)
English baritone, composer, and conductor of mixed Polish-German descent. His compositions include large-scale religious works, three operas, several chamber works and song cycles. He was a friend of Brahms, a distinguished singing teacher, and was one of the first conductors of the Boston Symphony Orchestra. He was knighted in 1914.

HENSELT, Adolf von (1814–1889)
Bavarian pianist and composer. He was a pupil of Hummel and from 1838 was court pianist and teacher at St. Petersburg. He is remembered for his smaller piano pieces and many excellent studies.

HENZE, Hans Werner (b. 1926)
Distinguished German avant-garde composer whose eclectic style still puzzles his contemporaries. After absorbing the influences of Stravinsky, Hindemith and Blacher in the neo-classical 1st Symphony and the *Chamber Concerto*, he employed serial techniques in his first opera. In 1952 he emigrated to Italy and grafted on to his style the operatic lyricism of his adopted country, resulting in five further operas including *The Bassarids* (1966). Following this, his compositions were aimed at the popular sociological needs of Marxism, especially the régime in Cuba. His latest works have included a vast and brilliant 6th Symphony (1971) and several concertos and ballets.

HÉROLD, Louis Joseph Ferdinard (1791–1833)
French operatic composer who produced his first opera in 1815. Two symphonies and three string quartets were written in Italy, and on returning to Paris in 1816, 13 of his operas were produced. His most famous comic opera *Zampa* appeared in 1831 followed by *Le Pré aux Clercs* (1832). He died of consumption.

HERSCHEL, William (1738–1822)
German astronomer and musician who became Astronomer Royal to George III after discovering the planet Uranus. He came to England as an oboist in the band of the Hanoverian Guards, then became an organist in Bath where he wrote a symphony and two concertos.

HESELTINE, Philip (Peter Warlock) (1894–1930)
English composer, musical editor and writer. After Eton and a year at Oxford, he came under the influence of Delius and van Dieren, both of whom he helped by his journalism and arrangements. His work on early music included the English Ayre, Gesualdo, Locke and Purcell while his own compositions include *The Curlew Serenade for Delius's 60th Birthday*, and such exquisite songs as *Sleep* and *Yarmouth Fair*. It is possible he committed suicide.

HILLER, Ferdinand von (1811–1885)
German pianist, conductor, and composer who was on intimate terms with Chopin, Liszt, Rossini and Berlioz. His numerous compositions are in the Mendelssohn-Spohr tradition and include six operas, three symphonies, several concertos and chamber works. Only a few of his 30 smaller piano pieces are heard today.

HILTON, John (1560–1608)
Organist of Trinity College, Cambridge, whose madrigal *Fair Oriana* was included

in *The Triumphes of Oriana* (1601). The popular anthem *Lord for Thy Tender Mercies' Sake* (once ascribed to Farrant) was probably by him and his seven-part *Call to Rememberance* is still in the cathedral repertoire.

John II (1599–1657)
Organist of St. Margaret's Westminster and composer of *Ayres or Fa-las for Three Voices* (1627). He also wrote church and consort music, and *Catch that Catch Can, or A Choice Collection of Catches, Rounds and Canons for Three or Four Voyces*, (1652).

HINDEMITH, Paul (1895–1963)
Prolific German composer and many-sided executant. At 21 he was leader of the orchestra of the Frankfurt opera house and soon became a virtuoso viola player, touring with a string quartet until 1929. He was also a good pianist and competent player of all orchestral and several early instruments. As a composer, he seems to have been largely self-taught, at first working through the late Romantic influences of Brahms, Strauss and Reger, but later (1918) adapting a more linear and dissonant style. He always composed at high speed and the neo-classical climate of the 1920's encouraged his facile craftsmanship and the concept of *Gebrauchsmusik* — 'music for use'. From this period date the seven *Kammermusik* works (mostly concertos for different combinations) and a satirical, jazz-like, one-act opera which, together with his 'back to Bach' counterpoint and extended tonality theories, gave him the reputation of an *enfant terrible*.
In 1927 Hindemith joined the teaching staff of the Berlin Conservatoire and his brilliant reputation as a performer and teacher was only dimmed by the organised opposition of the Nazi Party led by Goebbels and Hitler himself. The spate of educational *Gebrauchsmusik* had to be dropped in favour of commissions such as the *Philharmonic Concerto* (1932). His best-known work, the opera *Mathis der Maler*, was not produced until 1938 in Switzerland; the symphony of the same title appeared in 1934. His exile from Germany started with three years of concert tours and then, from 1940 to 1953, he was a professor at Yale University. Here he became involved in much practical research into early music which clearly influenced his later works.
His compositions during this period included first the huge series of sonatas for almost every instrument, and such concertos as the one written for Benny Goodman (for clarinet and orchestra). His earlier handbook on musical composition, together with his contrapuntal approach, found expression in *Ludus Tonalis* (1943), a kind of 20th century version of *The '48'*. The heavy series of professional engagements and new compositions continued after his return to Europe in the last decade of his life resulting in an opera on the life of the astronomer Kepler, *Die Harmonie der Welt* (1957) and the final a capella *Mass* (1963).
It would be idle to claim that the whole of this immense outlay has become part of the regular repertoire, but it is certainly true that Hindemith's place as the leading German composer of the 20th century has never been more secure. From the second *Trio* (1933) consummate craftmanship and vibrant musicality are rarely absent from his music.

HODDINOTT, Alun (b. 1929)
Prolific Welsh composer and Professor of Music at the University of South Wales. His compositions include several symphonies, 10 concertos for various instruments, music based on folk music and some chamber works. His romantic textures are rarely tonal, and his musical style owes much to his rhythmic originality.

HOFFMAN, Ernest Theador Amadeus (1776–1822)
German writer and composer (although a civil servant for most of his life) he wrote several operas of which *Undine* (1816) was most successful. His writings are marked by fantasy and humour. His inspiration comes from various sources, including Weber, Schumann and Offenbach.

HOLBORNE, Anthony (d. 1602)
English composer who published 57 pieces for the cittern in 1597, and 65 consort pieces two years later.

HOLBROOKE, Joseph Charles (1878–1958)
Successful English composer of orchestral and chamber music together with several operas and ballets often on Celtic themes and sometimes in Wagnerian style. The orchestral variations on *Three Blind Mice* are still popular.

HOLLINS, Alfred (1865–1942)
Blind English pianist and organist whose colourful organ compositions, once very popular, are still played.

HOLMES, John (fl. 1605)
English organist of Winchester Cathedral who contributed a madrigal to *The Triumphes of Oriana*.

HOLST, Gustav Theodore (1874–1934)
English composer of Swedish descent. His early training was in amateur circles in Gloucestershire and later as a composition pupil of Stanford at the RCM. As a result of neuritis he became a professional trombonist, but for a time was a pianist-repetiteur with Carl Rosa Opera Company as well as organist at Covent Garden. From 1903 his professional activities veered towards teaching, especially at St. Paul's Girls' School and Morley College ('for working men and women'). His compositions soon showed the influence of the Hindu epics in the opera *Savitri* (1908) and the cold intensity of the *Rig-Veda* seemed to accentuate his leaning towards thin, clear textures. The earlier influence of folk music in the *Cotswold Symphony* (1902) continued through his life, not least in his friendship with Vaughan Williams. These aspects of his style were brought together in the ever-popular suite *The Planets* (1915). His great *Hymn of Jesus* (1917) showed a kind of cerebral mysticism and a movement towards linear writing and novel rhythmic frameworks. This composition also shows plainsong added to his eclectic style. The stark and bare quality of *Egdon Heath* (1927), based on Hardy, seems to sum up the spiritual isolation of his last decade but also exemplifies the intensity and mastery of his technique.

HONEGGER, Arthur (1892–1955)
Swiss composer whose life was mainly spent in France. His early works, influenced by Debussy and Ravel, were sufficiently striking for him to be hailed in 1920 by the critic Henri Collet as a worthy member of 'Les Six'. His apparent interest in the common things of life and in the unpretentious aesthetic of Satie proved to be misleading and the influence of Stravinsky led to the famous *Pacific 231*, a sound picture of a steam locomotive (1923). The oratorio *King David* (1921) was far removed from the satirical modernism of 'Les Six' and *Joan of Arc at the Stake* (1938) emphasized his seriousness of intent.
Much of Honegger's work was for the theatre, ballet, radio and films although five symphonies date from 1931, 1942, 1946, 1947 and 1951. His songs and chamber music appeared at intervals between the two World Wars.

HOOK, James (1746–1827)
English song writer associated with Vauxhall Pleasure Gardens. Among his 2,000 songs and glees, *Sweet Lass of Richmond*

Hill has remained popular.

HOPKINS, Anthony (b. 1921)
English composer and personality. He has been particularly successful as a writer and radio speaker about music and his activities have covered educational work and conducting. Among his smaller pieces are several operas, the most popular of which is *Three's Company*.

HOPKINS, Edward John (1818–1901)
English organist and composer of hymns and church music. He was a pupil of Walmisley and organist of the Temple Church for 55 years. He also wrote extensively about the organ, and edited several collections of madrigals.

HOROVITZ, Joseph (b. 1926)
Composer who emigrated from Vienna to England in 1938, was educated in Oxford, at the RCM and under Nadia Boulanger. His early musical activities included work as a pianist and conductor of incidental and ballet music, and later of London orchestras. He has written several concertos for different instruments, notably one for euphonium/bassoon with brass band, five string quartets and music for children and jazz groups, besides choral works such as *Samson* (1977) also with brass band.

HOVHANESS, Alan (b. 1911)
Prolific American composer of Armenian descent who was for a time organist of the Armenian cathedral in Boston, Mass. Practically all his music before the 2nd World War has been withdrawn and destroyed and his reputation was made in this 'Armenian' period up to 1948. His interests widened geographically to include Eastern music of India and Japan. Amongst his many commissions *Mysterious Mountain* (1959) is best known in America and is remarkable for its unfashionable melodiousness and harmonic concordance. The *Magnificat* (1959) has been equally popular and includes the 'free buzzing' of string writing *senza misura*. He has written for almost all combinations; works include 15 symphonies and several concertos.

HOWELLS, Herbert (1892–1983)
English composer who became a composition pupil of Stanford after earlier experience at Gloucester Cathedral. His early works include a piano concerto, piano quartet and a prize-winning *Phantasy String Quartet*. After joining the RCM teaching staff, his works tended to be in a recognisably national style while his activities included teaching (in succession to Holst) at St. Paul's Girls' School from 1936, and much adjudicating. From the outbreak of war to three years later, his compositions were more identified with cathedral music and choral societies. *Hymnus Paradisi* has proved a popular work and the long series of settings of the Anglican canticles from *Howells in G* (1919) through to the services for King's College Cambridge, Gloucester, New College Oxford, Canterbury, St. John's Cambridge, St. Paul's Worcester, Westminster Abbey, St. George's Chapel Windsor, York and Hereford are unique and unparalleled even by 18th century standards. His organ compositions too are remarkable in their fastidious integrity and the many songs are still regularly heard. The orchestral works have been less successful, but Howells' rich style is a true part of the English 20th century tradition, even if the spiritual timelessness can occasionally become rather static and amorphous.

HUMFREY, Pelham (1647–1674)
English Restoration composer who was one of the 'first generation' of choirboys at the Chapel Royal. Together with Blow and Turner he was chosen by 'Captain Cooke', and later sent to study abroad at

the expense of King Charles II. He returned to England and was, according to Pepys, 'a regular monsieur'. He became royal lutenist, and from 1667 a Gentleman of the Chapel Royal.

Apart from some songs and stage music, all his extant compositions are for the church. He was largely responsible for the introduction into England of Lulli's string sinfonias into the verse anthem, as in *By the Waters of Babylon*.

HUMMEL, Johann Nepomuk (1778–1837)

Hungarian pianist, conductor and composer. His first public appearance was at the age of 10 with Mozart, and the following year he made a triumphant tour as a piano virtuoso. As the teacher of Liszt, and as the acknowledged rival of Beethoven as an improviser, he was largely responsible for the new 19th century style of pianistic virtuosity; in 1828 he systematised his teaching in his famous *Klavierschule*. He was less successful as a *Kapellmeister*, but his various posts included Eisenstadt (Prince Esterházy) and Weimar. He left 12 stage works, three masses and a lot of tasteful and often delicate chamber music.

Besides occasional performances of his several piano concertos, and his many brilliant solo pieces, his trumpet concerto is now deservedly popular.

HUMPERDINCK, Engelbert (1854–1921)

German operatic composer remembered for *Hänsel und Gretel* (1893). After leaving the Cologne Conservatory, he met Wagner in Naples and returned with him to Bayreuth to help in the first production of *Parsifal* (1880–1881). As a result of this experience, Humperdinck rewrote the simple setting of Grimm's story using Wagnerian techniques but keeping the charm of the catchy children's songs. The opera was immediately popular but never again paralleled. Humperdinck spent most of his later years as a professor in Berlin.

HURLSTONE, William Yeates (1876–1906)

English pianist and composer of distinguished chamber music; sonatas for cello, clarinet, and bassoon are still performed. His early death was due to asthma.

I

IBERT, Jacques (1890–1962)
French composer trained at the Paris Conservatoire who lived in Rome from 1937 to 1955 later becoming the Director of the Paris Opéra and Opéra-Comique (for two years). His compositions are mostly light, fastidious, and in the Impressionist tradition. He is remembered especially for the short piano piece *The Little White Donkey* from *Histoires*, but also wrote several operas, ballets, works for orchestra such as *Divertissement* (1930), a *Flute Concerto*, chamber music and songs.

INDY, Vincent d' (1851–1931)
See *D'Indy*.

INGEGNERI, Marco Antonio (1547–1592)
Italian church composer, from 1572 choirmaster of Cremona cathedral. His 27 *Responsoria* for Holy Week were until recently attributed to Palestrina; other works are two books of masses and three books of motets. Monteverdi was at one time a pupil of his.

IRELAND, John Nicholson (1879–1962)
English composer born into a literary family and trained at the RCM under Stanford. From 1904 until 1926 he was organist of St. Luke's, Chelsea where he wrote *Greater Love Hath No Man* (1912) and the *Service in F* (1907–20). Although he wrote the later *Service in C* (1941), church music never became his most characteristic medium. His reputation grew from the *Phantasy Trio* (1908), the piano piece *Island Spell* (1912), and the immensely popular song *Sea Fever* (1913). The important *Piano Sonata* (1920) and several successful chamber and orchestral works culminated in the magnificent *Piano Concerto* (1930), the *Legend* for piano and orchestra (1933) and the cantata *These Things Shall Be* (1937).
Throughout his life the flow of songs and small piano pieces (such as *Rosemary*) continued. He wrote over 20 'school-songs' for unison and two-part choir, and several very popular unaccompanied part-songs. Ireland was a highly successful teacher of composition, his pupils including Moeran, Searle and Britten. His musical style seems to be inspired by pre-history and post-Romantic poetry such as Housman, the chromaticism of Scriabin, and the sophistication of French textures. In a generation that included Holst and Vaughan Williams, he was a leading English composer and did much to release British music from its Germanic traditions.

ISAAC, Heinrich (1450–1517)
Although regarded as the first great German composer (through his parentage), Isaac's life and musical output are international. From Flanders he entered into service with Lorenzo de' Medici ('The Magnificent') in Florence. In 1496 he was appointed court composer at Innsbruck by the Emperor Maximilian while his later life was spent mainly in Florence. He set several of Lorenzo's texts — 22 German, five French, 10 Italian and five Latin secular poems; he left 58 instrumental pieces in three-five parts (including the four-part setting of *Innsbruck, ich muss dich lassen*, later adapted to *O World, I Now Must Leave Thee*) and 29 pieces of Hausmusik. His church music included 23 masses, 49 motets and the monumental *Choralis Costantinus* which contained 58 'Offices' for the whole ecclesiastical year.

IVES, Charles (1874–1954)
Influential American composer whose

background was the small town atmosphere of New England. Main influences were Emerson and Thoreau, the town band directed by his father and hymn tunes, often 'wrongly' harmonised. The urge to experiment aurally withstood the academic influence of Yale, and Ives' music never found the stylistic integration expected in the European concert hall. He soon became a successful businessman and an assiduous amateur composer of startling originality; as a consequence many of his works waited many years for their first performance. (The 2nd Symphony (1901) for instance, with its strange mixture of Beethoven, Dvorák and New England, was first heard only in 1951.) Since 1950 Ives has become a cult figure as a representative of genuine American music and the 3rd and 4th Symphonies, the *Concord Sonata* for piano, the 114 songs, and *The Unanswered Question* for chamber orchestra have become generally known, if not universally popular. Many of Ives' modernities such as dissonant linear counterpoint, polytonality, polyrhythms and tone clusters have become standard techniques since 1950, though the difficulties in performing his works still make many of them a serious challenge.

J

JACKSON, Francis (b. 1917)
English organist and composer of church music and organ music. He was organist of York Minster (1946–82) and has written successfully both for his own instrument and for the Anglican rite; the *Toccata, Hymn and for Fugue* and the *Communion Service in G* are well known.

JACKSON, William (1730–1803)
English organist and composer known for his *Te Deum in F* which has only disappeared from cathedral lists relatively recently. He was organist at Exeter cathedral, a composer of ballad-operas and harpsichord sonatas and was responsible for some anthems and services. He was also a minor landscape painter.

JACOB, Gordon (b. 1895)
English composer and teacher. He was a pupil of Stanford and after early experience in conducting and teaching theory, he became an acknowledged expert on orchestration, both by virtue of his text-books and his facility in the well-known radio show ITMA. His own compositions are marked by clarity of texture and natural flow. His orchestral works include two symphonies (1929 and 1944), a sinfonietta (1942), and several suites and concertos of which perhaps that for trombone is best known.

JANÁCĚK, Leŏs (1854–1928)
Czech composer from northern Moravia on the Polish border who was brought up in amateur musical circles and later in the atmosphere of church music at the Augustinian monastery of Brno. He became distinguished as a singer, pianist, and organist in Prague (1874–76) and then in 1878 and 1879 moved on to Leipzig and Vienna. On his return to Brno the next year he became involved in Moravian folk music and became active as the founding director of the Brno Organ School from 1881 to 1919. He was less successful with his compositions, both in gaining recognition and finding his own individual style.
It was not until 1904, when *Jenufa* was triumphantly produced in Brno that he became thoroughly committed to composition, and not until the opera's belated success in Prague in 1916 that he became a major figure in Czech music. From then on his youthful revolutionary spirit took no account of age: the romantic *Mr. Broucek's Excursions* (1914) showed a new angularity and bite. The fiery, pantheistic *Glagolithic Mass* (1926) and the brilliant *Sinfonietta* (1926) belong more to the world of Stravinsky than Dvorák, while his 10 operas culminated in *From the House of the Dead* (1928) where the primitive harshness of Dostoievsky is musically realised, and a new economy of texture is added to the jerky rhythmic vitality of a truly 20th century composer.

JANNEQUIN, Clement (c. 1475–1560)
French composer of chansons, little of whose life is known. The *Chansons* are in four parts and often of a descriptive and imitative nature as in *La Chant des Oiseaux*, *La Bataille* and *La Chausse*. His only church music consists of two masses, each based on one of his chansons, and the late settings of the Proverbs and Psalms in French. On the basis of these last works, it has been suggested that Jannequin became a Huguenot towards the end of his life.

JÄRNEFELT, (Edvard) Armas (1869–1958)
Naturalised Swedish conductor and com-

poser of Finnish birth. He was Director in turn of the Opera Houses at Helsinki and Stockholm. He is remembered almost entirely for the charming orchestral *Praeludium* and the *Berceuse*. Järnefelt was the brother-in-law of Sibelius.

JEFFRIES, George (d. 1685)
English composer of church music. He was a Gentleman of the Chapel Royal and organist to Charles I at Oxford during the Civil War, and left a large quantity of English church music (mostly with a basso continuo). Some stage works, several 'symphonies' for five-part strings and some instrumental three-part fantasias are also extant.

JENKINS, John (1592–1678)
Lutenist and violist to Charles I and Charles II. He composed 19 five-part fantasias in the 'old' English style, many lighter string pieces which he called *Rants* (and which helped to form Restoration taste), and *12 Sonatas for Two violins and a Base with Thorough Base for the Organ or Theorbo* (1660); these were the first English trio sonatas. Other works included songs, rounds and popular tunes in Playford's *Musick's Handmaid* (1678).

JENSEN, Adolf (1837–1879)
German song writer in the Schumann tradition. He wrote about 160 songs and some shorter piano pieces which are still performed.

JEUNE, Claude le (1528–1600)
Franco-Belgian composer of metrical psalms. Besides this Huguenot activity, he also wrote chansons, madrigals, motets and instrumental fantasias.

JIŔAK, Karel Boleslav (1891–1972)
Czech conductor and Musical Director of the Czech Radio from 1930 to 1945 who moved to the USA in 1948. His works include five symphonies, some chamber music and song-cycles.

JOACHIM, Josef (1831–1907)
Great Austro-Hungarian violinist of Jewish extraction and friend and disciple of Brahms. Besides providing models of interpretation in the classics for succeeding generations, he was active as a conductor and composer. His works are in the Schumann tradition and include several violin concertos and overtures, and cadenzas to most of the standard violin concertos (up to Brahms).

JOHNSON, Robert (c. 1583–1633)
English composer and lutenist to James I from 1604 until his death. The ayres which he wrote for plays performed at the Blackfriars and Globe theatres are his best-known works. Two of the most popular written for this medium are *Where the bee sucks* and *Full fathom five*, written for *The Tempest* in 1611.

JOHNSON, Robert Sherlaw (b. 1932)
English pianist, scholar and composer. After training at Durham University and RAM, he was a pupil of Nadia Boulanger and attended some of Messiaën's classes at the Paris Conservatoire. His book on Messiaën (1975) is a standard work, and he has been prominent in performances of Messiaën's music. He has held academic posts at Leeds, York and Oxford Universities.
His own music is marked by rhythmic luxuriance and atmospheric sonorities e.g. the two piano sonatas (1963 and 1967) and the two chamber pieces, *Triptych* (1973) and *Quintet* (1974). He has also written for the voice, electronic tape and piano in *The Praises of Heaven and Earth* (1969) and *Green Whispers of Gold* (1971) as well as more conventional choral combinations. *Anglorum Feriae* (1977) is a larger-scale cantata and *The Lambton Worm* (1978) is his first opera.

JOLIVET, André (1905–1974)
French composer, a pupil of Varèse and

with Messiaën a member of the group *La Jeune France* (1936). Apart from touring as a conductor and lecturer, he was Musical Director of the Comédie Française from 1945 to 1959. He has written an opera, two ballets, incidental and radio music, although most of his works are for orchestral and chamber combinations as in *Suite Delphique* for wind, ondes martenot, harp and percussion (1942).

JONES, Robert (fl. 1610)
English lutenist and composer who contributed to *The Triumphes of Oriana* and published his *First Set of Madrigals of 3, 4, 5, 6, 7 and 8-parts, for Viols and Voices or Voices alone; or as you please* (1607). His lute songs are in five books of ayres (1600 to 1611) and he is known to have been involved from 1610 to 1615 in training the 'Children of the Revels to the Queene within Whytefryars'. Otherwise, little is known of his life. He must not be confused with the Robert Jones who was present with the Chapel Royal at the 'Field of the Cloth of Gold' (1520). He also composed a mass and magnificat.

JONGEN, Joseph (1873–1953)
Belgian pianist, organist and composer, widely travelled and resident in England 1914–19, but from 1925 active as a conductor in Brussels. His compositions include several concertos, a considerable amount of chamber music and works for the piano and organ, of which the organ *Sonata Eroica* (1930) is still heard.

JOSEPHS, Wilfred (b. 1927)
English composer of film and television music, who has also written three symphonies, several concertos, chamber and ensemble music.

JOSQUIN DES PRÉS (c. 1440–1521)
The greatest of the Flemish composers of the early Renaissance. He is said to have been a pupil of Okeghem and to have been primarily concerned in his earlier style with absorbing and refining the canonic techniques of his master. Smooth expressive vocal lines and euphonious vertical harmonies in comparison with those of Okeghem are features of his works. From 1486 to 1494 he was a member of the Papal Chapel in Rome, later in the service of Louis XII of France and finally Provost of Condé. His later works were widely recognised as unsurpassed examples of Renaissance balance and inspiration and were eclipsed only by the generation of Lassus, Victoria and Palestrina; the 20th century revival of his music is still only in its infancy. Josquin's prolific output includes three books of masses, more than 100 motets and many secular chansons.

JOUBERT, John (b. 1927)
South African composer involved academically in England. He has written important works for the Anglican rite including the popular *O Lorde, the Maker of Alle Thinges*, and has also produced a symphony and concertos for piano and violin.

K

KABALEVSKY, Dmitri (b. 1904)
After a liberal education, Kabalevsky trained in mathematics and then in the early years of the Russian Revolution became a composition student of Miaskovsky. His early works are for the piano: between 1927 and 1929 he wrote his first Piano Sonata, String Quartet and the Piano Concerto. All three pieces are influenced by the chromaticism of Scriabin, and established the composer in the Soviet Union.
In the 1930's Kabalevsky became identified with the political ideology of the period although he did not join the Communist Party until 1940. He was also prominent as a writer and teacher. Much of his musical output was in incidental music for the stage, radio and films, but this decade saw his first three symphonies and 2nd Piano Concerto; most of these works had political programmes. His first opera, *Colas Breugnon* (1938) has a socialist theme and is written in the style of French popular music.
After the outbreak of the 2nd World War his music aimed to represent the strivings of the Russian people in such works as *The People's Avengers* (1942). The policy of socialist realism has led to such sunny works as the *Violin Concerto* (1948) and *Piano Concerto* (1952), which are repertoire pieces in the USSR. More recent works include *Leninists* (1959) and *Three Songs of the Cuban Revolution* (1963); both are recognised as typical of the composer's maturity. In Europe Kabalevsky is better known for his non-programmatic works such as the 2nd Symphony and the many children's pieces such as the early *Sonatina*, the songs for children's choir, and *The Little Puppets*.

KALKBRENNER, Friedrich Wilhelm (1785–1849)
German pianist, teacher, and composer of several operas, symphonies, piano sonatas and concertos. He is remembered now for his smaller piano pieces and famous teaching 'method'.

KARG-ELERT, Sigfrid (1877–1933)
German pianist, organist and (mainly) organ composer. He is unusual in writing extensively for the harmonium, only discovering the organ via this instrument. His forte as a composer was in miniature impressionist pieces which often combine extreme chromaticism and romantic colour, with baroque contrapuntal techniques. His large-scale works are generally ignored nowadays but his 66 Chorale Improvisations, Op. 65 and Op. 66, are still often played.

KEISER, Reinhard (1674–1739)
German composer of operas and oratorios. Most of his life was spent in Hamburg attempting to establish German opera. Mattheson says that his 'smooth and graceful' melodies fell upon the ear 'like charmed accents after the dull pedantries of the contrapuntists of the day'. From 1704 to 1728 he often averaged four operas each year. His oratorios date mainly from his last decade and include a famous setting of the *Brockes Passion.*

KELLY, Bryan (b. 1934)
English composer, trained at Oxford, at RCM, and under Nadia Boulanger. Besides several relatively short orchestral and band pieces, he has written extensively for chorus, children and church, including the major *Stabat Mater* (1970) and *Let There be Light* (1973).

KELWAY, Thomas (d. 1749)

English organist and composer of church music. He was organist of Chichester Cathedral from 1726, but is now only remembered for his *Evening Service in B minor*.

KENT, James (1700–1776)
English organist of Trinity College, Cambridge, and Winchester Cathedral and College. At the end of his life 12 pleasing but mediocre anthems were published, of which *Hear my Prayer* became very popular.

KERLL, Johann Kaspar (1627–1693)
German organist and composer first in Munich and then at St. Stephen's, Vienna. His numerous operas have not survived but several masses have been found in manuscript and a number of organ and harpsichord works have been published in modern times.

KERN, Jerome David (1885–1945)
American popular composer, remembered for *Sally* (1920), *Sunny* (1925) and especially for *Show Boat* (1927), with its bass solo *Ol'Man River*, which had a long run in various American cities and at Drury Lane. His fluent melodic flair and elegant craftsmanship are also evident in his many film scores.

KETÈLBEY, Albert (1875–1959)
English composer, who was director of Colombia Gramophone Company and music editor for Chappell. He had a tremendous success with his popular songs, especially *In a Monastery Garden*. He also wrote a comic opera, a *Concertstück* for piano and orchestra and a piano quintet.

KHATCHATURIAN, Aram (1903–1978)
Soviet composer of Armenian origin. His music studies started in Moscow when he was 20 and he soon showed his fascination with bright oriental colours and rhythms, together with an awareness of Debussy and Ravel. This involvement with his cultural origins in Armenia continued throughout his life.
Larger works such as his *Piano Concerto* (1936) and the popular *Violin Concerto* (1940) led to recognition abroad as well as in the USSR. The more aggressive idiom of the 2nd Symphony (1943) and *Cello Concerto* (1946) led to official censure in the Party Decree of 1948.
Gradually he became more involved as a teacher in Moscow, as a composer of film scores and as an international conductor. His ballet *Spartacus* (1956) is generally hailed in the USSR as his masterpiece.

KING, Charles (1687–1748)
English singer, organist, and composer. He followed Jeremiah Clark at St. Paul's Cathedral as choirmaster (with Maurice Greene as organist). His tuneful Services in F and C led to Greene's comment that King was a serviceable man. Both these settings remained popular well into the 20th century.

KIRBYE, George (d. 1634)
English madrigal composer. In 1597 he published the *First Fruites of My Poore Knowledge in Musicke*, 24 madrigals in four, five and six voices. He contributed to the *Triumphes of Oriana* in 1601. *Vox in Rama* is still in the liturgical repertoire.

KNUSSEN, Oliver (b. 1952)
The son of a professional double-bass player who was educated at the Menuhin School, where his 1st Symphony was written. Two further symphonies followed, the 3rd (1979) being especially successful. He has recently been prominent as a conductor.

KODÁLY, Zoltán (1882–1967)
Hungarian nationalist composer. He went to Budapest in 1900 and worked his way

through the influences of Brahms and Debussy before finding his musical salvation in the scientific collection (with Bartók) of Hungarian folk music. His early works up to 1922 attracted little notice and he was suspended from the Budapest Academy from 1919 to 1922 for revolutionary sympathies.

Psalmus Hungaricus (1922) established him while the increasingly personal language of Bartók tended to alienate public support. *Hary János* followed in 1925 and two sets of dances — *Marosszék* (1930) and *Galanta* (1933) — led to the *Concerto for Orchestra* (1940). During the 2nd World War Kodály managed to stay in Hungary and retain his dignity under the Nazis; from this period comes the almost Italianate but deeply moving *Missa Brevis* (1944).

Kodály's educational compositions have had a far-reaching influence, both in Hungary and more recently in England, through their emphasis on unaccompanied singing.

KOECHLIN, Charles (1867–1950)

French composer who was a pupil of Massenet and Fauré at the Paris Conservatoire. He was first known as a composer of songs but from 1920 onwards he produced much neo-classical orchestral and chamber music in an individual but limited style. Several of his critical and pedagogic works are still widely consulted. He shares with Roussel and d'Indy the unusual distinction of exercising more influence on his pupils than on the public at large.

KREBS, Johann Ludwig (1713–1780)

German organist and composer — the best known of Bach's pupils. Besides some large-scale Lutheran settings, he wrote effective works for his own instrument of which the *Fantasia and Fugue in G* is still played, and works for clavier and flute.

KREISLER, Fritz (1875–1962)

Famous Austrian violinist and composer. In 1888 he gave up his brilliant touring career to study medicine and art and was later commissioned into the Austrian Army. He resumed his musical career in 1899 and made a brilliant debut in London in 1901. After several visits, he lived in New York from 1915 to 1924 and eventually returned to Europe in 1938 as a French citizen.

As a player he recorded the 'standard' performance of such works as Beethoven's Violin Concerto and as a composer he is remembered for many deft and light works such as *Caprice Viennois* and *Liebesfreud.* He also made many arrangements of earlier composers such as Martini and Pugnani. (Many of these published transcriptions were acknowledged as original pastiches by Kreisler.) His operetta *Apple Blossoms* enjoyed wide popularity in 1919.

KŘENEK, Ernest (b. 1900)

Austrian composer, who after writing several impressive late Romantic works under Schreker in Vienna and Berlin, was attracted to the atonal world of Schönberg. He was also influenced by Bartók and Mahler (his father-in-law). He was involved in opera and after several pioneering ventures (including jazz) he produced the famous *Jonny Spielt Auf* (1927); this story of a black jazz violinist and white woman is in a mixed style and aroused much hostility especially among the Nazis. Since then he has not managed to repeat its undeniable popular success. He returned to Austria in the 1930's and became more deeply immersed in the serial techniques of Berg and Webern, continuing to compose prolifically in this style after his move to America in 1938. His instrumental works include six symphonies, four piano concertos, seven string quartets, sonatas, and concertos for several other instruments.

KREUTZER, Rodolphe (1766–1831)

French violinist and composer, remembered as the *dedicaté* of Beethoven's most famous violin sonata (though he is said not to have played it). He wrote more than 40 operas and ballets, but it is with his 40 *Etudes ou Caprices pour le Violon* that his fame rests. These pieces are still the basis of modern string technique and are fluent and musical in their conception and workmanship.

KUHLAU, Friedrich (1786-1832)
German flautist and composer. He wrote six popular operas in Copenhagen where he had fled to avoid conscription in Napoleon's army. His many works for two, three and four flutes, and for flute with other instruments, are almost equalled in popularity by his piano sonatinas.

KUHNAU, Johann (1660-1722)
Bach's predecessor as Cantor of St. Thomas, Leipzig, and famous for his set of biblical sonatas for the clavier (he is said to be the first to write three-movement sonatas for the instrument). He was very interested in literature and published translations from five languages. His church music — largely based on chorales — enjoyed wide popularity in its day.

KULLAK, Theodor (1818-1882)
German pianist and pupil of Czerny. Apart from his didactic work *Octave School*, which is still used, his compositions are mainly of salon type, but include many transcriptions, and a *Grand Concerto* in C minor (Op. 55).

L

LALANDE, Michel Richard de (1657–1726)
French composer of church music at the court of Louis XIV where he first taught the King's daughters, then was appointed master of chamber music and lastly (in three month spells with three others) Director of the Royal Chapel. His music consists mainly of 42 motets with orchestral accompaniment, and some ballet music for the court.

LALO, Édouard (1823–1892)
French composer of Spanish antecedents, now remembered mainly for *Symphonie Espagnole* (1875) — the result first of his activities as an orchestral and chamber viola player, and secondly of the inspiration from the famous Spanish violinist Sarasate. In 1876 he began his opera *Le Roi d'Ys*. The success of the opera in Paris, where it was staged in 1888, was enormous, but it has never been in the international repertoire. Apart from his skilful orchestration, Lalo was considered to have combined the colourful French tradition with some of the externals of Wagner's structural technique.

LAMBERT, Constant (1905–1951)
English composer, conductor and critic, famous for *The Rio Grande* (1929) which uses jazz idioms in a setting of Sacheverell Sitwell for chorus, piano and orchestra. Lambert had earlier become involved with ballet at the invitation of Diaghilev, and *Horoscope* (1938) has had several subsequent revivals. Perhaps his most striking work was *Summer's Last Will and Testament* (1936), subtitled 'a masque'. As a writer, he produced the well-known *Music Ho!* (1934). This work is marked by an imaginative and entertaining sparkle, though the writer has proved to be far from the avant-garde group with which he was identified in the 1920's.

LAMBERT, John (b. 1926)
English composer and teacher who trained at RAM and RCM and under Nadia Boulanger in Paris. After four years as Director of Music at the Old Vic, he began his influential teaching of composition at RCM (1963). His own compositions have become progressively more experimental and perhaps owe something to Lutoslawski and Ligeti. His recent *Seasons* (1982) is unusual in requiring a full orchestra; most of his works tend to be for small combinations, like *The Golden Sequence* (1966) which is for two voices, organ and strings and *Sea Change* (1981) for chamber ensemble and electronics.

LAMPE, John Frederick (1703–1751)
An orchestral bassoonist of German origin who became one of John Wesley's converts and who set many of Charles Wesley's hymns. He had previously written stage music and songs for London theatres.

LANDINO (Landini), Francesco (c. 1325–1397)
Famous blind Italian composer of the Ars Nova period. He was a noted poet and player on the lute and portative organ. He spent most of his life in Florence.

LANIER (Lanière), Nicholas (c. 1588–1666)
English singer, composer and painter of French extraction, who was in the service of the Prince of Wales from 1604 and of the King from 1626. He composed music for the flute and wrote masques with Campion and Ben Jonson (in one of these last he is said to have introduced the new Italian

style recitativo into England).
Charles I also commissioned Lanier to buy pictures for him in Italy and as a portrait painter, but he spent most of the Commonwealth period in the Low Countries. He was reinstated as Master of the King's Music in 1660. He composed New Year Songs in 1663 and 1665 and songs by him are found in several publications of the decade.

LARSSON, Lars Erik (b. 1908)
Swedish composer, critic and professor, who has held a series of influential musical posts in Stockholm and Uppsala. His works include symphonies (1928, 1936, 1945), several concertos, an opera and chamber music.

LASSUS, Orlandus (Orlando di Lasso) (c. 1532–1594)
Great Flemish composer who, with Palestrina, marks the climax of the High Renaissance. He was cosmopolitan both in his life and compositions holding posts in Rome, Antwerp and Munich besides being 'at home' in Paris. His prolific output of vocal music (over 1200 works) includes madrigals in Italian, French and German together with over 500 Latin motets, 18 masses and a few instrumental pieces. His best-known work is the setting of the *Seven Penitential Psalms* (1563–70).

LAWES, Henry (1595–1662)
Member of the Chapel Royal from 1626 and reinstated after the Civil War. He is remembered as the composer of the music for Milton's *Comus* (Ludlow Castle 1634). Many of his songs were published during the Commonwealth.

LAWES, William (1602(?)–1645)
Elder half-brother of Henry (and like him a member of the Chapel Royal) who was killed in the Royalist army at the Siege of Chester. He collaborated with Davenant in a masque and left many songs, catches and psalm-settings including the well-known part-song *Gather ye Rosebuds*. He is remembered most for the startling originality of his 66 string pieces in *The Royal Consort* which certainly influenced Purcell.

LECLAIR, Jean Marie (1697–1764)
French violinist and composer, remembered for his advanced technique on the violin and the graceful musicality of his concertos, trios and solo sonatas for the instrument. He had some early experience as ballet-master in Turin and wrote several ballets and an opera for the Paris Opéra. He died the victim of an unexplained assassination.

LE FANU, Nicola (b. 1947)
The daughter of Elizabeth Maconchy. She studied at Oxford, the RCM, in Rome and at Harvard. More recently she has taught at several schools, at Morley College and at King's College, London. Her compositions have been partly descriptive, as in the orchestral piece *Columbia Falls* (1975) and partly balletic as in *Downpath* (1977), a chamber opera for two singers and a dancer, in which she was responsible for both the libretto and choreography.

LEFÉBURE-WÉLY, Louis James Alfred (1817–1869)
French organist and composer, famous for his improvisations and his interest in the harmonium. His compositions cover a wide range of music from opera to chamber music, but even his organ music, after an enthusiastic reception in his lifetime, is now quite forgotten.

LEHAR, Franz (1870–1948)
Hungarian composer, trained in Prague, and from 1902 based in Vienna. At 20 he became the youngest bandmaster in the Austrian Army and wrote an opera in the then new Mascagni style (which was rejected by Mahler at the Vienna Opera).

He soon found his métier in operetta and his third attempt in the style was the world-famous *Merry Widow* (1905). Although 30 similar works followed, Lehar never quite repeated his phenomenal success but, with Tauber as his principal tenor, many of his operettas received repeated performances in England and America between the wars — *The Land of Smiles* (1931) was particularly successful. He was the last Viennese Waltz-King.

LEIBOWITZ, René (1913–1972)
Polish-French serial composer, whose compositions, critical writings and teaching were influential in furthering the cause of Schönberg and his school. His most characteristic works are the *Chamber Concertos* for violin, piano and 17 instruments (1942), for nine instruments (1944), and the *Chamber Symphony* for 12 instruments (1948). Pierre Boulez was at one time a pupil.

LEIGH, Walter (1905–1942)
English pupil of E.J. Dent at Cambridge and Hindemith in Berlin who was killed in the North African campaign. His compositions were largely for West End theatres but include light opera and chamber music, together with an often-performed *Concertino* for harpsichord and strings (1936).

LEIGHTON, Kenneth (b. 1929)
English composer and academic who, since studying at Oxford and Rome has held posts at Leeds, Oxford and Edinburgh Universities. His orchestral works have included two symphonies and three piano concertos. He has written extensively for organ, piano and chamber combinations besides producing important church music and many smaller choral pieces.

LEMARE, Edwin Henry (1865–1934)
English organist and organ composer. Lemare was famous as a recitalist and for the exciting transcriptions of orchestral works (many by Wagner) which he made for his programmes. His own compositions, once popular, are no longer heard.

LEO, Leonardo (1694–1744)
Italian composer of 60 operas, oratorios, and six cello concertos; his keyboard music is still occasionally played.

LEONCAVALLO, Ruggiero (1858–1919)
The famous composer of *Pagliacci* (1892), which with Mascagni's *Cavalleria Rusticana* has become the most popular 'double bill' of all times. Leoncavallo's earlier operas never reached the stage, and after this opera he never repeated his success. *La Boheme* (1897) suffered by comparison with Puccini's setting of the same story, while *Zaza* (1900) is now rarely heard outside Italy.

LESUER (Le Sueur), Jean Francois (1760–1837)
Self-taught French composer who first achieved notoriety by his attempts to introduce dramatic effects with full orchestra into the services of Notre Dame. After 1792 he became an operatic composer with Romantic subjects like *Ossian* (1804) and musical director for Napoleon I. His later years were devoted to teaching his pupils including Berlioz and 11 other winners of the *Prix de Rome* at the Paris Conservatoire.

LEXEU, Guillaume (Henri) (1870–1894)
Belgian pupil of Franck and d'Indy whose works continue to be performed, especially the sonatas for piano (1891), the Violin and Piano Sonata (1892) and the *Suite for Cello and Orchestra* (1892).

LEY, Henry George (1887–1962)
English organist and composer. Most of his compositions are relatively simple

pieces of church music which are still often heard. As organist of Christ Church, Oxford, and Eton College, he was the foremost player of his generation.

LIADOV, Anatol (1855–1914)
Russian composer who was a pupil of Rimsky-Korsakov and is now remembered for pianistic miniatures. The influence of Chopin blends with Russian qualities, partly acquired in his researches into the folk music of various districts. Some of this piano music was orchestrated for the ballet, as in *Russian Fairy Tales*. Liadov's output was small but did include four symphonic poems on Russian subjects.

LIGETI, György (b. 1923)
Hungarian composer who, while writing in the folk song idiom required by the authorities, privately explored avant-garde techniques. On moving to Vienna in 1956, he was prominent as theorist in ISCM circles and as a stylistic innovator in *Apparitions* (1960). This work like *Atmosphères* (1961) and the organ *Volumina* (1962), abandoned melody, harmony and rhythm as separate concepts in favour of continuous fluid changes of texture. He also produced the electronic *Artikulation* (1958). Influential later works have been the *Requiem* (1965), the choral *Lux aeterna* (1966) and the orchestral *Lontano* (1967). His notation is relatively conventional and some of his works have satirized the Cage School. Micro-intervals occur in his later string writing.

LINLEY, Thomas (1732–1795)
English composer of ballad operas including *Robinson Crusoe* (1781) and *Tom Jones* (1786) performed at Drury Lane Theatre.

LINLEY, Thomas (1756–1778)
Infant prodigy on the violin and the son of the above, he was a pupil of Boyce and (in Italy) of Nardini and a friend of Mozart. He joined with his father for *The Duenna* (1775) and wrote a number of pieces for various mediums.

LISZT, Ferencz (Franz) (1811–1886)
Great Hungarian pianist, conductor and composer, who after appearing as a child prodigy, became a pupil of Czerny and Salieri in Vienna and met Beethoven and Schubert. In 1823 the family moved to Paris where his career as a virtuoso pianist was soon established. He visited England and wrote the original version of the *Transcendental Studies*. He had a one-act opera performed at the Paris Opéra in 1825. There followed on his father's death a period of religious involvement and an unsuccessful love affair, and then a period of study based on his meetings with Berlioz, Paganini and Chopin — during which period he supported himself mainly by teaching. His affair with the Comtesse D'Agoult lasted from 1834 for five years during which three children were born (including Wagner's future wife, Cosima). Liszt's career as a travelling virtuoso was resumed from their homes in Switzerland and Rome, and this period marks the composition of the Paganini studies and the early books of *Années de Pélérinage*.
In Kiev, in 1847 he met Princess Sayn-Wittgenstein with whom he formed a lifelong liaison. She persuaded him to give up his life as a travelling virtuoso in favour of composition. Most of his major works were written during the next 12 years e.g. the *Faust* and *Dante* Symphonies, the two piano concertos, the first 12 symphonic poems, the great B minor Sonata and various choral works and songs. During this period he also conducted many first performances at the Weimar Opera House, including Wagner's *Lohengrin*, Schumann's *Manfred* and Berlioz' *Benvenuto Cellini*. His pupils now included von Bülow and Tausig. His intended marriage to the Princess was forbidden by the Pope in 1861, and Liszt took

the four minor orders of the Roman Catholic Church though he never became a priest (most of his church music belongs to this period). His later years were divided between concert tours, teaching the leading musicians of the next generation such as Weingartner, friendship with younger composers like Borodin and Debussy and an unfortunate quarrel with Wagner owing to Cosima's desertion of her husband, von Bülow, and her two illegitimate children. He appeared in London in his final year and died at Bayreuth.

Liszt's playing was legendary and his numerous transcriptions did much to make known the music of both contemporaries and of Bach and Schubert as well as transforming a hitherto empty piece into a genuine art-form. His harmonic language looks forward to the 20th century with its colourist and non-functional use of chords, while his transformation of Berlioz' *idée fixe* into Wagner's leitmotif technique even suggests Schönberg's serialism. It is not too much to say that our whole modern conception of the 'Artist' derives from this flamboyant yet introspective composer of the famous *Hungarian Rhapsodies.*

LITOLFF, Henry Charles (1818–1891)
English pianist, publisher and composer who from 1835 to 1841 was resident in France and later for three years a conductor in Warsaw. He was a pupil of Moscheles and a very successful pianist. In 1851 he took over the Meyer publications in Brunswick, transferred the business to London in 1860 and brought out the first popular-priced editions of the Viennese classics. His compositions belong mainly to Paris and his later years. Of his 115 (often large-scale) works only his shorter piano pieces are heard today — especially the well-known *Spinnlied.*

LLOYD, Charles Harford (1849–1919)
English organist and composer, who first followed S.S.Wesley as organist of Gloucester Cathedral. Later he moved to Christ Church, Oxford, to Eton College, and, lastly to the Chapel Royal. His well-written compositions were all either festival cantatas or church music; the latter are still occasionally performed.

LLOYD WEBBER, Andrew (b. 1948)
Outstandingly-successful English composer of musicals from *Joseph and His Amazing Technicolour Dreamcoat* (1967), to *Jesus Christ Superstar* (1970), *Evita* (1976) and *Cats* (1981).

LLOYD WEBBER, William (1914–1982)
The father of Andrew and himself a distinguished organist, educationist and composer. After holding several important posts he was prominent in his later years as a professor at the RCM and after 1964 as Director of the LCM.

As a composer, his reputation depends on a long series of unison and part songs together with some successful cantatas, anthems and organ pieces.

LOCATELLI, Pietro Antonio (1695–1764)
Italian violinist and composer who was a pupil of Corelli. He developed a virtuoso technique with his caprices and études. His sonatas and concertos are still performed.

LOCKE, Matthew (c. 1630–1677)
English stage composer who collaborated with Davenant during the Commonwealth in the *Siege of Rhodes* (1656) and was later credited with the music to his production of *Macbeth* (1672). He was appointed Composer-in-Ordinary to Charles II and wrote numerous anthems for the Chapel Royal, although he became a Catholic convert. His six keyboard suites and the 'lessons' in the teaching treatise *Melothesia*

are still played.

LODER, Edward James (1813–1865)
English composer of songs and ballad operas (the latter being forgotten), but some of his settings such as *The Brooklet* (the same text as Schubert's *Wohin*) are still occasionally heard.

LOEFFLER, Charles Martin (1861–1935)
Alsatian composer who after stays in Russia, Hungary, Switzerland and a period in Berlin under one of Joachim's assistants, lived in America from his 20th year. His compositions seem to owe much to French Impressionism with their polished technique, but are insufficiently individual to have retained their popularity. *La Mer de Tintagiles* (1905), a symphonic poem using a viola d'amore, is still occasionally heard.

LOEILLET, Jean-Baptiste (1680–1730)
Belgian harpsichordist, flautist, oboist and composer who worked in London from 1705 to 1710 and was largely responsible for popularising the German or transverse flute at the expense of the English block-flute or recorder. Most of his sonatas for flute and/or oboe with continuo were published in London.

LOEWE, Carl (1796–1869)
German composer of 150 ballads for voice and piano as well as 145 opus numbers which include symphonies, concertos, oratorios and five operas. His settings of *Edward* and *Erlkönig* were better known than those of Schubert to his contemporaries and the 17 volumes of his songs are still popular in Germany.

LORTZING, Gustave Albert (1801–1851)
German operatic composer, actor, singer and librettist who achieved success with *Undine* (1845) and whose comic operas are still popular in Germany with their rather four-square, folk-like melodies, e.g. *Czar und Zimmerman* (1837).

LOTTI, Antonio (c. 1667–1740)
Venetian composer, who also produced four operas and much church music in south Germany (1717–19). Most of his life was spent at St. Mark's where he wrote many masses and motets. During his earlier years in Venice, 17 of his operas were successfully produced at La Fenice Opera House. His pupils included Marcello, Alberti and Galuppi.

LULLY, Jean Baptiste (1632–1687)
French composer of Italian origin, famous for his ballet music and operas. He workd in Paris as a kitchen-boy and was largely self-taught as a guitarist and violinist. His gifts were discovered by the King's cousin who employed him and he was made leader of a small string band in the household. Louis XIV, then only 14, made him part of his staff with the triple function of ballet-dancer, violinist and composer of popular ballets de cours. An expert and unscrupulous courtier, he soon reformed the famous '24 violins' of the King's Band by severely restricting their individual freedom of improvisation, and then succeeded from one court appointment to another. In 1661 he was naturalised as a Frenchman and became 'Composer to the King's Chamber Music'.
From 1664 he began to collaborate with Molière, a partnership which culminated in *Le Bourgeois Gentilhomme* (1670). The collaborations were spoken drama with overture, songs and ballet. The proportion of music increased as a result of Cardinal Mazzarin's enthusiasm for Cavalli's operas. When it was clear that French opera was a real possibility, Lully seized his chance and brought out *Les Fêtes de l'Amour et de Bacchus* (1672) and then followed it with about 20 operas and ballets in collaboration with the poet

Quinault. Lully even became the King's 'Secretaire du Roi' and was soon extremely rich; he had popularised the opera with the French court and people. He abandoned the Italian *secco* recitative in favour of accompanied declamation and arioso using the note-values of French speech; he set the style of the French Overture (slow-quick movements); above all he disciplined players, singers and dancers so that French style of performance became a respectable alternative to the Italian.

LUTHER, Martin (1483–1546)
Great German reformer who was also a trained musician. In order to encourage congregational singing, he wrote and adapted the words and melodies of many popular chorales of the day such as *Ein' feste Burg* and *O Welt ich muss dich lassen*. He played the flute and lute and also wrote a short treatise on music.

LUTOSLAWSKI, Witold (b. 1913)
Leading Polish composer who was pressurised to try and write in a Nationalist style up to 1956. His 1st Symphony (1947) was withdrawn after criticism that it was 'formalistic'. The *Concerto for Orchestra* was rather more fortunate thanks to its overtones of Bartók, and is now a repertoire piece. With the opening of the cultural frontiers in 1956, Lutoslawski was fascinated by the serialists on the one hand and Cage's use of chance in music on the other. In 1961, he used orchestral alaetoric techniques for the first time in *Jeux venitiens* and in most of the succeeding works such as *Trois Poèmes d'Henri Michaux* (1963) where each of the two conductors synchronise carefully-calculated chance procedures.
Lutoslawski is one of the most cosmopolitan of modern composers and much in demand as a conductor, lecturer and teacher.

LUTYENS, Elisabeth (1906–1983)
English composer educated at the RCM and the Paris Conservatoire who later adopted serial techniques. She has written much for film and radio and several major works for unusual combinations as well as six string quartets and six chamber concertos. Her best-known works are *Valediction* for clarinet and piano, *Four Nocturnes* (1954) and the wind quintet (1961).

LVOV, Alexis Feodorovich (1798–1870)
Russian violinist, composer and conductor, remembered as the composer of the Imperial Russian National Anthem (used in Tchaikovsky's *1812 Overture*). He also played in a string quartet and wrote three operas, a violin concerto and much church music for the orthodox service.

M

McCABE, John (b. 1939)
English composer and pianist, trained at the RMCM and in Munich. His many orchestral works include three symphonies, three piano concertos, the *Concerto for Orchestra* (1982) and two violin concertos. He has also been prolific in works for wind and brass ensemble for organ, for piano and most chamber combinations. His choral works include *Stabat Mater* (1976) and important cathedral commissions.

MacCUNN, Hamish (1868–1916)
Scottish composer and conductor. A pupil of Parry at the RCM, he conducted for the Carl Rosa Opera Company and followed Sullivan at the Savoy Theatre. He composed several operas and musical comedies, as well as a number of cantatas, but only the overture *The Land of the Mountain and Flood* (1887) and one or two songs are still occasionally performed.

MacDOWELL, Edward Alexander (1861–1908)
New York composer and pianist of mixed Scottish-Irish descent. He studied for a time at the Paris Conservatoire and under Raff in Germany; Liszt gave his early compositions encouragement. In 1888 he returned to America where he remained for the rest of his life. After an unsatisfactory period as the first music professor of Columbia University, his time after 1904 was divided between composition, concert tours and private teaching.
Although he is usually described as America's first major composer, his affinities were rather to the Celtic and Scandinavian style of Grieg. He himself denied any Nationalist intention, even in a work such as the *Indian Suite* (1897). The parallel with Grieg is, however, a fair one: he not only dedicated the last two of his four piano sonatas to Grieg but was also particularly fond of colourful harmonies and haunting melodies as in *To a Wild Rose* and *To a Water Lily*, two of the short piano pieces in *Woodland Sketches* (1896) which have always been almost embarrassingly popular. He is remembered for the subtle and cosmopolitan *Sea Pieces* (1898) and songs rather than the ambitious symphonic poems or the two brilliant earlier piano concertos.

MACHAUT (Machault), Guillaume de (c. 1300–1377)
French composer and poet who after various European posts was made a canon of Rheims Cathedral in 1333. He wrote 23 motets (usually isorhythmic), and was also supreme as a 14th century poet. Together with Vitry he was one of the two outstanding secular composers of the time. Most of his ballades, rondeaux and lais, (almost 120 pieces in all) are for solo voice with two independent instrumental lines.
Historically, Machaut is also important as the composer of a four-part mass (the earliest complete setting of the choral sections of the mass) which has received regular performances in recent years.

MACKENZIE, Sir Alexander Campbell (1847–1935)
Scottish composer and conductor. At the age of 10 he was sent to Germany to study the violin. He moved to London in 1862 hoping to further his career with his father's former teacher, Sainton. The latter suggested he entered for the King's Scholarship at the RAM, which he did, and was successful. At the RAM he studied harmony and counterpoint, piano, and the violin with Sainton. During this time he earned his living as a violinist in theatre

orchestras.
In 1865 he returned to Edinburgh and during the next few years became well known as a conductor. He also arranged concerts, taught, and occasionally appeared as a violinist.
In 1879 he moved to Florence and began to devote his time to composition. *The Bride*, a cantata, was the first in a long line of successful compositions. With the oratorio *The Rose of Sharon* (1884), his reputation of being a leading English composer was confirmed.

In 1888 Mackenzie became principal of the RAM, which appointment he held for the next 36 years. He was knighted in 1895, and during the remainder of his long life worked to promote new works from home and abroad.

MACONCHY, Elizabeth (b. 1907)
English composer of Irish parentage and pupil of Vaughan Williams. Her main compositions are a group of one-act operas and several orchestral and chamber music works: the oboe quintet (1933); two symphonies; a concerto for viola; concertinos for bassoon and strings, clarinet and strings, and for piano and strings; a clarinet quintet, and nine string quartets.

MADERNA, Bruno (b. 1920)
Italian composer and conductor who after the 2nd World War was identified with Boulez and Berio in the avant-garde movement. He was largely responsible for the electronic music centre of the Italian Radio and later became Director of Milan Radio.
As a conductor he specialised in such works as Berg's *Wozzeck* and performances of composers like Nono. His own works include *Quadrivium* for large orchestra, *Serenata* for 11 instruments, *Composizione in Tre Tempi* (1954) for chamber orchestra, *Syntaxis* (1957) for four different electronic timbres, an opera, and several concertos.

MAHLER, Gustav (1860-1911)
South German composer and conductor who gave his first piano recital at the age of 10. His childhood was marked by several family tragedies which he never forgot. The popular music of Vienna too was implanted in his mind from earliest days and the marches and bugle calls of a nearby barracks.
He had a successful period at the Vienna Conservatoire from 1875, and by 1888 he had sufficiently established himself as an operatic conductor (including a spell with Nikisch in Leipzig) to be appointed artistic director at the Budapest Opera House. Although Mahler originally became a conductor to support his family, he never earned enough from his compositions to give up conducting; all composing had to be done during his annual holiday. Nevertheless, he was the outstanding conductor of his generation, admired by Brahms, Bruckner and Richard Strauss, and was the teacher of Bruno Walter and Mengelberg. In 1897 he formally left his Jewish faith to adopt Catholicism in order to accept the directorship of the Vienna Imperial Opera, and during the next 10 years he became world famous in spite of his dictatorial style of control. He finally spent three seasons at the New York 'Met' where he collapsed during his third year. Throughout his conducting career he was assiduous and always successful in his productions of Wagner's music dramas and Wagner's shadow is often felt in Mahler's music.
Mahler's compositions derive first from the 19th century lieder tradition. His song cycles (usually with orchestral accompaniment) proceed from *Lieder eines fahrenden Gesellen* (1880) through to *Kindertotenlieder* (1905), and finally to *Das Lied von der Erde* which, like his 9th Symphony, was posthumously conducted by Bruno Walter.

Beethoven's influence on the composer was perhaps stimulated by Mahler's first published work — a piano arrangement of Bruckner's 3rd (Wagner) Symphony (1878). Mahler's arrangement of movements in his own symphonies owes something to Beethoven's 9th (he uses voices in Symphonies 2, 3, 4 and 8) but mostly the order grew naturally from the implied but usually unexpressed programme. On the other hand his orchestration, as in Wagner's *Siegfried Idyll*, is basically soloistic. In spite of the enormous scale and sometimes loose construction of works like the purely instrumental Symphonies 5, 6 and 7, his approach becomes more and more contrapuntal, and certainly led to the 'chamber symphony' of his successors.
This is equally true of the even larger '*Symphony of a Thousand*' (No. 8) with its use of the *Veni Creator* and the end of Goethe's *Faust*. Mahler was above all the poet of death and seems, in the concluding Adagio of the 9th, to speak for the whole 20th century. His 10th Symphony was left unfinished but has recently been performed in a completed version by Deryck Cooke.

MALIPIERO, Francesco (1882–1973)
Venetian composer and scholar. He spent some time in Berlin and Vienna but soon returned to his home town. During the 1st World War he retired to compose in Asolo. His music was influenced equally by performances of Wagner, the 1913 performance of Stravinsky's *Rite of Spring* and his discovery of 17th century manuscripts of early Italian music. Malipiero progressed to opera from ballet — perhaps his most important work was the avant-garde production of *Sette Canzoni* (1918).
Among his later works are *Favola del Figlio Cambiato* (with Pirandello, 1933) which fell foul of the Fascist authorities; and successful operas on both Shakespeare's *Julius Caesar* (1936) and *Anthony and Cleopatra* (1938). During the last 30 years of his life he produced over 20 other stage works.

MARAIS, Marin (1656–1728)
French pupil of Lully active as a singer and bass violist who became conductor of the Opéra. His compositions include *Alcyone* (1706) and several other operas, but he is now remembered principally for his chamber music: trio sonatas for flutes, violin and bass viol (1692), and viol pieces (1701, 1711, 1717 and 1725).

MARCELLO, Benedetto (1686–1739)
Important Italian composer for strings and church music. The latter compositions are in eight volumes and include free poetic paraphrases of 50 psalms for one to four voices with figured bass, and (usually) two violins and cello obbligato (published in 1724 and 1726). He also wrote instrumental concertos and sonatas, as well as several operas. He was a successful librettist, translator (of Dryden), lawyer and politician.

MARCHAND, Louis (1669–1732)
French organist and composer. He was brilliant enough to be appointed organist at Nevers Cathedral at fourteen, and was soon renowned as a virtuoso player and improviser. He lost the King's favour by his 'tantrums' and during his exile in Dresden is said to have competed with Bach. He returned to France and Du Mage and Daquin became his pupils.
Marchand's organ and harpsichord compositions are relatively few and marked by both daring chromaticism and ill-matched dance figurations.

MARENZIO, Luca (1553–1599)
Italian madrigal composer who was in service in Rome and Poland and finally in the Papal Chapel from 1595. The 17 Italian books of his madrigals were introduced into England in his *Musica Transalpina*

(1588). He also wrote several volumes of motets and 'Sacri concerti'.

MARSCHNER, Heinrich August (1795–1861)
German operatic composer. He was joint Kapellmeister with Weber in Dresden in 1823, and was associated with German Romantic Opera in settings of Sir Walter Scott such as *Der Templer and die Judin* (*Ivanhoe*, 1829). His most famous work was *Hans Heiling* (1833) which probably had some influence on the young Wagner. As well as many other operas, Marschner wrote chamber and piano music.

MARTIN, Frank (1890–1974)
Swiss composer who studied in Rome (1921–23) and taught in Geneva (1933–39). He lived in Amsterdam (1950–52) and taught in Cologne (1952–58) before returning to Switzerland. His earlier works tend to be impressionist, but he later adopted a free form of serialism. He wrote ballets, operas and incidental music, but most of his output has been choral and orchestral (usually for chamber orchestra). The two oratorios *Golgotha* (1949) and *Pilate* (1964) have been particularly successful, as have the Organ *Passacaille* (1944) and the violin sonatas (1915 and 1931).

MARTIN, Easthope (1885–1925)
English composer of drawing-room songs such as *Come to the Fair*.

MARTINI, Giovanni Battista (Padre Martini) (1706–1784)
Famous Italian composer, theorist, and teacher of J.C.Bach and Mozart among others. His compositions include a mass, a requiem, three oratorios and keyboard works. He was ordained in 1722, collected, according to Burney, a library of 17,000 volumes, and was one of the earliest musical historians.

MARTINON, Jean (1910–1976)
French composer and conductor and a pupil of Roussel. He was first heard as the composer of *Stalag 9* which he wrote as a prisoner of war in Germany. His later works have included four symphonies, an opera *Hecuba* (1949), a cello concerto (1965) and chamber music.

MARTINU, Bohuslav (1890–1959)
Czech composer, who after being expelled from the Prague Conservatoire earned his living playing second violin in the Czech Philharmonic Orchestra. As a composer he was always prolific but largely self-taught. In 1922 his ballet *Istar* was produced and he had a few lessons from Suk before moving to Paris in 1923 where he married and lived until the outbreak of the 2nd World War. He had lessons with Roussel and became part of the cosmopolitan scene of Stravinsky, Picasso and the futurists and neo-classicists. His music continued to flow unabatedly, and became more and more dissonant, dynamic and motoric, but was often wildly impracticable. He began to concentrate more on setting Czech words and subjects: the 2nd Piano Concerto and the 4th String Quartet were obviously Nationalist, and his opera *Juliette* (1938) was performed in Prague. This period culminated in the outstanding *Double Concerto* (1938) which seemed to foreshadow the tragedy of War.
After frightening experiences under the occupation, he escaped without scores to America and within five years had written five major symphonies, two concertos and the *Memorial to Lidice*. He returned to France after the War but, owing to the Communist take-over, never to Czechoslovakia. Several of his many new Czech works, however, were performed there. From 1955 until his death he taught in Rome; he also became an American citizen.
His last compositions included three symphonic poems: *The Frescoes of Piero della*

Francesca, the 5th Piano Concerto, several stage works, the large-scale music drama *Christ Recrucified* (well-known in the film version *He Who Must Die*) and many more Czech works.

Martinu was a late developer but belonged to the main Dvorák-Janácek tradition of Czech music. Like Bartók, he remained an exile.

MASCAGNI, Pietro (1863–1945)
Italian operatic composer who was immortalised by his first opera — *Cavalleria Rusticana* (1889). Mahler considered his second — *L'Amico Fritz* (1891) — its superior, but it is now never heard outside Italy. The bold and obvious colouring and passion of *Cavalleria Rusticana* are perhaps the natural result of the spasmodic and undisciplined teaching that Mascagni received. In later years there followed several operas, varying from operetta to grandiose music drama. The last, *Nerone* (1935), was designed as a tribute to Mussolini which led to Mascagni's appointment as conductor at La Scala on Toscanini's resignation. The later operas are no longer heard and Mascagni ended his life in obscurity and disgrace because of his political sympathies.

MASSENET, Jules Emile Frédéric (1842–1912)
French operatic composer, whose *Manon* (1884) and *Werther* (1892) have retained their places in the operatic repertoire. Massenet entered the Paris Conservatoire at eleven and was a pupil of Ambroise Thomas. He was consistently successful as a student, was hardworking and had an instinctive awareness of what the public would accept. He used the Wagnerian leit-motif in an easily recognisable way and developed a lush Romantic orchestral style; he had the ability to produce discreetly erotic music contrasted with colourful stage music of a mildly innovatory nature. Massenet became part of the 'mainstream' of French music as Professor of Composition at the Conservatoire, and certainly influenced Debussy even if the avant-garde group under d'Indy reacted against him.

Although some operatic successes of Massenet seem to depend on either a great singer (e.g. *Don Quichotte*, 1910) or the French theatrical tradition where the original word declamation is all important (e.g. *Thaïs*, 1894), there has been a series of recent successful revivals and *Manon* and *Werther* are hardly likely to be forgotten.

MATTHESON, Johann (1681–1764)
Versatile German writer, singer, player and composer. He was first a treble in the Hamburg opera chorus, later a leading tenor, and five of his operas were staged before 1705. Later on his harpsichord and organ playing became more important although much of his time was spent in translating books on law and politics. After holding a post as tutor to the English envoy, he was cantor and a canon of Hamburg cathedral until deafness forced his resignation. His writings and compositions continued and the latter included 24 oratorios and 12 flute sonatas. He was influential in the development of the church cantata and wrote many text-books.

MATHIAS, William (b. 1934)
Welsh composer, pianist, conductor, and University Professor at Bangor since 1970 who studied at the RAM with Lennox Berkeley. His works date from the *Clarinet Sonatina* of 1957 and he has provided repertoire works for harp, organ and church choirs. His major works include *Concerto for Orchestra*, three piano concertos, a symphony and wind quintet, the choral *This Worldes Joie* and the opera *The Servants* (1980).

MEDTNER, Nicholas (1880–1951)
Russian composer and pianist who, after

studying under Arensky and Taneiev at the Moscow Conservatoire, left Russia in 1921 and became a conservative champion of German Romanticism in his playing and compositions in France, Germany and America. He lived in England from 1936 and left piano concertos, about 100 songs, and important piano miniatures such as the many *Fairy Tales*.

MÉHUL, Étienne Henri (1763–1817)
French operatic composer who in his operatic reforms is regarded as the follower of Gluck. Although he achieved distinction as a child pianist and organist, it was not until 1790 that his long run of 30 stage works brought him professional eminence. His best known work is the colourful opera *Joseph* (1807).

MELLERS, Wilfred Howard (b. 1914)
English musicologist whose compositions include cantatas, choral works and songs. His writings include *Man and his Music* and *Caliban Reborn*.

MENDELSSOHN-BARTHOLDY, Felix Jakob Ludwig (1809–1847)
Celebrated German Romantic composer. Among his many talents developed in a liberal education was his ability as a child prodigy, as a pianist, and composer. He was compared with Mozart and encouraged by Goethe, Moscheles, Hummel, Cherubini and Rossini. His teenage compositions established his mature style and the *Octet* (1825) and the Overture to *A Midsummer Night's Dream* (1826) have never been surpassed. He had already made aquaintance with the works of Bach and, after experience gained from his father's music making, he conducted the first revival of the *St. Matthew Passion* in his 20th year. The same year he visited England and Scotland and his musical 'water-colours' included the famous *Hebrides* Overture and the first of the eight books of *Songs Without Words*.
In Germany he became active as a conductor in revivals of Beethoven and Handel, and his first oratorio *St. Paul* (1836), the *Italian Symphony*, the *Ruy Blas* Overture and the two piano concertos were all heard. Meanwhile, Mendelssohn's reputation in England continued to grow under the distinguished patronage of the Prince Consort. The symphony entitled *Hymn of Praise* (1840), the *Scottish Symphony* (1842, dedicated to Queen Victoria), the organ works and most popular of all, *Elijah* (1846), owe much to English taste and encouragement.
His work in Germany at Leipzig and later Berlin continued to absorb his energy and the *Violin Concerto* (1844) belongs to this environment. His early death was mourned throughout Europe, but his reputation continued to grow throughout the century — in England it eclipsed even that of Handel.
Besides the juvenile symphonies and string quartets, large-scale orchestral, chamber, piano and vocal works appeared throughout his life, and few of these are not marked by fluent sensitivity and superb technique. Only the darker aspects of life are unrepresented and his music seems to portray his cloudless earlier life. The later works are marred perhaps by the worthy sense of moral purpose that was such a feature of the 19th century bourgeoisie, and this is probably the reason for the lack of critical esteem in the earlier years of the present century.

MENOTTI, Gian-Carlo (b. 1911)
Italian theatrical composer, resident in America since 1927 and trained in Milan and Philadelphia. Most of his works were written for the opera house though their success has sprung from their theatrical effectiveness (he writes his own librettos) rather than their Italian lyricism. His best-known works have been *The Medium* (1946), *The Telephone* (1947), The *Consul* (1950) and *Amahl and the Night Visitors*

(1951). These (and several others) have had long runs on Broadway, television and international opera houses, but only *Amahl* seems to have the musical substance to survive its melodramatic origins; it has become a classic of nativity operas and has received many amateur performances. Menotti's other works include concertos for piano and violin and a song cycle for Elizabeth Schwarzkopf.

MERBECK(Merbecke, Marbecke), John (c. 1510–c. 1585)
English reformation composer. While a singer and (from 1541) organist of St. George's Chapel Windsor, he wrote a five-part mass and was then active as a reformer. He was condemned for heresy in his *Concordance* in 1543 but reprieved as 'only a poor singing man' who was needed to help in 'the englishing of the services'. In 1550 'the booke of Common praier noted' — his unison setting of the sung parts of the 1549 Prayer Book — appeared, and in the same year the third version of the *Concordance* was at last published. The former is partly an adaption in mensural rhythm of lively plainsong originals, but also includes some virile settings of the new English text. It was soon superseded by later prayer books but has been generally used in the English church during the century following 1870. Merbecke's later years seem to have been largely spent as a preacher and pamphleteer.

MERCADANTE, Saverio (1795–1870)
Italian operatic and church music composer whose most famous work *La Vestale* (1840) was influential as a 'reform opera' on Verdi. He wrote approximately 60 operas and was also active as a player, as *maestro di capella* at Novara Cathedral, and from 1840 as director of the Naples Conservatiore.

MERKEL, Gustav (1827–1885)
German organist and composer of nine sonatas, many chorale preludes and teaching material for his instrument. Most of his mature life was spent in Dresden as Court organist at the Conservatoire. He was a composition student of Schumann.

MERULO, Claudio (1533–1604)
Italian composer of motets, masses, and madrigals, but now remembered mainly for his idiomatic keyboard music. The organ toccatas have lately received an increasing number of performances. He also produced an opera *La Tragedia* (1574) in madrigal style.

MESSAGER, André (1853–1929)
French composer and conductor who was a pupil of Saint-Saëns and for a time organist of Saint Sulpice, Paris. He had many successes in light opera and ballet including *La Béarnaise* (1885) and *Les p'tites Michu* (1897). His activities as a conductor spread from the Opéra Comique to Covent Garden.

MESSIAEN, Olivier Eugène (b. 1908)
French composer, organist and teacher, who during a brilliant studentship under Dupré and Dukas at the Paris Conservatoire, published the organ *Le Banquet Céleste* (1928) and the piano *Préludes* (1929) in a startlingly original style. The series of organ works continued after his appointment to L'Église de la Trinité (a post he still holds) in 1931, with *L'Ascension* (1932) and *La Nativité* (1935). The many influences on his music — the harmonic styles of Franck, Debussy and Wagner's *Tristan und Isolde* and the rhythmic and melodic feeling of plainsong — were soon to be systematised in a pamphlet and extended by still wider study. While he was a prisoner of war in 1941 he wrote his *Quatuor pour la fin du temps* with its non-metrical concepts and hynotic slow tempos. He worked under the umbrella of the Catholic faith and in

the endeavour to express its theology in sound; his experience of oriental rhythms and colours, single line bird-song and an almost static sense of time-duration has led to such works as *Visions de l'Amen* (1943) for two pianos; such enormous works as *Vingt regards sur l'enfant Jésus* (1944) — over two hours for solo piano; the symphonic *Turangalîla* (1946–48); and the 'Hindu' *Cantéyodjahâ* (1949) for solo piano.

By this time, his 'analysis' classes at the Paris Conservatoire included such pupils as Boulez, Stockhausen and Xenakis, and work on the music of Schönberg and Webern led to experiments with total serialism (of rhythm, dynamics and 'attack' besides pitch) in *Quatre études de rythme* (1949–50) for piano, the electronic *Timbre-Durées* (1952) and the organ *Messe de la Pentecôte* (1950). This compositional idea was widely taken up during the next decade and led to the aleatoric reaction associated with the element of 'chance' in the music of John Cage.

The series of large-scale works has continued with the orchestral *Chronochromie* (1960) and the 'open air' *Et exspecto resurrectionem mortuorum* (1964); the piano *Catalogue d'oiseaux* (1956–72), the organ *Méditations sur le Mystère de la Saint Trinité* (1969), and the choral *La Transfiguration de notre Seigneur Jésus Christ* (1970).

Of Messiaën's originality and influence there can be no doubt, but reactions to his music are still highly individual. He certainly sums up French musical technique from Fauré onwards and has opened many doors to his contemporaries and pupils. In spite of the many 'parental' influences on him, there is a characteristic 'Messiaen' sound in all his works and a sense of inevitability even in his complexities. Perhaps because of his strongly personal philosophy, his attempt to express the wholeness of life in music may seem pretentious to some; others may find his scores bound by the lushness of the salon, and the over sweetness of the ondes martenot. For his power, sincerity and serenity, musicality and fluency, intellectual insight and projection, there must be unanimous respect.

MEYERBEER, Giacomo (1791–1864)
Cosmopolitan composer of German-Jewish origin, several of whose operas remain in the continental repertoire. As a pianist he was a child prodigy and later a fellow student with Weber studying composition under Abt Vogler. After limited success with a comic opera in Stuggart, he was enraptured by Rossini's *Tancredi* (1815) in Venice and produced a successful series of Italian operas in a similar style. *Il Crociato in Egitto* (Venice, 1824) was written in Berlin, where he was urged by Weber to throw in his lot with the new German Romantic opera. He soon became more involved with French opera, however, and most of his later life was spent in Paris.

After several rather fallow years, *Robert le Diable* (1831) was the first opera in a new style in which Italian vocal melody, brilliant German orchestration and the French dramatic sense were combined in a series of 'world' successes. *Les Huguenots* (1836) and *Le Prophète* (1843) followed; he continued to work on the six-hour *L'Africaine* from 1838 until his death (its performance took place in Paris the following year, 1865). Meyerbeer had some success at the Opéra Comique in 1854 with *L'Étoile du Nord* but relatively little with his later German operas. He was, however, active in Berlin in 1844, conducting Weber's *Euryanthe* and Wagner's *Rienzi*, but Wagner was soon bitterly critical of the bombastic musical emptiness of his style, a judgement which has been endorsed by posterity. Nevertheless, *Rienzi* owes much to Meyerbeer's 'grand opera' style.

MIASKOVSKY, Nicholas

(1881–1950)
Russian symphonic composer who studied with Glière, Rimsky-Korsakov and Liadov. Of his 24 symphonies, the first six are in the Romantic tradition of Glazunov, and for the most part rather introspective although he used revolutionary songs in the sixth, which has remained in the symphonic repertoire. The composer described symphonies 7–12 (1922–32) as transitional, and felt that the later ones marked his turn towards Soviet social themes. His works continued to be acceptable to the Soviet authorities and Symphony 21 was awarded the Stalin prize of 100,000 roubles.

MILFORD, Robin (1903–1959)
English composer who studied under Holst and Vaughan Williams and whose smaller-scale works are sometimes performed. Much of his output was choral and included two oratorios. He also wrote a symphony, concerto grosso, violin concerto and two ballets.

MILHAUD, Darius (1892–1974)
Prolific French composer who was associated in 1919 with 'Les Six'. The light, flippant and sometimes vulgar style associated with this group is hardly characteristic of the rest of Milhaud's output; his works from the 1920's seem to combine the dryness of the neo-classical movement with experiments in polytonality and jazz, juxtaposed with warmly lyrical and poetical passages. Much of this period was occupied with works for the theatre such as *Le boeuf sur le toit* (1919), the ballet *La Création du Monde* (1923) and the opera *Christophe Columb* (1928).
He was also active during these years as a conductor and piano soloist in his own works and this early familiarity with America was continued after the fall of Paris in 1940 by a long engagement teaching in California which lasted until 1971 (though he also spent some of the years in a similar capacity at the Paris Conservatoire from 1947).
The flow of operas and ballets continued into later life, and after the orchestral pieces for jazz groups and such works as *Saudades do Brazil* (1921), he wrote a series of 12 symphonies mainly for American orchestras (1940–62). In addition, there were five piano, three violin and two cello concertos as well as works for more unusual combinations, such as the *Concerto for battery and small orchestra* (1930) and the popular *Percussion Concerto* (1949). His chamber music includes 18 string quartets, many sonatinas for different combinations, several piano suites and sets of songs.

MILNER, Anthony (b. 1925)
English academic musician and choral composer who has been active in Morley and King's Colleges in London. His best known pieces are his unaccompanied *Mass* and *Te Deum* for chorus and orchestra. He has also written a chamber symphony, a string divertimento, wind quintet and an oboe quartet.

MILTON, John (c. 1563–1647)
The father of the great English poet, one of whose madrigals was included in *The Triumphes of Oriana* (1601). Several other madrigals and psalms were printed by Leighton (1614) and Ravenscroft (1621).

MOERAN, Ernest John (1894–1950)
English composer and collector of Norfolk folksongs. He was a pupil of John Ireland at the RCM, his compositions reaching a wider public with his two *Orchestral Rhapsodies* (1924). His *Symphony* (1938), *Violin Concerto* (1942), *Cello Concerto* (1945), the *Oboe Quartet* (1946) and *Cello Sonata* (1947) all established him as a fastidious craftsman and sensitive poet in the English folksong tradition. His *Sinfonietta* (1944) is perhaps his most popular work.

MONCKTON, Lionel (1862-1924)
Successful English composer of musical comedies and particularly remembered for *The Arcadians* and *The Quaker Girl*. He was also for a time music critic for the *Daily Telegraph*.

MONIUSZKO, Stanislaw (1819-1872)
The most important Polish composer after Chopin. His 300 songs have been compared by his countryman with those of Schubert. He was active in Warsaw as organist, operatic conductor and professor at the Conservatoire. Of his 15 operas, *Halka* (1858) is said to mark the beginning of Polish national opera and four others are in the permanent operatic repertoire of his own country. More recently *Halka* has been performed in Germany, Switzerland and Finland. Besides important choral works, the symphonic poem *Bajka* (Winter's Tale) is also a Polish repertoire piece.

MONK, Edwin George (1819-1900)
English organist and church music composer remembered mainly for hymn tunes and chants. From 1859 to 1883 he was organist of York Minster.

MONK, William Henry (1823-1889)
Remembered as the composer of *Abide with Me* (Eventide) and as an editor of the important first edition of *Hymns Ancient and Modern*. He was related to E.G. Monk (above) and active in London at King's and Bedford Colleges.

MONTE, Filippo di (1521-1603)
Flemish composer of 600 madrigals and 24 masses. He was Kapellmeister to the Emperors Maximilian II and Rudolf II in Vienna and Prague, and from 1568 was a famous singer. In 1583-84 he exchanged letters and compositions with William Byrd in England. His madrigals have been compared with those of Lassus, and his church music with that of Palestrina. Few of his 300 motets have survived.

MONTEVERDI, Claudio (1567-1643)
Great Italian composer who welded together the traditions of the High Renaissance with the new operatic style of the *Camerata*. As a result of the early teaching of Ingegneri, the cathedral organist in Cremona, he had three sets of sacred madrigals and canzonettas published before he was 20. At the age of 24, he was appointed to the important court at Mantua where the more progressive influence of the director, de Wert, led to the composition of revolutionary madrigals in books III, IV and V (1592-1605). By this time, Monteverdi had married one of the singers in the Duke's establishment and been promoted to the position of *maestro di capella* in 1602. His new musical style brought him both fame and notoriety; the fifth book of madrigals included a preface which defended his new composing practice against the attacks of the conservative Artusi. (This book included a *basso continuo* and cadences with unprepared dominant seventh 'in the French manner'.) 1607 was the year of his first opera, *Orfeo*, and that of his wife's death. Nothing is known of the opera's reception at Mantua. The drama unfolds largely in the melodic declamatory style of Peri. This is often highly characterised by chromatic passages, whilst there are many 'set pieces' in the style of the earlier Italian madrigal composers and in the style of the French airs and ballets de cours. For the first time indications are given of contrasting colours in the rather mixed collection of instruments available at that time. The next opera *Arianna* (1608) only survives in the famous Lament but the *Ballo delle Ingrate*, again in the French style, is known to have been performed before the same large and enthusiastic Mantua audience.

Opinions differ on the details of the *Vespers*, also from this period. This enormous work is either for a liturgical performance culminating in one of the *Magnificat* settings or is a convenient collection of separate sacred pieces in Monteverdi's two contrasted styles. At all events its publication in 1610 seems to have been directed towards an appointment in Rome which never materialised. Instead Monteverdi was appointed to a similar position at St. Mark's, Venice in 1613, where he spent most of the remainder of his life.

Only *Il Combattimento di Tancredi e Clorinda* (1624) survives from the early Venetian stage works but several more collections of the newer style 'cantatas' appear in the later volumes of 'madrigals' and the long series of sacred pieces continued. An important set-back occurred in 1630 with first the Sack of Mantua, with which Monteverdi was still connected, and then a recurrence of the plague in Venice; in 1632, Monteverdi took holy orders. By this time his musical fame had spread throughout Europe, thus attracting composers like Schütz, and pupils such as Cavalli, on visits to Venice. Happily Monteverdi's last two operas, perhaps stimulated by the first public opera house (1637), are both extant. *Il ritorno d'Ulisse* (1641) and *L'Incoronazione di Poppea* (1642) lead on naturally to the later bel canto operas of the 18th century with their da capo arias and recitativo secco, and are a wonderful testimonial to the forward-looking vitality of the 75-year-old composer.

MOREAU, Jean Baptiste (1656–1733)

French church musician and composer who moved from Dijon Cathedral into service with Louis XIV. He wrote divertissements for the court and musical interludes for the plays of Racine. He is especially remembered for his choruses for *Esther* (1688) and *Athalie* (1691). He was also a well-known singing teacher of his day.

MORLEY, Thomas (1557–1602)

Most famous English madrigal composer. A choirboy of St. Paul's Cathedral (where he later became organist), he became the pupil of Byrd and was choirmaster at Norwich Cathedral 1583–87. Although, like Byrd, he seems to have been a Papist sympathiser, he became a Gentleman of the Chapel Royal and was granted a printing monopoly by the Queen in 1598. He is perhaps best known for his editing of *The Triumphes of Oriana*, which was only published in 1603 after his death. This included single contributions from most of his contemporaries, perhaps originally as a tribute to the Queen.

His own madrigals, ballets and canzonets take *Musica Transalpina* — a translated collection of the lighter Italian *fa-la-la* madrigals by such composers as Gastoldi — as their starting point and Morley was particularly successful in this genre.

Madrigalls to Foure Voyces (1594) was the first English publication in this style and it was followed by similar collections *to Five Voyces* (1595), *The First Book of Canzonets to Two Voyces* (1595), *Canzonets to Five and Six Voyces* (1597) and *The First Booke of Ayres* (1600) which included *It was a Lover and Lass.*

His church music is less well-known but includes several 'services', *Nolo Mortem Peccatoris* and the verse anthem *Out of the Deep.* The 1600 *Book of Airs* included a lute part and there are a number of his virginal pieces (pavans, galliards and variations on songs) in the *Fitzwilliam Book.* He also published *The First Booke of Consort Lessons made by Divers Exquisite Authors for Six Instruments* (1599) and the English 'teaching book' — *A Plaine and Easie Introduction to Practicall Musicke* (1597) in dialogue form.

MORNINGTON, Earl of (Garrett Colley Wellesley) (1735–1781)

Professor at Dublin University 1764–74 and founder of the Academy of Music there. Mainly self-taught, he is remembered as the composer of an Anglican chant and many glees. His son, the Duke of Wellington, actually opposed the publication of an edition of the glees in 1834.

MOSCHELES, Ignas (1794–1870)
Czech pianist, teacher and composer. After appearances as a child prodigy in his own works, he studied in Vienna under Albrechtsberger and Salieri. He taught Mendelssohn and was one of the first teachers at the new Leipzig Conservatory (1846) founded by Mendelssohn. Besides extensive tours as a pianist, he conducted the Royal Philharmonic Society in London from 1845.
His piano compositions include eight concertos, sonatas and studies. He also wrote chamber music. He was associated with the Beethoven era and did not claim to understand the music of Chopin and Liszt. His improvisations were especially famous.

MOSKOWSKI, Moritz (1854–1925)
Polish pianist and composer remembered for his popular salon pieces, concert pieces, waltzes, etc. He also wrote an opera, an orchestral symphonic poem, concertos for piano and violin besides many songs. He lived in Berlin until 1897 and then Paris, where he was active as a conductor.

MOUTON, Jean (c. 1470–1522)
French pupil of Josquin des Près, and the teacher of Willaert. He was musician to Louis XII and Francois I in Paris. His works, all famous in their time, include nine masses, 75 motets and psalms and some chansons.

MOZART, Leopold (1719–1787)
Austrian violinist, composer and the father of Wolfgang Amadeus. He became Vice-Kapellmeister and Court Composer to the Archbishop of Salzburg and wrote symphonies, concertos, piano sonatas and church music. He is, however, more famous for his *Violin School* (1756).

MOZART,
Wolfgang Amadeus (1756–1791)
The son of Leopold and probably the greatest composer and musician that Austria has produced. His earliest compositions were written down by his father and date from his fifth year. With his talented older sister, he was taken to play in Munich and Vienna in 1762 and welcomed to the heart of the aristocracy. Tours further afield followed in succeeding years and more and more early works were heard in Belgium, Paris and London as well as at the principal German courts. By this time, the boy had become a better keyboard player than his sister and also a competent violinist; besides improvising in competitions and sight-reading before George III, he was composing his first symphonies. In his 12th year, his German operetta *Bastien und Bastienne* was produced. At Salzburg the Archbishop had tested him by keeping him in isolation for a week while composing church music. In London he had met Abel and J.C. Bach and had some singing lessons from the famous male soprano Manzuoli. Leopold was still directing his son's education and the youthful tours culminated in an Italian visit in 1769 where wide recognition greeted his precocious musicality; he produced several opera seria and a number of symphonies.
His return to Salzburg was less successful and a permanent lucrative appointment eluded him. The new Archbishop was much less sympathetic and severely restricted his touring. He continued to compose prolifically — string quartets, five violin concertos and another opera during 1775 and the *Haffner Serenade*, three more masses and six violin sonatas in 1776. Mozart's next tour was only allowed provided that Leopold stayed in Salzburg. The

earlier successes were not repeated in either Germany or Paris; however, a youthful infatuation with the singer Aloysia Weber eventually led to his marriage to her sister Constanze and the more immediate composition of several important concert arias. His return to Salzburg in 1779 was marked by the first of the mature symphonies (K338), the *Sinfonia Concertante* for violin and viola, and in 1780 he composed his great opera seria *Idomeneo*. Following its production in 1781 in Munich, the break with Salzburg and its Archbishop forced Mozart into financial independence and poverty for the rest of his life. His meeting with Haydn in 1785 led to the composition of six quartets which were dedicated to the older composer. The death of Leopold later in the same year was another blow to Mozart. His various operatic ventures did not come to much until he met the librettist Da Ponte, whose adaption of the banned *Marriage of Figaro* by Beaumarchais led to Mozart's greatest success in 1786. This opera buffa was followed in 1787 in Prague by *Don Giovanni*, another big success.

The rest of his life was marred by continued poverty, but in spite of this Mozart poured out the late masterpieces by which he is most remembered: the last three symphonies in E flat, G minor and C major (the '*Jupiter*'), the six string quartets dedicated to the King of Prussia and his last Italian opera buffa *Così fan tutte* (1790). Throughout his life he had written piano sonatas and concertos either for his own use as a performer or for his pupils. By 1785 the piano concerto had become Mozart's greatest contribution to instrumental music. Even the form was largely his own and the last eight of these concertos together with such chamber works as the G minor string quintet form his personal musical testament.

During the last few months of his life he returned to writing Italian opera seria in *La Clemenza de Tito*, and the German Singspiel 'pantomime' opera, *The Magic Flute*. This, with it mixture of naive humour and the most profound human emotions, brings to the surface the idealism prompted by Mozart's freemasonry. In this work, and others such as the *Clarinet Concerto*, his music seemed to transcend personal tragedy at the end of his life. He became obsessed with the mysterious commission of the *Requiem*, which he was never to finish; his health weakened and he succumbed to partial paralysis and early death. His pauper's grave was unmarked.

The last word on Mozart's musical achievement is unlikely ever to be written. Each generation takes from his sublime masterpieces what is relevant to its spiritual needs. The appeal of his music continues to change — the music itself endures.

MUFFAT, Georg (1653–1704)
German organist in Strasbourg and Salzburg. He left a considerable amount of organ music and concerti grossi.

MUFFAT, Gottlieb (1690–1770)
The son of Georg above, and an organist in Vienna. He composed music for organ and harpsichord, some of which was used by Handel.

MUNDY, John (d. 1630)
The son of William (below), and also a Gentleman of the Chapel Royal. He became organist of Eton College and succeeded Merbecke at St. George's, Windsor. *Songs and Psalmes* (1594) were published by him and he contributed to the *Triumphes of Oriana*. There are several keyboard pieces by him in the *Fitzwilliam Virginal Book*.

MUNDY, William (c. 1529–c. 1591)
English composer, and Gentleman of the Chapel Royal from 1564. Remembered as the composer of *O Lorde, the Maker of All Things*.

MURRILL, Herbert Henry John (1909–1952)
Oxford-trained musician who was active in London theatres with a jazz opera *Man in Cage* (1930) and much incidental music. He also wrote orchestral and chamber music, and became Head of BBC Music in 1950.

MUSGRAVE, Thea (b. 1928)
Scottish composer, educated at Edinburgh University, who later studied with Nadia Boulanger at the Paris Conservatoire. Her compositions include opera, ballet, several cantatas, three chamber concertos, a clarinet concerto (1968) and various orchestral, chamber and piano pieces.

MUSSORGSKY, Modeste Petrovich (1839–1881)
Russian Nationalist composer. He was a natural musician and a good pianist and singer whose early professional life was spent in the army. Encouraged by Dargominsky and Balakirev, he resigned from the army in 1858 in order to devote his time to music though he was slow to show any marked individuality in composition. His private income largely disappeared in 1861 with the liberation of the serfs and the consequent fall in land values. He began to express peasant life in some highly original songs and started work on an opera which was abandoned after two years. By 1869, however, he had completed his best-known work, the opera *Boris Godunov*. It was successfully produced in 1874 after it had been rewritten. The work, however, was still uncompromising in its originality and was shunned by the musical establishment. By this time, Mussorgsky had had to take a job as a clerk in a government office and was drinking heavily. On his death the opera *Khovanstchina* was left unfinished.
His most popular instrumental works are the orchestral tone poem *A Night on the Bare Mountain* (1867) and the piano work *Pictures at an Exhibition* (1874). His songs entitle him to be called the 'Russian Schumann'. His musical style derives directly from the rhythms of Russian speech and folk song and the direct simplicity of dramatic realism. His genius was recognised but his music's lack of sophistication and surface smoothness led such composers as Rimsky-Korsakov to rewrite several of his works after his death. This 'editing' for performance included a bowdlerised version of *Khovanstchina* and a very popular abridged version of *Boris Godunov* which held the stage until 1928; only since then have the two original versions become generally known again. In his direct dramatic effects, Mussorgsky anticipated many 20th century effects such as harmonic and melodic use of the whole tone scale, changing rhythmic metres and bare orchestral textures. He is recognised today as the most important historical figure in Russian Nationalism.

N

NARDINI, Pietro (1722–1793)

Italian violinist and composer. He was a pupil of Tartini, and worked in Stuttgart and at the court of the Duke of Tuscany. Among much violin music, he left six concertos, six sonatas for two violins and six violin duos. He also wrote six string quartets and six flute trios.

NARES, James (1715–1783)

English organist and composer; appointed to York Minster in 1734 and to the Chapel Royal in 1756. Apart from the anthem *The Souls of the Righteous* and other church music, he published three collections of harpsichord pieces as well as catches and glees.

NAUMANN, Johann Gottlieb (1741–1801)

German composer active at Dresden and in Sweden. He had lessons with Tartini and Padre Martini and wrote many operas and much church music. He is best known, however, as the putative composer of the *Dresden Amen* which became the most important leitmotif in Wagner's *Parsifal*.

NICHOLSON, Richard (c. 1570–1639)

The first professor of music in Oxford University (1626) who left several madrigals and anthems which have been published in recent years.

NICHOLSON, Sidney Hugo (1875–1947)

English organist and founder of what is now the Royal School of Church Music. His compositions were almost all for the church and included some excellent hymn tunes. He wrote several operettas for his own choristers including *The Boy Bishop* and *The Children of the Chapel*.

NEILSEN, Carl August (1865–1931)

Denmark's greatest composer began his professional life as a military bandsman at 14. After studying at the Copenhagen Conservatoire (1884–89) he earned his living as a violinist in the Royal Theatre Orchestra there. His 1st Symphony was played by this orchestra under Svendsen and by 1902 he had conducted his opera *Saul and David* and 2nd Symphony (*The Four Temperaments*) there also. In 1905 his most famous 'Danish' work, the opera *Maskarade*, was produced and from 1908 to 1914 he was permanent conductor of the Royal Theatre Orchestra. From 1915 he was able to spend more time on composition. His 3rd Symphony (*Sinfonia espansiva*) had been heard in 1912 and the symphonic cycle continued with No.4 (*The Inextinguishable*, 1918), No. 5 (1922) and No.6 (*Sinfonia semplice*, 1926). These six symphonies invite comparison with those of Sibelius in Finland. Both composers started in the world of Brahms and both breathe the spirit of 19th century Nationalism. Both composers later became trend setters of the 20th century but Nielsen never had the advocacy of international conductors. His practice of 'progressive tonality' made less immediate impact than did Sibelius' 'syncretic' approach to musical form. It is, however, through this cycle of symphonies that Nielsen's music has become such an important part of the modern concert repertoire.

Neilson also wrote much incidental music as well as concertos for violin (1911), flute (1926) and clarinet (1928). Much of his chamber music belongs to his student period but four string quartets date from 1888 to 1906 and the wind quintet from 1922. One of his last works was the large-scale organ work *Commotio*. Several cantatas bring to an end another side of his creative genius.

NICOLAI, Karl Otto Ehrenfried (1810–1849)
German operatic composer who studied in Rome and wrote several pieces in the Italian style (1838–41) before directing firstly the Vienna Court Opera and then, in 1847, the Berlin Opera. Today he is remembered almost entirely for his German opera, *The Merry Wives of Windsor*, which was produced only two months before his death.

NIETSCHE, Friedrich (1844–1900)
Important German philosopher, author of *Also sprach Zarathustra*, and, for some time, a disciple of Wagner. He later became one of Wagner's most bitter opponents criticising his movement away from the Teutonic ideal in favour of the 'Mediterraneanising' of music.
He was an assiduous amateur composer and left songs, piano pieces, and *Hymne an das Leben* for chorus and orchestra (1887).

NOBLE, Thomas Tertius (1867–1953)
English organist and composer who resigned his post at York Minster in 1912 to become organist of St. Thomas', 5th Avenue, New York. His best known composition is the setting of the *Evening Canticles* in B minor but he wrote several other settings of services and a number of unaccompanied anthems. There are also several larger-scale works such as the incidental music to *The Wasps* and the burlesque *Jupiter*.

NONO, Luigi (b. 1924)
Together with Berio, he is the best-known Italian composer of the post-war period. His compositions take as their starting point the serial music of Webern. These avant-garde pieces were prominent in the early 1950's in the festivals at Darmstadt under the direction of his old teacher Scherchen. Most of these compositions were in the tradition of 'protest' — both sociological and political. These include *La victoire de Guernica* (for chorus and orchestra, based on Picasso, 1954), the opera *Intolleranza* (1960), *Sul ponte de Hiroshima* (for soprano, tenor and orchestra, 1962) and *Non consumiamo Marx* (for voices and tape, 1969).

NOVELLO, Ivor (1893–1951)
British actor, playwright, composer and manager. His first song was published at the age of 15. *Keep the Home Fires Burning* was one of the best known of all the songs in the 1st World War. Later he was very successful with light musical shows in the West End of London such as *Glamorous Night* (1935) and *The Dancing Years* (1939).

NOVELLO, Vincent (1781–1861)
Italian-born founder of the London publishing company and an important practising musician. He was organist at various Roman Catholic churches, pianist, viola player and conductor. Besides editing works by Purcell, Handel, Haydn, Mozart and Beethoven, he composed much sacred music, many glees, and hymn tunes, some of which are still used.

O

OBRECHT, Jacob (c. 1453–1505)
Netherlands composer of church music. Although he visited Italy, his active life was divided between Utrecht, Cambrai, Antwerp Cathedral and Bruges. He was ordained by the year 1480. Twenty volumes of his compositions appeared in the early 20th century.

OCKEGHEM, Jean de (c. 1425–1495)
Flemish composer who was a pupil of Dufay (and perhaps Binchois) and the teacher of Josquin des Près. He was in the service of the French Charles VII in 1454 as a chaplain but from 1459 most of his life was spent at Tours.
From a historical aspect, Ockeghem's compositions are noted for the ingenuity of their canonic techniques in such works as *Missa cujusvis toni* and *Missa prolationum*. His contrapuntal facility was as evident in the famous 36-voice motet as was his musicality in the relatively simple *Mimi Mass*. All are distinguished by the vitality of their rhythms and vocal lines and it is with justice that Ockeghem is regarded as the founder of the New Netherlands School.

OFFENBACH, Jacques (1819–1880)
Famous German-Jewish composer of nearly 100 French operettas. His father was nicknamed Offenbach from his town of origin and his seventh son was something of a child prodigy as a composer and cellist. After a year at the Paris Conservatoire, he made his living for a time mainly as a cellist touring and playing in salons. From 1849 he was conductor at various Parisian theatres where he wrote, at first, incidental pieces. From 1855 he was manager of the Théâtre des Bouffes-Parisiens where he became famous for his successful productions of such works as Bizet's *Doctor Miracle*. His own first success followed with *Orpheus in the Underworld* in 1858. His other masterwork, *Tales of Hoffman* was not produced until after his death; many more of his operettas are now proving modern successes, such as *La Belle Hélène* (1865), *La Vie Parisienne* (1866) or *La Périchole* (1868).

ONSLOW, George (1784–1853)
French pupil of Dussek, and Cramer in London. He is remembered almost entirely for his use of the double-bass in his 34 string quintets and 36 string quartets. This is said to have been occasioned by the famous Dragonetti having to deputise for an absentee 2nd cellist. He also wrote three comic operas, four symphonies and much other chamber music.

ORFF, Carl (1895–1982)
Munich composer whose early activities included keyboard and cello playing and childhood compositions based on intuition rather than teaching. He also worked as an operatic repetiteur and conductor. After the 1st World War he composed several suites of incidental music. In 1924 he became interested in gymnastic dancing and the training of amateurs in percussion orchestras. The result of this experience was the famous *Das Schulwerk* in the field of musical education with its invention of 'teaching' instruments. In the meantime he had become the conductor of a Bach Society and made some arrangements of the music of Monteverdi.
Orff only recognised his compositions from *Carmina Burana* (1937) onwards and certainly this is his best-known work. It is marked by the combination of primary rhythmic patterns and ostinati, free rhythm monodies, simple static chord-like

textures and short melodic motifs. Much of his later music is designed to be seen and thus *Die Bauerin* (1945) has important parts for speakers and uses verbal declamatory rhythms. However limited his musical techniques, the primitive force is often very powerful in its impact.

ORR, Buxton (b. 1924)
English composer, who was first trained as a doctor and then became prominent as a composer of film and theatrical music. He was also the conductor of the London Jazz Composer's Orchestra. His works included several brass band works such as the concertos for trumpet and trombone, a one-act opera, much light and educational music, the orchestral *Triptych* (1977), and his music-theatre piece *Unicorn* (1981).

ORR, Robin (b. 1909)
Scottish musician who has been equally influential as an academic (Professor successively at Glasgow and Cambridge) and as a composer. His works include two symphonies (1965 and 1971), the opera *Full Circle* (1967), choral music including the *Festival Te Deum* (1950) and *Spring Cantata* (1955) as well as several song cycles.

ORTIZ, Diego (fl. 1550)
Spanish composer who is credited with being the first to use 'divisions' (variations) in his published pieces for bass viol and keyboard. Some of his motets were also printed in lute tablature.

OUSELEY, Sir Frederick Arthur Gore (Bart) (1825–1889)
Brilliant English academic who, after he was ordained, became Professor of Music at Oxford in 1855. He was a ready improvisor and prolific composer of church music. Little of this is heard today except *How Goodly are thy Tents* and the eight-part O *Saviour of the World*. He is more important for his text-books, his editing of the music of Gibbons and his generous endowment of St. Michael's, Tenbury, as a 'cathedral' musical foundation.

P

PACHELBEL, Johann (1653–1706)
German organist and composer of church and keyboard music who had considerable influence on J.S. Bach. He was a pupil of Kerll and held posts at Stuggart and Nuremberg. His most famous works are *Hexachordum Apollinis* — six sets of variations (1699) and many chorale preludes (mainly published in 1693 and usually consisting of fugal treatment of each successive line of the tune). His six suites for two violins and continuo are still occasionally heard.

PADERWSKI, Ignacy Jan (1860–1941)
Famous Polish pianist and composer, who became for a year, in 1919, the first Prime Minister of the reconstituted Polish state. Considering his later eminence, he was a relatively slow developer as a pianist. His first composition dates from his sixth year and his first work was published when he was 18. From 1890 onwards he became internationally known as a performer. During a busy life he managed to compose a piano concerto, an opera and symphony as well as many shorter pieces of which the *Minuet in G* is the most often heard. His *Symphony* (1907) expresses the epic story of the Polish people and, partly because of his speeches, he became an obvious representative of an independent Poland at the Versailles Conference. He later appeared in the film *The Moonlight Sonata* (1938).

PAISIELLO, Giovanni (1740–1816)
Italian composer of opera buffa, whose *Barber of Seville* (1782) was only eventually superseded by Rossini's setting of 1816. He wrote the music for Napoleon's coronation. His output included symphonies, concertos, string quartets, much church music and more than 100 operas.

PAGANINI, Niccolo (1782–1840)
Great Italian violin virtuoso and composer for this instrument. The legend of his playing and his life started during his childhood when his mother saw an apparition telling of her son's future greatness. He was soon believed to have sold his soul to the devil in return for his technical mastery. His dissolute habits encouraged these legends and he paid the price with some bad health. His Violin Concertos owe something to the style of his friend Rossini. Paganini is perhaps best known for the famous theme from one of his 24 *Caprices* for unaccompanied violin which was used by Brahms and Rachmaninov, among others, as the theme for sets of variations.

PALESTRINA, Giovanni Pierluigi da (1525–1594)
Great Roman composer of the Counter-Reformation. From 1544 to 1551 he was organist and choirmaster of his native cathedral at Palestrina near Rome, after which, on the Bishop becoming Pope Julius III, he was called to the Sistine Choir in Rome. The next Pope, Marcellus II, soon applied pressure with a view to simplifying the style of church music so that words would always be audible. This movement led to the composition of his *Missa Papae Marcelli* in the new style. When a 'third' Pope, Paul IV continued the musical reformation by expressing his disapproval of married singers, Palestrina left the Sistine Chapel to succeed Lassus at St. John's, Lateran. In 1561 he moved to Santa Maria Maggiore, where he had been a choirboy, but in 1570 he was reinstated in his old post at the Sistine Chapel. Soon after the death of his wife and two sons in an epidemic he entered the priesthood, but

in 1571, having presumably renounced his orders, he married again. Palestrina is known to have been active in business ventures until he retired to his native town a year or two before his death. Apart from a few keyboard *Ricercari* and about 100 madrigals, all Palestrina's compositions are for the church. Of the many masses the best known are *Assumpta est Maria* (à 6), *Dum complerentur* (à 6), *Aeterna Christi munera* (à 4) and the *Missa Brevis* (à 4). The motets are even more numerous and often form the basis of the 'paraphrased' masses of the corresponding names, such as *Tu es Petrus* or *Alma Redemptoris*. Palestrina wrote in the unaccompanied *a capella* style favoured in the Sistine Chapel compared with the instrumentally supported style which was associated with St. Mark's, Venice. His technique was extremely polished, and the 'expressive' roughness, found in earlier more expansive composers such as Josquin, was refined into smooth succinct vocal lines, in which all dissonances were 'prepared and resolved'. (This smooth *Palestrina style* was to become the basis of later academic teaching via Padre Martini.) Such a work as *Stabat Mater* (1590) for double choir has received the homage of Burney and Wagner in recent centuries and well epitomises the achievements of the *Prince of Music* in a well-filled field.

PALMGREN, Selim (1878–1951)
Finnish pianist, conductor and composer who was for a time a pupil of Busoni. His first opera was produced in 1910 to his own Swedish libretto (it was revived in Finnish in 1929). From 1912 he was involved in extensive European and American tours and was often joined by his first wife, the singer Maikki Järnefelt. His many songs were performed either by her or his second wife, the singer Minna Talvik. Most of his other compositions consist of small-scale piano pieces which are marked by a smooth melodic and harmonic originality and owe something to Finnish folk rhythms. He also left five piano concertos, stage and choral works, and some orchestral pieces.

PANUFNIK, Andrzej (b. 1914)
Polish conductor and composer who, after holding conducting posts in Cracow and Warsaw, settled in England in 1954 and was conductor of the City of Birmingham Symphony Orchestra from 1957 to 1959. His compositions are in an advanced style and are mainly orchestral: *Tragic Overture* (1942), *Sinfonia Rustica* (1949), *Piano Concerto* (1962), *Katyn Epitaph* (1967). There are also piano and choral works and pieces based on Polish folk songs.

PARADIES, Pietro Domenico (1707–1791)
Italian harpsichordist and composer who is chiefly remembered for the *Toccata in A* — a movement from one of his 12 sonatas. Three of his operas were produced, the last being after his move to London in 1747 where he became a very successful teacher of singing and harpsichord.

PARKER, Horatio William (1863–1919)
American composer, teacher, and church musician. His first music lessons were from his mother who taught him piano and organ. Later he studied in Boston, and in 1880 took the first of many appointments as a church organist. From 1882 to 1885 he studied in Germany, and here wrote his first major compositions.
Returning to New York in 1886, he spent the next seven years teaching and playing, and it was during these years that he achieved his first recognition as a composer. Much of his church music was published at this time, and in 1893 the cantata *Dream-king and his Love* won the National Conservatory prize. Frequent performances of *Hora Novissima* brought the composer into prominence, and his

standing as a respected composer was confirmed with his receiving the honorary degree of Master of Music from Yale University in 1894. The following year he accepted the Battell Professorship of the Theory of Music at Yale, holding this position for the rest of his life.

Commissions from England at the turn of the century led to more popularity across the Atlantic, and he accepted the honorary degree of MusD from Cambridge University in 1902.

Apart from the early years, Parker's *main* contrapuntal output was in the field of choral music, although the symphonic poem *A Northern Ballad* and the *Concerto for Organ and Orchestra* were both popular with American orchestras.

Although he was considered one of the most highly-respected composers of his day, Horatio Parker's popularity has declined considerably since his death.

PARROT, Ian (b. 1916)

British academic and composer. His works range from opera to a Symphony (1946) and chamber music. He has also written works for chorus and piano.

PARRY, Sir Charles Hubert (1848–1918)

English composer, writer and administrator, who, with Stanford, is considered to have led the 'Second English Renaissance' in the 1880's. He took his MusB while still at Eton and studied with Sterndale Bennett and Macfarren at Oxford. He interrupted his studies, however, to spend three years in business. His early successes were largely at the Three Choirs Festival where the *Scenes from Shelley's Prometheus Unbound* (1880) was recognised as a new departure in choral music. *Blest Pair of Sirens* (1887) confirmed his status as a composer and after the oratorio *Job* (1892), and several honorary degrees, he succeeded Sir George Grove in 1894 as Director of the RCM and was appointed Professor of Music at Oxford in 1900. He was knighted in 1898 and made a baronet in 1903. He was unusually prolific in his compositions: five symphonies, witty incidental music for three of Aristophanes' comedies, significant works for various chamber combinations, more than 100 songs, and important works for the organ repertoire. But it was in choral music that he was most influential. Besides much church music, he set the words of many of England's greatest poets and inspired a new generation of English composers. *Jerusalem* (1916) remains as a second national anthem. In a more rarified style the six motets forming *Songs of Farewell* (1919) are a national heritage.

His influential books and addresses such as the *Art of Music* (1893) were largely responsible for the 'German' outlook in English music which is still with us. As a result of his teaching and example, English music again assumed its rightful place in Europe.

PARRY, Joseph (1841–1903)

Welsh composer, who after having gained some musical experience when his family emigrated to the USA, returned to Wales and distinguished himself at an Eisteddfod in 1862-63. A public appeal made it possible for him to study at the RAM for three years. While there he won various prizes and was awarded a Mus.D. at Cambridge. Later he became Professor of Music at Aberystwyth.

His works include several operas, oratorios and cantatas, orchestral and chamber works although it is in his part songs that his greatest influence lies. He is chiefly remembered today for the hymn tune *Aberystwyth* (Jesu, Lover of my Soul).

PARSLEY, Osbert (1511–1585)

English singer and composer who was a lay-clerk at Norwich Cathedral. He left some Latin motets and services for the newer English rite.

PARSONS, Robert (d. 1570)
English composer who became a Gentleman of the Chapel Royal in 1563. He left some church music (services and English anthems) together with several instrumental *In Nomines.*

PASQUALI, Nicolo (d. 1757)
Italian violinist and composer who lived mostly in Edinburgh from 1740 and published songs in 1750. Two sets of sonatas — for violin and continuo and two violins, viola and continuo respectively — were published in London as well as 12 Overtures 'for' (with) French Horns, being published in Edinburgh. He also wrote *Thoroughbass made Easy* and *Art of Fingering the Harpsichord.*

PASQUINI, Bernardo (1637-1710)
Italian keyboard player and composer who was a pupil of Cesti and a student of the works of Palestrina. He was prominent as an organist in Rome and also harpsichordist at the opera house at the time when Corelli was 'leader'. His operas and oratorios share some of Handel's characteristics but his many harpsichord pieces have proved to be historically more significant. Among his pupils were Durante, Muffat and Gasparini.

PATRICK, Nathaniel (d. 1595)
English composer who was organist of Worcester Cathedral from 1590. He was succeeded by Tomkins. Little of his music has survived apart from two services for the Anglican rite.

PATTERSON, Paul (b. 1947)
English composer, who trained at the RAM and with Richard Rodney Bennett. He has been associated with the avant-garde by virtue of his activities as a performer and teacher of electronic music; but he considers himself 'very much a *motivic* composer' in an older tradition. He has also been involved with school and amateur music: *The Canterbury Psalms* (1981) for King's School, Canterbury and *Messa Maris* (1983) for the Three Choirs Festival. Contrasted with these have been *Brain Storm* (1978) for four voices and live electronics, and *At the Stoll Point of the Turning World* (1980) for the Nash Ensemble.

PEARSALL, Robert Lucas de (1795-1856)
English composer, who after showing unusual facility as a child, practised as a lawyer until he was 30 and then recommenced the study of music in Germany, where he remained for most of the rest of his life. Apart from orchestral and choral music, much church music (for both Anglican and Latin rites) and some theoretical writings, he was most remarkable for his enthusiastic rediscovery of the English Madrigal School, and for his own 60 or so compositions in this style. The *a capella* arrangement of *In Dulci Jubilo* retains its popularity today.

PEERSON, Martin (c. 1572-1651)
English organist and composer. He is first mentioned in connection with a setting of words of Ben Jonson as part of a masque played before the King and Queen in 1604. He is also said to have written 'many lessons for the virginals, which is his principle instrument' though only four pieces in the *Fitzwilliam Book* have survived. He is thought to have become organist at St. Paul's Cathedral in 1613 and to have held this post until his death.
His works comprise approximately 30 English a capella anthems, about 10 Latin motets and some secular madrigals. Most important are the string *Fantasies* and *Almaines* and the two collections for 'Voyces and Vials': *Private Musicke or the First Booke of Ayres* (1620) and *Mottects or Grave Chamber Musique* (1630); the last is described as 'Containing Songs of five parts... some full, and some Verse and

Chorus... with an organ part; which for want of organs, may be performed on Virginals, Base lute, Bandora or Irish Harpe'.

PEETERS, Flor (b. 1903)
Belgian organist and composer. He has held many academic and playing appointments in the Low Countries and is well known as an international recitalist. His most influential compositions have probably been the many organ chorale preludes based equally on Plainsong and Lutheran chorales. He has also written a sinfonia, a *lied*-symphony, organ concertos and concert pieces as well as *Ars Organi* — an organ method in three volumes.

PENDERECKI, Krzystof (b. 1933)
Polish composer whose maturity coincided with the more 'liberal' attitude in Polish culture after 1956. His first international achievement was the well-known *St. Luke Passion* (1966) with its even more popular *Stabat Mater*; this work uses choral speech, spatial polyphony, 'splintered' words, highly dissonant choral clusters together with modal and tonal harmonies. Starting as a serial composer, Penderecki has absorbed the various practices and innovations of his contemporaries and elders such as Lutoslawski, Nono, Ligeti and Xenakis. His religious humanism lightens the more uncompromising aspects of his style.
Perhaps his most famous works are the *Threnody to the Victims of Hiroshima* (1960) for 52 strings, and the opera *The Devils of Loudon* (1970). His output also includes two string quartets, a cello concerto, *Psalmus for Tape* (1961) and such works as *Capriccio for Oboe and Strings* (1965).

PEPUSCH, John Christopher (1667–1752)
German theorist, organist and composer who lived in London from 1700, where he was active as a player and composer for the stage. In spite of his successful work with Gay on the *Beggars Opera* (1728), the music he wrote for several masques brought him little lasting fame. He is more remembered for his learned treatises than for his many odes, sonatas and concertos.

PEPYS, Samuel (1633–1703)
Famous English diarist and enthusiastic musical amateur. His most famous song is *Beauty Retire*.

PERGOLESI, Giovanni Battista (1710–1736)
Prolific Italian composer, who, in a very short life, managed to make his mark in no less than three musical areas.
He is best known for the amazing posthumous popularity of *La Serva Padrona* (1733) which set the pattern for opera *buffa* for almost a century, by developing the tradition of the comic *intermezzo* originally performed between the acts of the opera *seria*.
Pergolesi's successful opera buffa attracted commissions from Naples, such as the Mass for double five-part choir and orchestra. The famous *Stabat Mater*, also intended for Naples, was a late work. His less successful opera seria are said to have encouraged him to write more extensively for instrumental combinations. Certainly the many sonatas and concertos with strings and bass, like the beautifully written harpsichord lessons and sonatas, anticipate later textures and procedures.
The picture of Pergolesi's output is complicated by the attribution of many works to him whose authenticity is doubtful. Opinions still differ as to his achievements, but there can be no doubt of the freshness of his style or the impact of *La Serva Padrona* in Paris in 1752. It was there that it was taken by one side in the 'Guerre des Bouffons' as representative of Italian music as opposed to the stately French tradition of Rameau.

PERI, Jacopo (1561–1633)
Italian composer and singer who is credited with writing the first opera for the Florentine *Camerata* in 1597. At that time he was in the service of the Medici as a singer and contributor to court *Intermedii*. The so-called *Camerata* group was active there in trying to revive the tradition of classical Greek tragedy. Urged on by the scholar Corsi, Peri set a libretto by the poet Rinuccini, in a new declamatory style — known as *stile rappresentativo*. This first opera, *Dafne*, has not survived but *Euridice* (1600) is the earliest extant opera. When the opera was composed it was more famous than the setting by Peri's rival Caccini. Although Peri also contributed the recitatives to Monteverdi's *Arianna* (1608), he never suceeded in equalling his own earlier works; nor did he ever reach Caccini's standard of *arioso* in the new monodic style.

PEROSI, Lorenzo (1872–1956)
Italian priest and prolific composer of church music. He was successively choirmaster of St. Mark's, Venice and in 1898 of the Sistine Chapel where he had considerable influence on Pope Pius X in his decree, *Motu Proprio* (1903). This dealt with the reform of Catholic church music, encouraging plainsong and Renaissance music at the expense of the prevalent Romantic style.
Perosi's own music was enormously popular at the time though it seems to modern taste to be an unintegrated mixture of earlier styles and uncharacterised Romanticism. Besides oratorios and organ music he wrote extensively for orchestral and chamber music combinations. From 1917 onwards much of his life was clouded by mental illness.

PERICHETTI, Vincent (b. 1915)
American composer and writer who has been active as a teacher of composition at the Julliard School since 1947. His compositions are tonally based, though often highly dissonant. They are often polytonal, melodic and rhythmically exciting. They include eight symphonies, four string quartets, songs, music for piano, band and small ensembles.

PÉROTIN-le-Grand (c. 1180–c.1236)
Famous composer of the Notre Dame School. His predecessor, Leonin, wrote his *Magnus Liber Organi* in melismatic and unmeasured two-part *organum* style above the prolonged notes of the plainsong melodies. Perotin revised this work, often increasing the part writing to three and four voices. He retained the sustained plainsong notes but used the newer troubadour rhythms in the added parts and often added free *clausulae* (without plainsong) in *conductus* style. In his music there is also a sense of major tonality 'radiance' in his chordal upper parts.

PFITZNER, Hans Erich (1869–1949)
German composer who opposed modernist tendencies in his writings and composed in the Romantic tradition. In Germany and Austria his operas, symphonic music and chamber music are still heard. Elsewhere he is remembered only for his opera *Palestrina* (1917), in the idiom of Wagner and Strauss, and composed to his own libretto.

PHILIDOR, Francois André (1726–1795)
French composer and famous international chess player. His music dates mainly from his return to Paris in 1754. It was there that his series of opéra comique was very successful, especially *Tom Jones* (1764) and *L'Amant Deguisé* (1769).

PHILIPS, Montague Fawcett (1885–1969)
English light music composer. He is chiefly remembered for the operetta, *The Rebel Maid* (1921) and his many songs and piano

pieces in an attractive and fluent style.

PHILIPS, Peter (c. 1560–c. 1629)
English Catholic organist and composer who spent most of his life after 1590 in the Netherlands. He was organist at Antwerp, and at the Chapel Royal, Brussels from 1611. Little is known of his early life in England. 19 of his virginal pieces are in the *Fitzwilliam Virginal Book* and two collections of madrigals (in the Italian style) were published in Antwerp in 1591 and 1603 (each being republished later). Subsequently he was ordained. Collections of motets and other church music appeared in 1612 and 1613 (together with reprints) and two collections with basso continuo in 1616, 1623 and 1628.
Like John Bull, Philips was known to Sweelinck and his music was appreciated throughout Europe. His best-known motet in England is *Ascendit Deus.*

PIATTI, Alfredo Carlo (1822–1901)
Italian cellist and composer. After extensive European tours he spent most of his later years in London where he exercised much influence on its musical life and composers. Besides editing and arranging much for his own instrument, his own compositions were very popular. They include two cello concertos, six cello sonatas, many songs with cello accompaniment, and light orchestral pieces.

PICCINI, Nicola (1728–1800)
Famous Italian operatic composer, who is today remembered as the figurehead of the anti-Gluck campaign in Paris from 1778 to 1780 although he himself never encouraged this rivalry. His early operas were performed in Naples and their success led to his celebrated opera buffa *La Cecchina* or *La Buona Figliuola* (Rome, 1760). When he was invited to Paris (on most favourable terms) by Marie Antoinette, his own setting of *Iphigénie en Tauride* in the agreed competition was brilliantly outclassed by that of Gluck. Piccini remained in Paris until the events of the Revolution forced his return to Italy, but he returned in 1798, where, in spite of support from Napoleon, he died in poverty.
Piccini was unusually prolific as a composer and is credited with over 120 operas. Despite the fact that his overtures, orchestration and ensembles were much admired, his obvious musical virtues hardly qualify him as a major rival to Gluck.

PIERNÉ, Gabriel (1863–1937)
French composer and conductor who was a pupil of Franck and Massenet at the Paris Conservatoire. From 1903 to 1932 he was associated with the Concerts Colonne as conductor. His compositions include operas, oratorios, ballets, symphonic poems and 'programme' overtures as well as chamber works, songs and organ pieces. His style is marked by fastidious and graceful melodic and harmonic invention.

PIERSON (Pearson), Henry Hugo (1815–1873)
English composer who spent most of his life in Germany. Apart from many songs, mainly to English words in a Mendelssohnian style, and the oratorio *Jerusalem* (Norwich, 1852), he wrote four German operas and several 'Shakespearian' overtures.

PIJPER, Willem (1894–1947)
Dutch composer, teacher and writer, who, as Director of the Rotterdam Conservatoire from 1930, was considered to be the leader of the Dutch 20th century school of composers. His works reflect his interests in French music and literature, and in the music of Mahler, Flemish folk song and even Stravinsky and Schönberg. His compositions tend to progress from the complexity of the 1st Symphony (1917) to the directness of the *Wind Trio* (1927) and include an opera, three symphonies, three

concertos, choral, chamber and incidental music.

PILKINGTON, Francis (c. 1562–1638)
English madrigal composer. Most of his life was based at Chester Cathedral first as 'chaunter', later minor canon, and precentor from 1623. His two major publications — *The First Booke of Songs or Ayres of 4-parts* (1605) and the *Second Set of Madrigals and Pastorals of 3, 4, 5 and 6-parts* (1624) are both designed for performance either as lute songs or as 'apt for violls and voyces'.

PISTON, Walter (1894–1976)
American composer and academic, and Professor of Music at Harvard University from 1944 to 1960. His own training was first in art at Massachussetts and then, after the 1st World War, in music, firstly at Harvard and then with Nadia Boulanger. His style is that of rather astringent Neo-Classicism. His music has the power of rhythmic complexity and the workmanship of linear contrapuntal strength. Most of his output is for orchestral or chamber combinations.

PIZZETTI, Ildebrando (1880–1968)
Italian composer and educationalist. An early interest in plainsong, Renaissance and Baroque Italian music led him away from the style of the popular Puccini and Mascagni towards the style of the avant-garde group of Malipiero and Respighi (1911). Later he became more of a reactionary in his work at Milan University (1924–36) and at the Accademia Sta. Cecilia (1936–60). His interests as a composer tended to be derived from Wagner, Moussorgsky and Debussy rather than from Stravinsky and Schönberg. He wrote most of his operatic plots himself basing them on Greek and Old Testament subjects, e.g. *Fedra* (1915) and *Debora e Jaele* (1922). Much of his later work was incidental music for theatrical classics, such as *Agamemnon* (1930), and orchestral works such as the *Violin Concerto* (1944) and the *Harp Concerto* (1960). His chamber and piano music and songs belong to his earlier period. His series of unaccompanied choral works continued with two *Composizioni Corali* (1961).

PLEYEL, Ignaz Joseph (1757–1831)
Prolific Austrian composer. From 1807 he was the founder-owner of a piano factory in Paris, this last activity absorbing all his energies. He was a favourite pupil of Haydn for five years and conducted in London. His works include 29 symphonies, five books of string quintets, 45 string quartets, 18 flute quartets, as well as many concertos and sonatas.

PONCHIELLI, Amilcare (1834–1886)
Italian operatic composer who is chiefly remembered for *La Gioconda* (1876), although several other operas are still in the Italian repertoire. His later years were partly spent as choirmaster of Bergamo Cathedral and Professor of Composition at the Milan Conservatoire.

POOT, Marcel (b. 1901)
Belgian composer and a pupil of Dukas. In 1935 he founded the 'Synthésistes' and championed their progressive ideas by his musical criticism. He taught at the Brussels Conservatoire where he became Director in 1949. His music is tonal, and Neo-Classical in its wit and precision, and includes operas, ballets, symphonies, chamber and piano music as well as film and radio scores.

POPPER, David (1843–1913)
Czech cellist and composer for his instrument. He was active as an international soloist and also played in the Vienna Court Opera and in the Hubay Quartet. He wrote four cello concertos, many études and three suites for cello and piano.

PORPORA, Niccolo Antonio (1686–1767)
Neapolitan singing teacher and composer. He wrote 53 operas, six oratorios, many solo cantatas, much church music, 12 violin sonatas and eight keyboard fugues. His work was praised by Handel and from 1729 Porpora set up in rivalry to him in London. Among his pupils were the singers Caffarelli (who, Porpora insisted, studied the same page of vocalises for five years), the famous castrato Farinelli and the composers Hasse and Haydn. In spite of his European reputation as a musician, he died in poverty.

PORTER, Cole (1893–1964)
American composer and lyricist of many popular songs such as *Begin the Beguine*. He also wrote outstanding musical comedies, of which the most famous was *Kiss me Kate* (1948).

PORTER, Walter (c. 1595–1659)
English composer who was a member of the Chapel Royal 1617–44 and Master of the Choristers at Westminster Abbey 1639–44. His madrigals and ayres are intended to be sung with instruments 'after the manner of Consort Musique'. He also wrote recitative in the style of Monteverdi, a pupil of whom he is said to have been at one time.

POSTON, Elizabeth (b. 1905)
English composer and pianist, who after nine years as an archaeologist, worked with the BBC (1940–45). She wrote criticism and programme notes, prepared broadcasting editions of 17th century music and wrote extensively for radio. Most of her compositions have been choral, vocal and for chamber combinations.

POTTER, (Philip) Ciprani (1792–1871)
English pianist, composer and conductor who did much to introduce Beethoven's music to England. He was principal of the RAM (1832–59). Many of his works were performed by the Philharmonic Society, notably four of his nine symphonies, four overtures and three piano concertos. He was also responsible for much piano music and many arrangements based on earlier Viennese composers.

POULENC, Francis (1899–1963)
French composer who was first known as a member of 'Les Six' (1920). This was a group of young, forward-looking composers, who were at the time bringing into their music aspects of the music hall and the ordinary vulgarities of city life. (This was a reaction to the seriousness of late Romanticism and the subtle atmospheres of Debussy's Impressionism). Apart from the advocacy of Satie and Jean Cocteau, the group found it had less and less in common.
Poulenc was largely a self-taught composer despite the efforts of several piano teachers (although he did attempt to learn basic technique under Koechlin for three years). He was essentially 'a natural' who improvised at the piano. His early works are still among his most popular: *Mouvements Perpétuels* for piano, and *Le Bestiaire*, a song cycle with instrumental ensemble. Stravinsky recommended Diaghilev to commission a ballet from him, the result being *Les Biches* (1924), Poulenc's first major work. He was perhaps most successful in his many songs and these owe much to his 25-year partnership with Pierre Bernac from 1935. The two musicians toured extensively and later Poulenc often appeared as soloist in works such as the *Piano Concerto* (1949). There are also a series of sonatas for various instruments culminating in the *Clarinet Sonata* (1962), as well as various works for unaccompanied choir from the *Mass* (1937) onwards. His later religious works include the *Stabat Mater* (1950) and the *Gloria* (1959), both requiring solo soprano and or-

chestra with mixed choir.
The most important aspect of his later years were his two operas: *Les Mamelles de Tirésias* (1944), a return to the frivolity of 'Les Six', and *Dialogues des Carmélites* (1957), a tragedy based on the period of the French Revolution. The strange mixture of his personality was never integrated into symphonic writings and he remained a rather conservative tonal composer who used an electrically-Romantic, harmonic vocabulary.

POWER, Lionel (d. 1445)
English contemporary of Dunstable who left much church music which is to be found in the Old Hall Manuscript and in various Italian collections. He set two complete masses for three voices.

PRAETORIUS, Michael (1571–1621)
German musical historian and composer whose family included over twenty musicians. Each member of the family used the same Latin surname (their actual surname was Schulz). His four-volume *Syntagma musicum* is a systematic study of music up to his own day. His many compositions are mainly hymns set to German and Latin words. These still appear in modern collections e.g. the carol *Es ist ein' Ros' entsprungen*.

PREVIN, André (b. 1929)
Conductor, composer and pianist. He first became known in Berlin as a jazz pianist and then achieved prominence in Hollywood as a composer, arranger and conductor of film music. In England he has become a household name as the conductor of the London Symphony Orchestra. His recent compositions include *Principles* (1980) and *Reflections* (1981).

PROKOFIEV, Serge (1891–1953)
Precocious Russian composer, who, after an international career, returned to the USSR in 1934. His last years from 1948 were clouded by Communist Party criticism.
As a child, Prokofiev composed fluently and came into contact with Taneiev, Glière, Glazounov, Liadov and Rimsky-Korsakov, but the early *Sinfonietta* (1909 rev. 1929) and even more so the 1st Piano Concerto (1911) seem to owe little to his predecessors. Both these and the 2nd Piano Concerto (1913) were bitterly criticised for their dissonant modernity. On the other hand the short piano pieces, *Visions fugitives* (1914) and his first mature orchestral work, *Scythian Suite* of the same year, have retained their popularity. The famous *Classical Symphony* was performed in the troubled days of 1918 and soon after its performance, Prokofiev escaped through Siberia to the USA.
In America he produced the *Love for Three Oranges* (1921) and appeared as a pianist. He then moved to Paris where he was active with the Diaghilev Ballet and as a touring concert pianist in the 3rd (1921), and 5th (1932) Concertos. The 2nd (1925), 3rd (1928), and 4th (Boston, 1930) Symphonies belong to this period and owe something to the advocacy of Koussevitsky.
Perhaps more important was the welcome he received on a concert tour as pianist and conductor in Russia in 1927. By this time his interest in Russian traditions and Soviet aspirations had been awakened. Apart from his 2nd Violin Concerto (Madrid, 1935) and the *Cello Concerto* (Moscow, 1938), his first characteristically Russian work was his *Russian Overture* (1936). This period was marked by the film scores, *Lieutenant Kije* and *Alexander Nevsky* (1938), the ever fresh *Peter and the Wolf* and the ballet *Romeo and Juliet* (1936). During the 2nd World War he composed the opera *War and Peace* (1941) and the 5th Symphony (1944).
Prokofiev himself described the elements of his style as (1) the Neo-Classical (2) Innovation (3) the *moto perpetuo* element

to be found in his piano writing especially in the virtuoso *Toccata* Op. 11 and the nine sonatas (4) the lyrical and (5) 'jest, laughter, mockery'. To these must be added an attempt to meet the Communist requirements of Zhdanov's Central Committee in more popular and simpler melody and rhythm. He seems to have met his critics willingly and to have been well on the way to producing a genuinely popular National art. Unfortunately the 6th Symphony (1947) was sharply attacked for its 'formalism' and his last opera *A Tale of a Real Man* (1948) was criticised for its inadequate treatment of a Soviet war hero.

PUCCINI, Giacomo Antonio (1858–1924)
Italian operatic composer who came from a family of church musicians. He moved from Lucca to study with Ponchielli in Milan (1880–83) and was subsequently relatively slow to establish himself despite the encouragement of Boito and the publisher Ricordi. His first international success was *Manon Lescaut* (1893) which was based on the story used by Massenet in his opera of the same name. The text, however, was considerably modified by various writers. None of Puccini's later works achieved the same immediate success as this first performance under Toscanini but opera-goers of today do not class it with its successors.
In 1896 came the first of his popular works, *La Bohème*, followed at four-year intervals by *Tosca* and *Madama Butterfly*. All these centred on the sweet suffering heroine in a variety of colourful scenes (often suggested by Puccini himself). The up-to-date music (influenced by Wagner and Debussy) is marked by brilliant orchestral and harmonic touches and also influenced by the warm melodic lyricism of Verdi. Most of the libretti are based on the sentimental melodrama of the magazines of the period, and it is a measure of the power of the music that such unlikely events seem real in the setting of the opera house.
Puccini's marriage, eventually solemnised in 1904, was threatened by a domestic tragedy five years later. Their maid, suspected wrongly by his wife of an affair with Puccini, committed suicide. The immediate effect was to reduce Puccini's will to compose and his next two works were less successful. In 1918 there followed the celebrated three one-act operas: *Il Tabarro*, *Suor Angelica* and the often performed *Gianni Schicchi*. His last work, *Turandot*, was not first performed until after his death and was completed by Franco Alfano.

PUGNANI, Gaetano (1731–1798)
Italian violinist and composer of nine concertos and 14 sonatas for his instrument. He was a pupil of Tartini and spent much of his time between 1754 and 1770 as an orchestral leader in Paris and London. He was also famous as a teacher (he taught Viotti). His works also include operas and much chamber and orchestral music.

PURCELL, Daniel (c. 1663–1717)
Younger brother of Henry and organist of Magdalen College, Oxford. He wrote a masque for Act 5 of his brother's *Indian Queen* (1695) and from 1695 to 1707 much stage music for London productions.

PURCELL, Henry (1659–1695)
Great English composer of church and stage music. Both his father and uncle were Gentlemen of the Chapel Royal and Henry was a choirboy there at its most famous period under Captain Cooke. Whilst there he was a pupil of Pelham Hunfrey and Blow. He succeeded Matthew Locke as composer to the King's violins in 1677 and then succeeded Blow as organist of Westminster Abbey two years later. Apart from his marriage, which was probably in 1681, little is known of his life. In 1682 however it is known that he became one of the three organists of the

Chapel Royal. Purcell's church music, like that of Blow, falls naturally into two types:
(1) The 'full' anthems in which the organ doubles the voices. It is in these pieces that the Tudor tradition of chromatic modality can still be heard, just as in the string fantasias. Good examples of this style are the eight-part excerpt *Hear my Prayer* and the famous funeral anthem *Thou Knowest Lord*.
(2) The 'verse' anthems and services, where the harmony is based on the basso continuo. Usually there are string 'symphonies' interspersed between the prevalent SSA and ATB (verse) sections. Of these fifty or so 'cantatas', well-known examples are *Rejoice in the Lord* (The 'Bell' Anthem) and O *Sing unto the Lord*. The same division similarly applies to the string fantasias and the later Italian-influenced trio sonatas such as the famous *Golden Sonata* for two violins and continuo.

As court composer, Purcell wrote about 20 'welcome' odes and songs, of which the two great odes *Hail Bright Cecilia* (1692) and *Come ye Sons of Art* (1694) are the best known. In a similar category are the many convivial catches, vocal duets and songs with continuo such as *Mad Bess* and *If Music be the Food of Love*.

The last 10 years of Purcell's life were spent mostly in theatrical activities. Before his death at 36, Purcell is thought to have contributed to no less than 500 London productions. Most important to us now are the so-called operas. Of these only *Dido and Aeneas* (1689) is completely 'operatic' in the sense of being continuously musical. This was written for the amateur young ladies at Mr. Priest's School in Chelsea — presumably with help from the Gentlemen of the Chapel Royal. It remains the first English operatic masterpiece with its famous *When I am Laid in Earth* written over a haunting five-bar ground bass.

The other five works are more properly 'semi-operas' in the sense that they also require a cast of actors with speaking parts e.g. Dryden's *King Arthur* (1691) and the Shakespearian adaption, *The Fairy Queen* (1692). The music is in the nature of the Italian intermezzo (the light entertainment, later becoming the opera buffa, between the acts of a tragedy or opera seria). In Purcell's case. These entr'actes are on a large scale and continue the action on the supernatural level, often incorporating elements from the Court Masque. The historical tragedy is that this viable English operatic tradition was destined to be lost within 15 years in favour of Handelian Italian opera.

Q

QUANTZ, Johann Joachim (1697–1773)
German flautist who taught Frederick the Great and wrote 300 flute concertos for him. He played several instruments and had wide experience as a player. From 1741 he was chamber musician and court composer to Frederick at Berlin and Potsdam. Besides 200 compositions for one and two flutes together with numerous trios and quartets, Quantz wrote an important flute tutor which is the source of much of our knowledge of 18th century performing practice. He also added a key to the instrument and invented the tuning slide.

QUILTER, Roger (1877–1953)
English song composer, who went to Eton and later studied in Germany. He wrote some polished settings of the songs in *Twelfth Night* and *As You Like It*, which were taken up by singers of the calibre of Plunket Greene. His texts were taken from many English poets from Shakespeare to Tennyson. His songs are quite distinctive in their melodic and harmonic felicity. His works also include three light operas and orchestral pieces such as *A Children's Overture* (1914) based on nursery tunes. He also wrote much choral music.

R

RACHMANINOV, Serge (1873–1943)
Generally regarded as the last of the great Russian Romantic pianist-composers, Rachmaninov belonged to the generation of impoverished landowners familiar from the writings of Tchekov. He was a talented child who found disciplined work hard. Together with Scriabin he studied composition under Arensky but it was Tchaikovsky who was his inspiration. Rachmaninov never left the cosmopolitan Moscow for the nationalism of 'The Five' at St. Petersburg. The opera *Aleko* (1892) dates from this period as does also the famous *Prelude in C sharp minor*; the former earned him a publisher and the latter made him famous overnight. He was soon in international demand as a pianist/conductor of his own works which by now included the 1st Piano Concerto (1891) and 1st Symphony (1895). The latter was poorly received in a weak performance under Glazounov. Rachmaninov, after a period of doubt, started a second career as an operatic conductor at the Moscow Imperial Grand Theatre in 1905–06. He was later offered the Directorship of the Boston Symphony Orchestra — an offer he refused. By this time he had completed two of his finest works — the ever-popular 2nd Piano Concerto (1901) and the 2nd Symphony (1907), neither of which he was ever to surpass. He had resumed his career as an imaginative and passionate virtuoso pianist in the grand tradition. From 1910 until the Revolution of 1917 he was in Moscow, where he was active as a conductor. He never returned to the Bolshevik regime and the rest of his life was divided mainly between American and European concert tours with periods at his home by Lake Lucerne. Rachmaninov never developed in the *conventional* sense. Apart from the superb achievement of the *Rhapsody on a Theme of Paganini* (1934), the 3rd Symphony (1936) and the last two Piano Concertos (1909 and 1927) cover much the same ground as their illustrious predecessors — but with less success.

RAFF, Joseph Joachim (1822–1882)
Prolific German composer who was associated with Mendelssohn and Liszt and was an early champion of the music of Wagner. By 1856 he was an established piano teacher and for the last five years of his life, Director of the Frankfurt Conservatoire, where MacDowell was a student. His 'celebrated' *Cavatina* is still heard today but his operas, 11 symphonies and the rest of his 214 works with an opus number have sunk into oblivion.

RAINIER, Priaulx (b. 1903)
South African composer who studied at the RAM and with Nadia Boulanger in Paris. She has written mainly for chamber music combinations.

RAMEAU, Jean Philippe (1683–1764)
French composer, theorist and keyboard player. He visited Milan, where he is said to have joined a wandering group of players as a violinist. In France he was occupied (like his father) as organist in various cathedrals and Paris churches. His first book of harpsichord pieces had been published in 1705 but in 1715 he returned to his first post at Clermont Cathedral where he wrote the famous *Traité de l'harmonie* (which established the 'inversion' theory in chordal analysis as opposed to the older derivation from figured bass). This was published in Paris in 1722 and the second

book of harpsichord pieces in 1724. His first opera, the tragedy *Hippolyte et Aricie*, was performed in Paris. During the next 30 years, Rameau produced about 30 theatrical works: operas, pastorales, ballets, divertissements and comedies. None of these break new dramatic ground as did Gluck's works despite the influence of distinguished librettists like Voltaire. However, all are exquisitely fashioned court entertainments. During his last period Rameau published his six *Concerts* — the *Pièces de Clavecin en Concert* (1741) for two violins and harpsichord. These chamber pieces, like the earlier two books for solo harpsichord, are all given descriptive titles. The triviality of some of the titles often belies the musical value of the pieces. His style is more harmonic than contrapuntal, although, to his contemporaries, he seemed powerful and 'learned' in the Baroque rather than the newer Rococo style.

RAVEL, Maurice (1875–1937)

Brilliant younger contemporary of Debussy. He was born in Southern France of mixed Swiss and Basque descent. He entered the Paris Conservatoire and although he showed brilliance under Gédalge and Fauré, he soon disconcerted the academic authorities by his harmonic originality and by his imitations of the style of Chabrier and Satie. During his student period he wrote the famous *Pavane pour une Infante Défunte* for piano, which already showed the perfect balance achieved between classical restraint and human warmth so characteristic of the composer. He remained nominally at the Conservatoire until 1905, making repeated attempts (like Berlioz) to win the *Prix de Rome*. After a 2nd prize in 1901 — the year of *Jeux d'Eau* — his name was unmentioned in succeeding years. Considering the superb *String Quartet* in 1903, it was hardly surprising that his elimination in the preliminary round in 1905 provoked a public scandal which led to the replacement of Dubois as Director, by Fauré.

The series of piano works continued with *Miroirs* (1905), *Sonatine* (1905), and *Gaspard de la Nuit* (1908). His earliest song, a setting of the elusive poet Verlaine, dates from his student days and his song cycle *Schéhérazade* with orchestra appeared in 1903. Further songs, usually with piano accompaniment, appeared throughout his life. They were often marked by touches of irony and gentle malice.

Ravel normally composed at the piano and almost all his orchestral works exist in earlier keyboard versions. His acute ear and power of innovation made him a master of orchestration, whether in the brilliant scoring of Mussorgsky's *Pictures at an Exhibition* (1922), or his own *Rapsodie Espagnole* (1908) or the famous *Bolero* (1928). Such music lent itself to balletic treatment and *Daphnis and Chloe* (1912) and *Ma Mère l'Oye* (1912) were both commissioned by Diaghilev as ballets. Ravel left two operas, the one-act *L'Heure Espagnole* (1907) and *L'Enfant et les Sortilèges* (1925), both of which are still heard today. The two Piano Concertos (the 2nd for the left-handed pianist, Wittgenstein) are late works (1931). He never wrote a symphony.

Ravel stressed the necessity for restraint in his teaching and he succeeded in maintaining his own privacy. He never married and was something of a recluse so that he was a popular figure. His public appearances were effective in spite of his limited ability as a conductor (and he was hardly a virtuoso pianist). He suffered after his war-service with ill-health and was in effect an invalid from 1932.

The same restraint is apparent in his music. His superb technique as a composer is marked by the precision of Neo-Classicism and elusive sensibility. His harmonic fastidiousness fashioned an extension of tonality with its resonant use of chords of the 11th, together with pedal harmonies.

RAVENSCROFT, Thomas (c. 1590–c. 1633)
English composer today only remembered for his collection *The Whole Booke of Psalmes* (1607). This collection contains 100 tunes to metrical psalms of which 48 are by Ravenscroft. Several of these are in regular use in modern hymn books. He also left 100 rounds and catches, also published, several anthems and madrigals, as well as a theoretical treatise.

RAWSTHORNE, Alan (1905–1971)
English composer, who after attending the RMCM and studying with the pianist Egon Petri, spent several years on the staff of Dartington Hall. He was recognised as a composer when a work was performed at an ISCM Festival. Successive premières at Proms during and just after the 2nd World War earned him an enthusiastic following. Most of his music is atonal — but with strong tonal associations — and both rhythm and texture tend to be simple and direct. Apart from songs, most of his work is for orchestral and chamber combinations and includes five concertos and a symphony as well as music for film and radio.

REBIKOV, Vladimir (1866–1920)
Russian composer whose earlier work was in the Tchaikovsky tradition. He later introduced the whole-tone scale into more general use. He was particularly innovatory in his new combination of music and mime in the *Mélomimiques* for either piano or voice. Several of his operas and descriptive orchestral pieces were once popular.

REDFORD, John (c. 1485–c. 1545)
Remembered for the anthem *Rejoice in the Lord* (of doubtful authenticity) in the *Mulliner Book*. He also wrote extensively for organ as well as other church and dramatic music.

REGER, Max (1873–1916)
German composer, organist and pianist. He was involved academically at Munich (1901–06) and Leipzig (from 1907) and toured extensively. Largely due to the advocacy of Karl Straube, Reger is remembered nowadays mostly for his organ works, although he wrote extensively for orchestra, chamber combinations, piano and chorus. His textures are often thick in their polyphonic complexity and his extended tonality resulted in what seemed, to his contemporaries, to be awkward modulations. Although most of his works are on the grandiose scale they show tremendous technique. There are many more straightforward pieces, unusually for voice, which are direct in their simplicity. The best known of the organ works are the large-scale seven *Chorale Fantasias*. Simpler organ pieces include the beautiful *Benedictus*.

REICHA, Anton (1770–1836)
German composer and flautist who was a friend of Beethoven and Haydn and the teacher (in Paris) of Liszt and Gounod. His works include several operas, two symphonies and many chamber works (especially for flute), together with some theoretical works.

REICHARDT, Johann Friedrich (1752–1814)
German composer, conductor and writer. He was composer and conductor to Frederick the Great from 1775 until his dismissal in 1794 for sympathising with the French Revolution. He toured extensively while on leave during this period and attracted much opposition to his orchestral and operatic reforms. His music now takes second place to his letters describing the contemporary music of the period, though his orchestral and chamber music, and operas (especially Singspiel) were popular in their day.

REINECKE, Carl Heinrich (1824–1910)
German composer, conductor, pianist, violinist, teacher and writer. After earlier tours, most of his life was spent in Cologne and Leipzig. His many works include over 240 catalogued works: four symphonies, chamber and choral music and five operas. He also wrote many analyses and commentaries on Mozart piano concertos and Beethoven sonatas.

REINKEN, Jan Adams (1623–1722)
German organist and composer, whom Bach much admired and went to visit and hear play. His works are marked by improvisatorial *bravura* and brilliance of technique.

REIZENSTEIN, Franz (1911–1968)
German composer and pianist. He first studied with Hindemith and later with Vaughan Williams and the pianist Solomon. From 1934 he settled in England. His professionalism was apparent in his reputation as a concerto and chamber music pianist. His music was Neo-Classical — tonal and contrapuntal in outlook, but harmonically often strikingly original. Apart from the cantata *Voices of Night*, and three orchestral concertos, he composed mainly chamber music.

RESPIGHI, Ottorino (1879–1936)
Italian composer, who for several years earned his living as a violinist in several countries. During this period he had lessons from Rimsky-Korsakov and Max Bruch and became widely known as a result of his first two operas (1905 and 1910). From 1913 he lived in Rome where he was active as a teacher.
He was attracted to older Italian music and was responsible for some of the earlier performing editions of Monteverdi as well as several Baroque transcriptions. The three sets of *Ancient Airs and Dances* were very popular. The modality, however, of such a work as *Concerto Gregoriano* for violin (1922) is unconvincing in its highly coloured orchestral textures. Respighi is best known for his 'Roman' symphonic poems — *Fontane di Roma* (1917) and *Pini di Roma* (1924) where his subtle colouring takes precedence over the colder Neo-Classicism of his more extended chamber music. Of his nine operas, the last — *Lucrezia* — was completed by his wife, also a composer, after his death. In his operatic works he used 17th century style dramatic recitative, but never found the Italian lyricism for which he seemed to be searching.

REUBKE, Julius (1834–1858)
German pianist and composer, now remembered almost exclusively for his organ *Sonata on the 94th Psalm*. He was a favourite pupil of Liszt and this 'programme' piece is really an enormous Lisztian symphonic poem. It is generally recognised as the greatest Romantic organ work of the 19th century. From a composer who died so young, its intense maturity is phenomenal.
He also left a piano sonata and songs.

RHEINBERGER, Josef (1839–1901)
Prolific composer now remembered almost entirely for his organ works which include 20 sonatas each in a different key. From 1859 he was an organist, conductor and teacher in Munich. He composed several operas, symphonies, chamber and piano works, besides several choral settings of his wife's poems (credited to von Hoffnaas).
As a Roman Catholic, Rheinberger made no use of the Lutheran chorale, but the plainsong tones are used as part of a Brahmsian harmonic structure. His contrapuntal fluency seems to parallel that of Mendelssohn.

RIMSKY-KORSAKOV,
Nicholas Andreievitch (1844–1908)
Probably the best 'all-round' composer of the Russian 'Five', Rimsky-Korsakov was brought up as an amateur musician although as a child he showed clear signs of precocious fluency. Even after his introduction to Balakirev and Mussorgsky in 1861, his seniors by seven and five years respectively, he continued as a naval officer until 1884.
He was influenced by Glinka and Russian folk tunes at an early age and readily fell into association with the Nationalism of 'The Five'. Similarly, he was attracted early in his life to the glamour of orchestration. Under Balakirev's encouragement his 1st Symphony was performed in 1865. *Sadko* was produced in 1867 and *Antar* in 1868. These and several other works all used folk tunes (Russian, Serbian and even Arabic). Their harmony and scoring were extensively revised in later years.
Rimsky-Korsakov's first opera, *The Maid of Pskov*, was written at the same time as Mussorgsky's *Boris Godunov* and Darghomijsky's naturalistic *The Stone Guest.* Before its successful production in 1872, he had been appointed to teach composition and instrumentation at the St. Petersburg Conservatory. This, together with his post as Inspector of Naval Bands, stimulated him into making good his own musical academic shortcomings. The result was an earnest attempt at a more contrapuntal approach in several chamber works and the revision of his own earlier works. He also completed Darghomijsky's opera and edited Mussorgsky's operas. Once again he was saved from his academic preoccupations by Russian folk music in his collection (1877) and re-established his style in the operas *May Night* (1880) and *Snow Maiden* (1882).
By this time Rimsky-Korsakov was active as a conductor and teacher. With Glazunov he completed Borodin's unfinished opera *Prince Igor* and finished his own *Spanish Capriccio* in 1887 and *Scheherazade* in 1888 as well as a 'harmony' text-book and work on the later *Principles of Orchestration.*
The influence of Berlioz in *Antar* was followed by the influence of Wagner, in the operas *Mlada* (1892) and *Sadko* (1898). His later life was marked first by his 're-editing' activities which are now criticised for their 'impurity', (but largely responsible for the present popularity of 'The Five'), and secondly by illness. Also at this time he was temporarily dismissed from the Conservatoire, and his works were banned owing to his sympathy with the new students in the attempted coup of 1905. The succeeding storm resulted in the composition of his satirical opera *Coq d'Or* (1907). His pupils included Glazunov, Liadov and their followers, and the seminal figure of Igor Stravinsky. If his genius was less pointed than that of Mussorgsky and Borodin, his influence was wider, and forged a link between Liszt and the music of his own century.

RINCK, Johann Christian Heinrich (1770–1846)
German organist and composer and pupil of Bach's pupil, Kittel. He is remembered for a famous *Orgelschule* and also wrote church and chamber music.

ROBERTON, Sir Hugh (1874–1952)
Famous Scottish conductor of the Glasgow Orpheus Choir who is remembered mainly for his many arrangements of Scottish folk songs. He also wrote many original part-songs for his choir.

RODE, Jaques Pierre Joseph (1774–1830)
French violinist and composer for his instrument. He was a pupil of Viotti and, after a period as an orchestral player, soloist and teacher in Paris and St. Petersburg, was in 1813 associated with Beethoven in Vienna. He wrote 13 violin

concertos, 24 caprices, 12 études and a violin tutor.

RODRIGO, Joaquin (b. 1902)
Spanish composer who became blind at the age of three. He is famous for his *Concierto de Aranjues* (1940) for guitar and orchestra. He was a pupil of Dukas and was much influenced by Falla. During the Spanish Civil War (1936–39) he lived in Paris but has been Professor of Music at Madrid University since 1947. He has written other concertos — for piano (Lisbon, 1943), violin (Lisbon, 1944), cello (Madrid, 1949 and London, 1982), and harp (1954). All his works have been imbued with the spirit of the Spanish countryside, its history and people.

ROGER-DUCASSE, Jean Jules Amable (1873–1954)
French composer and musical educationalist who was a pupil of Fauré at the Paris Conservatoire. He later became an inspector of schools and teacher of composition. His music includes *Cantegril* (Opéra-Comique, 1931), and several orchestral, chamber and piano pieces.

ROGERS, Benjamin (1614–1698)
English organist of Eton College and Magdalen College, Oxford. Besides church music he wrote four-part *Airs* for violins and organ. Several of his instrumental pieces are included in *Courtly Masquing Ayres* (1662).

ROMBERG (Family)
German musical family whose most distinguished members were:

Andreas Jacob (1767–1821)
Violinist and composer whose works include 10 symphonies (one of which is a well-known *Toy Symphony*), 23 violin concertos and 33 string quartets as well as eight operas and operettas, church and choral music. He appeared in public at the age of seven with his cousin.

Bernhard (1767–1841)
Cellist and composer of six operas, 10 cellos concertos, 11 string quartets, and a cello tutor which was unusually comprehensive for its time. His professional life was divided between several countries but he lived mainly in Russia and in Vienna, where he performed with Beethoven.

ROMBERG, Sigmund (1887–1951)
Hungarian-American composer of operettas: *The Student Prince* (1924), *The Desert Song* (1926) and *The New Moon* (1928). He was trained as a civil engineer and moved to New York in 1913. He was also responsible for *Blossom Time* (1921), an adaption of Schubert's music.

RÖNTGEN, Julius (1855–1932)
Dutch composer, pianist and conductor who was trained in Leipzig where his father was a distinguished violinist. He taught in Amsterdam and became Director of the Conservatoire there in 1878. He wrote two operas, some choral music, concertos for piano and cello, as well as piano and chamber music, but is chiefly remembered for his editions of old Dutch music.

RORE, Cipriano de (1516–1565)
Venetian composer who succeeded Willaert at St. Mark's. He composed many madrigals and church music (including a St. John Passion). His contemporaries in both Italy and Flanders held him in high regard, especially for the innovations used in his madrigals.

ROSEINGRAVE, Thomas (1690–1766)
Most distinguished member of a family of English musicians. He met the Scarlattis on a visit to Italy in 1710 and, as a result, composed six Italian cantatas and an opera. He is remembered nowadays as the organist of St. George's, Hanover Square

in London and was the composer of voluntaries and fugues for organ on harpsichord which are harmonically astonishing for a contemporary of Handel. He also edited 42 of Domenico Scarlatti's 'lessons' writing eight of his own in a similar style. He ended his long life in Dublin suffering from a breakdown in mental health.

ROSSETER, Philip (c. 1575–1623)
English composer who combined with Campion in *A Booke of Ayres ... to be sung to the Lute ... and Base Violl* (1601). He also published *Lessons for the Consort ... set to sixe severall instruments* (1609). Little is known of his life except that, as a boy, he was one of the 'Children of the Revels to the Queen'.

ROSSINI, Gioacchina Antonio (1792–1868)
Italian operatic composer who, after a chequered childhood, was employed as a singer in churches and as a harpsichord player in the theatre at Bologna. His ability was soon recognised and he was elected to the local Accademia Filarmonica (1806). He had a successful period as a student at the Lilceo Musicale (1806–10) and his first opera, for Venice, was commissioned in 1810. His enthusiasm for the music of Haydn and Mozart led to his conducting *The Creation* in Bologna and to his first famous opera seria, *Tancredi* (1813). In the same year his comic opera *L'Italiana in Algeri* confirmed his reputation for a brilliant vocal writing-technique and orchestration, ironic and subtle humour, as well as dramatic tightness of construction. Operatic masterpieces followed: *Le Barbier de Seville* (1816) — his most celebrated work which triumphantly survived a disastrous first night — *Otello* (1816) — written in 20 days and only superseded by Verdi's *Otello* — *La Cenerentola* (1817), *La Gazza Ladra* (1817), *Mosè in Egitto* (1818) as well as several other successful works.
He married a Spanish soprano in 1822 and, after the opera *Semiramide* was produced in 1823 in Venice, he adapted several of his operas for the French stage e.g. *Moïse et Pharaon*, adapted from *Mosè in Egritto*. His Parisian career continued with *Le Comte Ory* (1828) and his crowning achievement *Guillaume Tell* (1829).
During the remaining four decades of his life, he never wrote another opera. This was partly due to ill-health but partly also to the political unrest of 1830 and 1848. He became a leading figure in the artistic and social world. He gave his name to the culinary masterpiece *Tornedos Rossini* and married a second time. He helped to reform the teaching at the Bologna Liceo and from time to time wrote more minor works such as the songs and duets of *Soirées Musicales* (1835), the *Stabat Mater* (which took him six years to write), and the popular *Petite Messe Solennelle* (1864) which is neither small nor particularly solemn.
Rossini has been called the 'Italian Mozart' and certainly bridges the gap between 18th century classicism and Bellini and Verdi. Elegance and humour are linked in his sublime bel canto, although such a style could hardly survive the advent of Meyerbeer and Wagner in Paris.

ROUSSEAU, Jean Jaques (1712–1778)
French-Swiss philosopher who was active in composition as well as other branches of music. He had little training but his pastoral, *Le Devin du Village* (1752), was included in the repertoire of the Paris Opéra until 1829. He also wrote the opera *Les Muses Galantes* (1747), fragments of *Daphnis et Chloé* (published 1780) in addition to about 100 duets and 'romances'.
For a while he earned his living as a musical copyist and invented a new system of notation. He defended Italian music against French music (1753) and wrote on music and musicians (often inaccurately)

for Diderot's *Encyclopédie* and his own *Dictionnaire de Musique* (1768).

ROUSSEL, Albert (1869–1937)
French composer, who, after a period in the navy from 1889 to 1894, studied with Gigout and d'Indy. He published several works including the popular ballet *Le Festinde l'Araignée* (1912). His earlier oriental period resulted in the composition of the opera *Padmavati* which was produced in 1923, after war service.
After his 50th birthday his music became more contrapuntal and neo-classical in outlook. His 2nd and 4th Symphonies were recognised as two of the most significant works to appear in Paris between the wars. He also wrote piano, chamber and vocal music, his last work being the opéra buffa, *Le Testament de la Tante Caroline* (1937).

RUBBRA, Edmund (b. 1901)
English composer and pianist who was a pupil of Holst and a member of a piano-trio. He was a critical writer on music and a most successful teacher of composition at Oxford and the GSM.
Rubbra seems to have been influenced mainly by polyphonic music of the English renaissance and early Baroque. The most obvious examples of this influence can be found in the two masses of 1945 (in English) and 1949 (in Latin). The same characteristic is present in his eight symphonies with their long linear interweaving and relative absence of contrasts of colour or shorter phrase lengths. His vocal writing, however, is marked by the directness of the *English Ayre* and his orchestral style became markedly simpler from the 3rd Symphony. Rubbra has written in most media but has been especially successful in his choral writing (unaccompanied motets and madrigals) and in the writing for orchestra e.g. *Dark Night of the Soul* (1935).
The string parts in his concertos and sonatas are unusually vocal and tonal for a 20th century composer, and Rubbra's individuality of style is inescapable in its unusual chromaticism. He was converted to the Roman Catholic faith. His mysticism tends to produce a rather unvarying slow pulse, while the rather monochrome orchestration will probably prevent him from receiving the popular acclaim that is his due.

RUBINSTEIN, Anton (1829–1894)
Russian pianist and composer. He toured extensively as an interpretative artist of the Lisztian school and wrote fluently in the German Romantic style. Few of his compositions have survived except *Mélodie in F* and several of his 125 songs. He also wrote 15 operas, four 'sacred' operas, six symphonies, five piano concertos, 10 string quartets and much piano music.

S

SAINT-SAËNS, Charles Camille (1835–1921)
Prolific French composer and virtuoso pianist and organist. His first compositions from his sixth year were already 'correct' and the same elegance was noted in his first piano recital at the age of 11. He studied composition at the Conservatoire in Paris with Halévy and his second organ appointment was at the Madeleine Church.
When he was 17 he met Liszt and it was perhaps his long friendship with Liszt that led Saint-Saëns to write programme music and symphonic poems. In 1853 and 1857 his 1st and 2nd Symphonies appeared. From 1861 to 1865 he became a teacher for the only time in his life, having Fauré, Messager and Gigout among his pupils.
In 1865 he wrote his first opera and in 1868 started work on his most famous biblical opera *Samson et Delila* which was not produced until 1877. Through works like *Danse Macabre* (1875) and his five piano concertos, (as well as three for violin and two for cello), Saint-Saëns helped to free French music from its domination by the theatre. Even more influential was the 'Organ' Symphony (No. 3, 1886) and *Le Carnaval des Animaux* (1886 but published posthumously). He established, with the new French concert orchestras, a French tradition which was marked by precision, balance, elegance and colour. This tradition was continued by Chausson, Lalo, Fauré and even Ravel.
Many of Saint-Saëns' works have been ignored, probably due to his facility and paucity of invention. His 169 opus numbers include 12 operas, many chamber and piano works as well as refined choral works and songs.

SALIERI, Antonio (1750–1825)
Italian composer and conductor who worked in Vienna (1770–78 and 1788–1824) and taught Beethoven, Schubert and Liszt. He was helped by Gluck in Paris whom he also imitated. In Vienna he was friendly with Haydn but sufficiently hostile to Mozart for the belief to become widespread that he murdered Mozart. This rumour was quite unfounded. His music has not survived but includes 40 operas as well as church, vocal and orchestral music.

SALZEDO, Carlos (1885–1961)
French-American harpist, composer and teacher who was trained at the Paris Conservatoire. He settled in New York in 1921. Most of his music involves one to seven harps and includes orchestral, chamber and choral works. He was prominent as a teacher at the Julliard School.

SAMMARTINI, Giuseppe (c. 1693–1750)
Italian oboist and composer who worked in London from about 1727, and was director of chamber music to the Prince of Wales. He left eight overtures, 12 concerti grossi, 12 violin sonatas and six sonatas for two flutes or violins, in addition to various other sonatas and concertos.

SARASATE, Pablo de (1844–1908)
Famous Spanish violinist who was noted for his purity of tone and charm of style. He wrote several popular pieces for his instrument such as *Zigeunerweisen* and *Jota Aragonesa*, and several sets of Spanish dances.

SATIE, Erik (1866–1925)
French composer whose mother was an English composer and pianist and whose father a Parisian music publisher. He com-

posed intuitively in an experimental style that did not please the Conservatoire in Paris. It did, however, impress Debussy in 1890, when Satie was a cabaret pianist in Montmartre. He made a second attempt to study composition firstly with d'Indy and then Roussel (1905-08). His reputation was that of a humorist. This was due to the inconsequential titles which he gave his piano pieces e.g. *Pièces en Forme de Poire* (1903). From 1910 he became the celebrated leader of a new group of young composers called, from 1920, *Les Six*.
His works are mainly for piano: *Gymnopedies* (1888) and *Gnossiennes* (1890) being the best known. He also composed several stage works: *Parade* (1917) and other ballets, incidental music, and two 'lyric drama' pieces.

SCARLATTI, Alessandro (1660–1725)
Sicilian composer whose creative life was divided between Naples (1684–1702 and 1709–19) and Rome (1703–09 and 1719–23). He studied with Carissimi in Rome from 1672; his first known opera was written in 1679. He was mainly occupied as Court conductor in Naples as well as choirmaster in Rome. Of his 115 operas, over 50 are partly preserved; of these the earlier ones are in the tradition of Luigi Rossi, Legrenzi and Stradella. They tend to be in relatively short movements, and dependent on contrapuntal textures. Scarlatti is important historically for the development of the techniques of opera seria. With *Teodora* (1693), and more so, *Tigrane* (1715), his successes were associated with magnificence and large-scale da capo arias. He established the 'Italian' three-movement overture, and the extended orchestra ritornello, and used 'accompanied' recitative as well as the older recitativo secco with harpsichord and bass. He is known to have written at least 20 oratorios, 10 masses, 46 motets in addition to 10 concerti sacri (with string and continuo accompaniment), and much other church music. It is, however, his enormous series of 600 solo cantatas (with continuo) and 60 others with strings and continuo, which are much more important. Few of these are known today, but the celebrated *Christmas Cantata* (1695) for soprano, strings and continuo is a good example of his five-movement structure consisting of a sinfonia and two pairs of recitative and aria. Also extant are 12 concerti grossi, as well as other chamber and keyboard works.

SCARLATTI, Domenico (1685–1757)
The sixth son of Alessandros' 10 children, who was a harpsichord virtuoso and composer and considered to be the source of modern keyboard technique. He met Handel in Venice in 1708 and later took part in a competition with Handel in Rome (1709). Honours were divided on their merit as harpsichord players but Handel was deemed the better organist. Both remained good friends and Handel 'used often to speak of this person with great satisfaction'. Most of Scarlatti's professional life was spent as *maestro di capella* in various aristocratic establishments. For these establishments he wrote a 10-part *Stabat Mater* (with continuo) as well as other church music. He also wrote 13 operas (mainly in Rome, 1710–18) and many chamber cantatas and arias. From 1721, in spite of extended visits to Italy, he was appointed to the Royal Chapel in Lisbon where he was cembalist to the King of Portugal and teacher of the Princesses. One of his pupils, however — Maria Barbara — took him with her to Madrid on her marriage in 1792 and, apart from short visits elsewhere, Scarlatti then remained at the Spanish court for the rest of his life.
It is astonishing that the 555 sonatas — *Esercizii per gravicembalo* as they are entitled in the only edition (of 30) published by the composer in 1738 — all belong to the end of Scarlatti's life; and

more than half of them belong to his last six years. Most of these short pieces extend the technique of the instrument and the harmonic language of the period in strikingly original directions. Almost all are in extended binary form — but even in this respect Scarlatti pointed the way to '2nd subject contrast'. The variety of styles, texture, and expression is seemingly inexhaustible, and transcends all baroque precedents.

SCHARWENKA, (Franz) Xaver (1850–1924)

German-Polish pianist and composer who studied with Kullak in Berlin and became a specialist in the interpretation of the music of Chopin. His compositions have much Polish national character and include a symphony, an opera, four piano concertos, some chamber music, and a large number of shorter piano pieces — of which his *Polish National Dances* are still heard. He and his brother, Philipp, who was also a prolific composer, taught piano at the Klindworth-Scharwenka Conservatory in Berlin and New York.

SCHEIDT, Samuel (1587–1654)

German organist and composer who was trained by Sweelinck in Amsterdam and then spent the rest of his life, in spite of the 30 Years' War, as Kapellmeister at Halle. He was famous in his lifetime for his choral compositions which included:
(1) varied settings of each verse of Lutheran chorales, (2) sacred concertos for up to twelve voices with instruments in the Venetian style, and (3) four books of *Geistlichen Concerten* for two to four voices with continuo.
Historically, however, he occupies a position in German organ music which is paralleled by Frescobaldi in Italy. Scheidt makes extensive use of the pedal organ and introduces violinistic phrasing-effects. Both his publications (1624 and 1650) contain liturgical organ works and some secular pieces. Apart from the more conventional variations and fugues, there are alternatim settings of alternative verses of plainsong melodies which express the words in short contrapuntal pieces with the addition of registration. The second publication consists of 4-part harmonisations of chorales which clearly influenced J.S. Bach's own chorale settings as to their metrical and tonal harmonic movement. The collection also includes the 'carol' O *Jesulein Süss.*
Together with Praetorious, Schein and Schütz, Scheidt was responsible for passing on the early Italian Baroque techniques to the German tradition that culminated in Bach. He also wrote dances, preludes and 'symphonies' for two violins and continuo.

SCHEIN, Johann Hermann (1586–1630)

German composer who from 1615 was one of J.S.Bach's predecessors at St. Thomas', Leipzig. He is mainly remembered for the relatively simple arrangements of 200 chorale-melodies in his *Cantional* (1627), (although many of these tunes and their texts are actually by Schein). His harmonies tend to be tonal and irregular in movement.
Like Praetorius, Scheidt and Schütz, Schein was influenced by Italian models in his publications, which include 5-part strophic songs and instrumental pieces (1609), Latin and German motets in Venetian style (1615), and 5-part instrumental dances (1617). He also wrote larger scale Sacred Concertos in the style of Viadana (1618) together with several collections of Italian-style madrigals for three vocal or instrumental parts, set to Pastoral German texts by Schein himself.

SCHMIDT, Franz (1874–1939)

Austrian composer who studied under Bruckner and was highly regarded in Vienna as being representative of the main

Romantic tradition between the wars. This was at a time when the historically more-important Schönberg was largely ignored. Although he was distinguished as a pianist, cellist and teacher and wrote major works for the opera house, four symphonies and chamber music, his reputation has never become international.

SCHMITT, Florent (1870–1958)
French composer who studied at the Paris Conservatoire with Massenet and Fauré. His works combine impressionist colouring with an architectural power and proportion. In spite of his high reputation in France, Schmitt has had a few performances elsewhere. His best-known pieces are *Anthony and Cleopatra* (1920) and *Salammbo* (1925), both being symphonic episodes which were originally incidental music. He also wrote much for the voice, piano, and chamber combinations.

SCHOBERT, Johann (c. 1720–1767)
Silesian harpsichordist who spent most of his life in Paris. He is remembered historically for his influence on Mozart in his Mannheim School style together with his idiomatic use of the keyboard in concertos and chamber music (as opposed to the continuo style). He wrote a Singspiel opera, six clavier concertos, many sonatas for piano solo, and chamber works with keyboard (especially violin sonatas).

SCHÖNBERG, Arnold (1874–1951)
German-Jewish composer who is a seminal 20th century figure by virtue of his innovations in atonalism and serial music. He was a self-taught musician who thrived on the Viennese amateur habits of chamber music playing, and always felt himself part of the Romantic tradition of Wagner, Brahms and Mahler. On his father's death in 1890 he worked in a bank to help support his family. He was introduced to Zemlinsky who both gave him theory lessons and work in making a piano arrangement of an opera of his own. Schönberg's early works such as the string sextet, *Verklärte Nacht* (1899) soon began to appear. The enormous *Gurrelieder* had to be put aside while his time was absorbed in more lucrative activities such as scoring other composers' operettas and providing music for cabaret and teaching. His first pupils included Webern, Berg and Wellesz, — Schönberg was to become one of the greatest teachers of his generation. Although his earlier works such as the unaccompanied *Friede auf Erden* (1907) were often highly contrapuntal later compositions soon became more and more chromatic, so that by the time of *Pierrot Lunaire* (1912), the tonality often seemed to be suspended for long periods. This, with such innovations as his use of *Sprechgesang* (speech-song) in the same work, caused several hostile receptions of these new works. This harmonic 'atonality' was paralleled by Schönberg's use of 'linear' harmony, chords of the 4th and whole-tone scale in the 'expressionism' of the 2nd String Quartet (1908), *Five Pieces for Orchestra* (1908) and the short piano pieces of Op. 11 and 19. Thanks to such conductors as Schreker, Busoni, and Sir Henry Wood, Schönberg's works soon began to be performed more widely.
When his recognition as a teacher provoked some anti-Semitism in Vienna, he accepted a post in Berlin, for which he had been recommended by Richard Strauss, but service in the German Army and ill-health considerably slowed down his achievements in composition.
Gradually he was drawn to serial technique — 'composing with twelve notes, related only to one another' — and the new system appeared first in the piano pieces of 1923. He used this technique for the rest of his life in such major works as the unfinished opera *Moses und Aron* (1932), the 3rd String Quartet (1927) and the *Variations for Orchestra* (1928).
Schönberg's personal life was sometimes

clouded during his first marriage to Zemlinsky's sister, and his public position was soon threatened much more seriously by the Nazi regime after 1933. He eventually settled with his second wife in Los Angeles, where he was professor at the University until his retirement in 1944. The most important works of this period were the 4th String Quartet (1936) and the *Violin Concerto* (1936). As a young man Schönberg had joined the Protestant Church; but as an American citizen he re-adopted the Jewish faith. Several of his last works use liturgical Hebrew texts as in the unaccompanied setting of *Psalm 130* (1950). Some of these works also have tonal 'overtones' though almost all are serial in construction. Probably best known is *A Survivor from Warsaw* (1947) for speaker, male-chorus and orchestra. The *Piano Concerto* (1942) and *String Trio* (1946) confirm the picture of a fluent composer, still trying new paths although his musical personality is consistently recognisable throughout his long life. His influence on his successors has been incalculable and the expressive emotion in his music is at last becoming more obvious than the intellectual permutations with which he was generally associated.

SCHREKER, Franz (1878–1934)
Austrian composer who was important for his conducting of new music and his consequent influence on Schönberg and Berg. In his own country, he enjoyed great popularity as a progressive composer between the wars. His best known works were those of his youth, the operas *Der ferne Klang* (1912) and the ballet *Der Geburtstag der Infantin* (1908) with their Straussian richness, subtle orchestral colour and sense of theatrical melodrama. Several operas followed later, all to his own texts, as well as orchestral and choral music and about 50 songs. His Directorship of the Berlin Hochschule from 1920 ended with the Nazi regime which caused his death.

SCHUBERT, Franz (1797–1828)
Great Viennese composer and prolific song writer. He was taught first of all by his family and then at choir-school by Salieri, though there is clear evidence that he was a 'natural' composer as a boy. Such was the poverty of his background that even manuscript paper was a luxury. He seems to have become a school teacher in order to avoid military service. At this time he wrote his first mass and opera and such songs as the immortal *Gretchen am Spinnrade* and *Der Erlkönig*. In one year (1815) he wrote *144* songs — eight on one day — his 3rd and 4th Symphonies, two more masses, two more unperformed operas and many piano pieces.
He gave up teaching in 1817 but had no fixed abode and often no piano. The never ending flow of songs continued, however, wherever he was staying. A rather distinguished social circle formed itself round him including the famous baritone, Vogl, and the poet, Schober. This *Schubertiad* was the composer's audience, and his father's amateur group the orchestra for which four early symphonies were written. At last, in 1818, he was gainfully employed during the summer as music teacher to the Esterházy family. Apart from one or two similar visits during the rest of his short life and some miserly payments from music publishers, Schubert's bohemian life continued. He had no suitable clothes in which to appear at a belated concert of his works near the end of his life. He suffered ill health (perhaps caused by syphilis) from 1823 onwards, and almost experienced starvation before he died of typhoid.
Although Schubert composed intuitively, he clearly tried to improve his technique. Of his 600 songs, 200 are revisions or new settings of the same poem and even at the end of his life he planned to begin studying Marpurg's textbook on Fugue. It goes without saying that Schubert was at his best in his spontaneous songs and shorter piano pieces; and there are few people

nowadays who would criticise the longer works of his maturity for their formal or academic shortcomings. In every medium (except perhaps opera where he had little success and few opportunities) he produced instinctive masterpieces: the *Death and the Maiden* Quartet, the *Quartetsatz* and two other mature works in the same medium, two *Piano Trios*, *The Trout Quintet*, *The Octet*, the *Arpeggione Sonata* and the three superb *Violin Sonatinas* of 1816. Even the 1st Symphony which he wrote for the Choir School in 1813 is interesting; Symphonies 2–6 date from 1815 to 1818. His last two symphonies have never been equalled — the *Unfinished* in its profound expression and technical fluency and the *Great C major* in its majestic and 'heavenly lengths'. Many of these works, like the latter, only reached the public some decades after Schubert's death. Sometimes this was because of their difficulty, sometimes due to the composer's shyness, but probably mainly through the absence of promotion. Schubert was always more concerned with his next work.

Schubert's piano sonatas have been generally under-rated. He was never a concert pianist though he was apparently an excellent accompanist of Vogl in his own songs. It is all the more surprising therefore that he extended the emotional and technical range of the instrument to such an extent. There are about 30 piano sonatas — some were published with different titles and at least six were unfinished. They include polished masterpieces like the popular A major work and several late works like the posthumous B flat which are as important historically as late Beethoven in their enormous scale and lyrical power. Schubert also wrote extensively for piano duet and the 'Grand Duo' is of epic symphonic proportions.

It is through his songs that Schubert has become immortal. With the exception of the *Unfinished Symphony* none of his music is better known than songs like *An die Musick*, *Ave Maria* or *Who is Sylvia?* Schubert's choice of text was sometimes indiscriminating from a literary standpoint — Goethe, and Schubert's friend, Mayrhofer, are both treated with equal insight and inspiration while the relatively undistinguished Müller is the source of the two sublime song-cycles, *Die schöne Müllerin* and *Die Winterreise*.

1828 saw the same flow of masterpieces as previous years: another operatic sketch, the *Great C major*, the great *Mass in E flat*, the last three piano sonatas, the poignant F minor *Fantasy* for piano duet, melodies such as *Ständchen* and much else. His short life ended with the sublime *String Quartet*, unequalled in its melody and integrated construction.

SCHUMAN, William Howard (b. 1910)

American composer of German-Jewish descent who learned musical notation at the age of 17 by jazz scoring. He heard his first symphony concert at the age of 19. This late start made the acquiring of a technique an urgent necessity. Luckily he became a pupil of Roy Harris in 1936, after submitting his first symphony to him for criticism.

Schuman's writing is generally linear rather than harmonic in conception. It is vigorous in its polyrhythms and dramaticlly intense in its long melodic lines. Each of his nine symphonies has been striking in its rather sombre power. Perhaps the best known is the 5th Symphony (for strings). He has also written many choral works, ballets, several string quartets and two concertos. His unorthodox approach to musical education has given him an unusual insight into its problems. From 1945 to 1962 he was president of New York's Julliard School, and from 1955 to 1969 he occupied influential positions at the Lincoln Centre.

SCHUMANN, Robert (1810–1856)
Great German Romantic composer who as a child showed literary imagination and cultural sensibility as well as ability as a pianist and improviser. It was not until he was 20 that he persuaded his widowed mother to allow him to give up his legal studies and train for a musical career. He became a piano pupil of Freidrich Wieck in Leipzig but within three years his pianistic ambitions were destroyed by an accident to his right hand. He then devoted most of his time to composition. Up until 1839, his output was mostly works for the piano. Descriptive cycles of short pieces like *Papillons*, *Carnaval* and *Faschingsschwank aus Wien* created a new feeling in their pianistic tone colours, passionate but elusive warmth, as well as the Romantic extravagance of their programmatic ideas. He was almost as successful in the three piano sonatas of the same period (especially the popular G minor sonata).
Schumann's literary abilities had, by this time, become important to his career. From 1834 to 1844 he was editor of a musical magazine which he had helped to found. In this magazine he set new standards of musical criticism from a technical standpoint, as well as making known the claims of the 'new music' which included music by Berlioz, Schubert, Chopin and even Bach.
His personal life was less successful. He had fallen in love with Clara, Wieck's daughter and star pupil (herself a composer). It was only after five years of wrangling as well as a law suit that her father allowed the marriage. In 1840, the year of his marriage, he wrote 140 lieder including the two song cycles *Dichterliebe* and *Frauenliebe und Leben*. Apart from their Romantic involvement and poetic range, Schumann's songs are remarkable for the equal importance of voice and piano. He seems to look ahead to the instrumental concepts of Wolf and Mahler. The superb and original *Piano Concerto* was given its first performance in 1841 by his wife Clara and the same year marked the beginning of his symphonic writing. The four symphonies have had periods of neglect during the last century. This is mainly due to the rather thick and unvaried orchestral textures. After several attempts at rescoring, the originals are again finding favour and a challenge to the skill of the conductor. Schumann proved rather inadequate as a conductor and teacher although he did direct choral music and even opera during the decade. More successful were his chamber works with piano: the three piano trios, the piano quartet and quintet, the three violin sonatas and the works for horn, oboe, clarinet and cello with piano.
From 1844 onwards Schumann's health deteriorated. His hallucinations and even the damage to his hand are nowadays recognised as being caused by syphilis and its treatment. From 1854 (after an attempt at suicide) he was confined to an asylum. Opinion is still divided on his later works. Certainly the songs and piano pieces never achieved the heights of 1830–40 and the *Violin Concerto* (1853) was held back by Joachim and has never been accepted. In that year he had the insight to welcome Brahms as 'he who should come' in a critical article in his magazine. The *Cello Concerto* (1850) is a standard repertoire work. Schumann's personality is as elusive as some of his music. Liszt and Wagner found him dull as a person and he seems to have been uxorious to a degree. The fiery Romanticism and occasional humour either belonged to his unrecorded youth or were part of the inner life of his music.

SCHÜTZ, Heinrich (1585–1672)
Most famous German composer before Bach, who was sent to Italy to study with Giovanni Gabrieli in Venice. This followed experience of music as a choirboy and preliminary training in law. He

published some madrigals in Italy before returning to Saxony to take up a position as organist first in Kassel and then in Dresden. Here he did much to introduce Italian ideas to Germany. The influence of Gabrieli is apparent in *Psalmen Davids* (1619) where Schütz uses the polychoral tradition in spatially contrasted groups of choirs, soloists and instruments. The Italian dramatic style of the *Camerata* is found in his *Easter Oratorio* (1623) where gambas accompany the declamatory solo voices in mixed arioso and recitative. The *Cantiones Sacrae* (1626) is a collection of contrapuntal Latin motets in four parts but with instrumental bass.

In the following year Schütz produced an opera (now lost) before returning to Italy, perhaps to study the music of Monteverdi. The *Symphoniae Sacrae* (1629) uses solo voices, choirs and instruments in Monteverdi's style. The unsettled state of Germany during the 30 Years' War caused him to spend some time in Copenhagen, Brunswick and Hanover before returning to Dresden in 1645.

All Schütz' extant music is for the church. Later publications tended to be in the simpler style enforced by the conditions of his employment. Both *Musikalische Exequien* (1636) — a kind of German Requiem in Italian style — and the *Seven Words from the Cross* (1645) are marked by simple expression. The second set of *Symphoniae Sacrae* (1647) is mainly for solo voices and instruments with German words; it included the famous *Saul, Saul, Why Persecutest Thou Me*? At the end of his life Schütz finally managed to integrate the German and Italian styles in the popular *Christmas Story* (1664) with its sets of obligato solo instruments to characterise the Shepherds, Wise Men etc. Finally he returned in style to the German Renaissance in the four unaccompanied Passions with their pseudo-plainsong narrative and simple choral settings. He was truly a many-sided composer.

SCOTT, Cyril Meir (1879–1970)

English composer and writer who is today remembered for some refined impressionist piano pieces like *Water-Wagtail* and *Lotus-Land* which were composed in the early years of this century. Part of his musical education was in Germany. After he returned to his native Liverpool as a piano teacher and occasional recitalist, he was regarded in Germany, and by such conductors as Richter and Beecham, as a major English composer. His early reputation was based on such major works as his operas (produced in Germany), two symphonies, several concertos, choral, and chamber music.

SCRIABIN, Alexander (1872–1915)

Russian pianist and composer who showed early promise but was rather an unsatisfactory pupil of Taneiev and Arensky. Nevertheless, he toured as a concert pianist playing his own works, and had a comprehensive contract with a publisher by the time he was 20. These early works are in the Chopin tradition and include his Piano Concerto, 1st Symphony and 1st Sonata as well as many other shorter piano pieces.

After a period as professor of piano at the Moscow Conservatoire 1898–1904, he devoted his time to composition and concerts in America and Europe, especially with the conductor Koussevitsky from 1908. By this time Scriabin had become fascinated by the mysticism of theosophy, Eastern religions and the unity of life. He developed an obsession for finding a perfect synthesis of the arts. Musically this led to his using 'mystical' chords, usually based on 4ths such as C, F sharp, B flat, E', A', D^2, as in the orchestral *Prometheus* (1911) — 'The poem of Fire' which combines projected colours with sound. Other similar ventures were his 3rd Symphony (1903) — 'The Divine Poem'— and *The Poem of Ecstasy* (1908).

The brilliance shown in his earlier piano music continued through 10 sonatas and almost 60 shorter pieces. The inevitable result of these 'mystical' chords was the gradual loosening of tonal feeling with the disappearance of key-signatures in the later works. On the other hand the 'diabolical' element and formal style belong to the Romantic tradition in its technical demands and sensuous colour.

SEARLE, Humphrey (1915–1982)
English composer and critic who was a pupil of John Ireland at the RCM and later of Webern in Vienna. His compositions from 1946 use serial technique and have included four symphonies, two piano concertos, a sonata and miscellaneous orchestral, choral and chamber works. His literary writings have dealt with Liszt and 20th century techniques.

SEIBER, Matyas (1905–1960)
Hungarian pupil of Kodály who, after a varied career as a cellist, conductor, jazz musician and teacher, settled permanently in London in 1935. His English activities included lecturing at Morley College, conducting his 'Dorian Singers' in Renaissance and modern works, music publishing and teaching composition. With such a wide range of experience, it is not surprising that his many compositions reflect an eclectic style: folk song arrangements, jazz, modal counterpoint, the 19th century influence via Kodály, Neo-Classicism, as well as serial and medieval techniques. His writings included books on jazz and an accordion tutor, and his compositions have ranged from incidental music and 25 film scores to three string quartets and many choral pieces such as the cantata *Ulysses* (1947).

SÉNAILLÉ, Jean Baptiste (1687–1730)
French violinist and composer of 50 sonatas for violin and continuo, which influenced such composers as Leclair and did much to introduce the Italian style of playing to the French. His father and early teachers were members of Louis XIV's 'vingt-quartre violons'. Later he was taught by a pupil of Corelli and Vitali.

SENFL, Ludwig (d.c. 1555)
Swiss composer whose life was spent firstly in the service of the Emperor Maximilian I (up to 1519) and then at Augsburg and Munich. His works include 'Lieder' and miscellaneous church music. There exists a letter to him from Luther on music (1530).

SERMISY, Claude de (d. 1562)
French singer and composer who was associated with Sainte-Chapelle in Paris from 1508 and was a canon there from 1533. Attaignant's publications 1529–35 include 92 chansons by Sermisy with 35 more appearing in 1548. 10 masses and some motets appeared in 1532 and 1556. Sermisy claimed to have been a pupil of Josquin.

SEROV, Alexander (1820–1871)
Russian composer and critic who was an admirer of Wagner, and hostile to the aims of 'The Five'. His first two operas *Judith* (1863) and *Rogneda* (1866), to his own libretti, enjoyed great success in Russia. His pupil and wife Valentina Bergmann (1846–1927) also wrote two operas and some piano music.

SESSIONS, Roger (b. 1896)
American composer who showed early promise as a musician and studied with Bloch. From 1925 to 1933 he lived mostly in Florence and Berlin and since then has been involved in teaching, firstly at Berkeley and then at the Julliard School in New York. Amongst his pupils have been Milton Babbit as well as other young American composers.
His music is eclectic in style and marked by naturalness of 'gesture', rugged rhymic vitality, and long but often syncopated melodic lines. His careful technique has recently been extended to include 12-note

procedures. Session's most important works are the eight symphonies, three concertos, three piano sonatas and chamber music.

SHAW, Geoffrey (1879–1943)
London composer and organist who was active in the reform of church music and by his work as an Inspector of Music. He was influential in musical education as well as amateur music. He is mainly remembered today for his part songs and simple, but musicianly, church music, and also for his editorial work in collaboration with his brother Martin (below).

SHAW, Martin (1875–1958)
English organist and composer who wrote for the amateur stage and extensively for voice and choir. He was particularly influential in introducing a rather austere but modern note into Anglican worship through his church music and his work with Vaughan Williams in the editing of *Songs of Praise* and the *Oxford Book of Carols*.

SHEPHERD, John (c. 1520–c. 1563)
English choirmaster of Magdalen College, Oxford and a Gentleman of the Chapel Royal. His work as a composer included several masses and many Latin motets which date from before the Reformation. Later, he also wrote 14 English anthems and several service and psalm settings. Little of his music is, as yet, available in modern editions.

SHIELD, William (1748–1829)
English composer of about 50 operas as well as several string trios and duos. He was a pupil of Avison in Newcastle but moved to London as an orchestral player in 1772. He became composer to Covent Garden and Master of the King's Music from 1817. His excellent songs are no longer heard so frequently.

SHOSTAKOVICH, Dmitri (1906–1975)
Russian composer and pianist who studied at Leningrad and became a brilliantly-successful pianist and composer in the international and liberal atmosphere of the city during the first decade of the Revolution. His 1st Symphony was played in Berlin in 1927 and in America in the following year. The 1st Piano Sonata shows the influence of Stravinsky and Prokofiev. After 1930 Shostakovich appeared only occasionally as a pianist performing his own works. Works written between 1927 and 1930 were less successful in their impact due, in the West, to the alleged triteness of their 'industrial' outlook and, in Russia, to their modernist 'formalism'. Apart from the 2nd and 3rd symphonies, this period included incidental and film music, ballets and the almost Wagnerian opera, *The Nose* (1928). Shostakovich's next opera *Lady Macbeth of Mtsensk District* (1934) met with a mixed reception abroad owing to its strange mixture of historical styles; set numbers and cantilena are merged with ideas from Berg's *Wozzeck* (produced in Leningrad 1927). In Russia it was denounced for its petit-bourgeois sensationalism, its leftish distortion and formalistic tendencies. In 1936, however, the opera was playing to packed houses in Moscow.
Shostakovich took the hint and withdrew his 4th Symphony which was not heard until 1961. He then began work on his 5th Symphony (1937) which he said was 'a Soviet artist's practical creative reply to just criticism'. Its immediate success led to a period of symphonic composition where the direct emotionalism of Tchaikovsky and Mahler seem to be dominant. The 5th Symphony is concerned with 'the stabilisation of a personality' and the 'heroic' period of the 6th and 7th (*Leningrad*) symphonies contrast with the sunny 1st String Quintet (1940).
Following the entry of Russia into the war,

Shostakovich became a national hero largely due to the tremendous success of the *Leningrad Symphony* as well as his patriotic activities. He and his family moved to Moscow in 1942 and the series of major works continued with the pessimistic 8th Symphony (1943) and the lightweight 9th (1945).

The more complex style which he adopted after the 2nd World War as in the 3rd Quartet (1946) and 1st Violin Concerto led once again to perverse Party reaction for his 'anti-People' and formalist proclivities. Shostakovich was banished from his post at the Moscow Conservatoire and was ignored for several years. Not surprisingly he turned to a more obvious style in his many film scores of this period, in the more approachable idiom of the *24 Preludes and Fugues* for piano (1951) and in the 4th and 5th String Quartets.

His 10th Symphony (1953) is tragic, large-scale, and intensely 'private' as compared with the massive and patriotic 11th (1957) which is based on events in the 1905 Revolution, and the 12th (*Lenin*). After this second recognition of the composer by the Party, each succeeding work was an international event. Symphonies 13 (1962) and 14 (1969) were in the nature of Russian cantatas while the 15th (1971) is almost humorous in its quotations from Rossini, Wagner and the composer himself. The 8th String Quartet (1960) is dedicated to the victims of Nazism while the 12th Quartet (1968) actually uses Schönbergian tone-rows in a D flat major context. Perhaps the most appreciated of his late works have been the two Cello Concertos (1959 and 1967) which were written for Rostropovich. Shostakovich's range is so wide that individual choice will value the international and personal or the popular and patriotic with equal enthusiasm.

His pupil and colleague Khatchaturian described him as 'the conscience of Soviet music'.

SIBELIUS, Jean (1865–1957)

Great Finnish nationalist composer and symphonist. He showed early promise in music and took naturally to the breadth of culture in the Swedish-speaking society that surrounded him. As a youth he was a keen violinist and despite his late start on the instrument (at the age of 15) he was serious enough to audition as a violinist for the Vienna Philharmonic in 1891. He was largely a self-taught composer who, in his 20's, came under the influence of the Finnish teacher Wegelius, and Busoni. He studied in Berlin and Vienna from 1889, where, besides learning basic contrapuntal skills, he absorbed the formal and orchestral procedures of Brahms.

On his return to Finland he found nationalist sentiment against the political control of the country by Russia at boiling point. Sibelius became politically involved and the influence on his music of the national epic *Kalevala* was added to the foreign folk-idiom of Tchaikovsky, Grieg, and the Celtic 'Ossian'. His large-scale *Kullervo* (1892) made him famous in Finland overnight. He claimed never to have used a Finnish folksong, but he found, on a visit to the remote area of Karelia, that the folksongs he heard were strikingly similar in idiom to his own music. This Nationalist period continued with the composition of *En Saga* (1892), the *Lemminkainen* legends which included the famous *Swan of Tuonela* (1893) and the even more popular *Finlandia* (1899) and *Valse triste* (1903). The influence of Tchaikovsky is still present in his 1st Symphony (1899) and the *Violin Concerto* (1903). His characteristic bleak hugeness and elemental power, however, are seen to take over in the impressive 2nd Symphony (1901) which is still his most popular symphony and one containing origianl principles of construction. By this time Sibelius was receiving a Government pension and from 1904 lived in a remote 'log cabin' with the added variety of some

foreign travel. This 'confirmed' his sense of musical direction and gave him welcome opportunities as a conductor of increasing the numbers of performances of his works in Europe and America. He moved away from romantic colour towards the rather naive Neo-Classicism of the 3rd Symphony (1907) and the spare and compressed lines of the 4th (1911). Here tonal ambiguity, and obsession with the tritone produce an 'international' style that was to become a seminal influence on the writings of 20th century composers.
In contrast to the grim fantasy of the 4th Symphony, the 5th (1915) marks a partial return to the hammer-blow grandeur of his earlier works, although the formal innovations continue. Symphony 6 (1923), like the tone-poem *Oceanides* (1914), seems to inhabit a different world again with its impersonal grandeur and the almost static coldness of its modal lines. Each of these works had long periods of gestation and were written in years of war and revolution until such time as Finland achieved her (temporary) independence.
Mystery still covers Sibelius' last 30 years. The series of major works end with the noble one-movement 7th Symphony (1924) and the powerful symphonic poem *Tapiola* (1925). All his life he had written lighter pieces for piano and chorus but even these ceased to be written after 1930. It is difficult to judge whether posterity will value more highly his nationalist intensity or his symphonic originality. Both are essential features of modern music.

SIMPSON, Robert (b. 1921)
English composer and pupil of Herbert Howells. His compositions include three symphonies, two concertos, three string quartets, other chamber music and some significant piano music. He has also written important books on Nielson and Bruckner.

SINDING, Christian (1856-1941)
Norwegian composer now mostly remembered for the popular *Rustle of Spring*. In his day he was an important Nationalist composer who wrote in the German Romantic tradition. He wrote three symphonies, two concertos and chamber music as well as various piano works, 200 songs and one opera.

SKALKOTTAS, Nikos (1904-1949)
Greek composer who studied in Germany with Kurt Weil and worked with Schönberg from 1927 to 1933. He returned to Greece and was involved with the recording of Greek folkmusic, his 36 *Greek Dances* (1936) being his best-known work. It was not until a committee was formed to promote his works after his death that he became internationally known. His works include a *Sinfonietta* (1948), several concertos and four string quartets. His style is markedly personal.

SMART, Henry (Thomas) (1813-1879)
London organist and composer, now remembered for his shorter organ pieces and occasionally for his flamboyant Anglican services and hymn tunes. He also wrote two operas, several cantatas and some distinguished part-songs. He was blind for the last 15 years of his life.

SMETANA, Bedřich (1824-1884)
First important Czech nationalist composer. He showed early precocity but was largely self-taught both as a pianist and composer. On moving to Prague at the age of 19 he managed to find work as a piano teacher and to have lessons in basic composition. He also heard and met Liszt, Berlioz and the Schumanns. He was an active partisan in the 1848 attempt to rid Prague of the Austrian Hapsburgs. Some early 'revolutionary' music dates from this period. His first published piano pieces were in 1851, and his early tragic *Piano*

Trio was written in 1855 in memory of his five-year-old daughter.

Partly for political reasons, Smetana left Bohemia in 1856. He went to Sweden where, for five years, he conducted and composed and became recognised as a pianist. There he met Liszt again and wrote several symphonic poems in the style of Liszt. After several concert tours he returned to Prague in 1863 and had to work as a music critic and choral conductor rather than as the operatic composer he now wished to be. At last, in 1866, his best-known (and second) opera, *The Bartered Bride*, was produced, and Smetana was appointed as conductor of the 'Provisional' Theatre. His work there was outstanding but he was soon being attacked for the 'Wagnerian' tendencies of *Dalibor* (1868). After two more operas and their mixed receptions he resigned as conductor in 1874. A more powerful factor in his resignation was the onset of total deafness which marred the last ten years of his life.

The two symphonic poems *Ma Vlast* were written in 1879 (the five movements being based on his country's traditions), and the two *String Quartets* in 1876 and 1883 — both programmatically autobiographical. His last three completed operas continued the series of new types of nationalist opera. He only became recognised in his country after his death in a mental home, probably of syphilis. During most of his life he had been disappointed at what seemed to be the lack of interest in the operas that followed *The Bartered Bride*. This has also been the case in international opera houses since his death. In his own country, however, he succeeded in producing a basic Czech repertoire for the new permanent National Theatre in Prague which opened in 1881. He was a patriot, a revolutionary, and the father of his country's music.

SMYTH, Dame Ethel (1858–1944)

English composer, trained in Germany, who became established with the *Mass* in D (1893). She later became better known for her operas, especially *The Wreckers* (1909) and *The Boatswain's Mate* (1916). Her activities for Woman's Suffrage resulted in *The March of the Women*. Nowadays her writings are more read than her music is heard.

SÖDERMAN, August Johan (1832–1876)

Swedish composer who lived in Germany. He is now remembered for a mass, and several operettas written for the Stockholm Court Opera, where he was chorus master and 2nd conductor. Many other of his choral works and songs are still performed there.

SOLER, Antonio (1729–1783)

Spanish priest, organist, and composer who called himself a disciple of Domenico Scarlatti. He left over 60 harpsichord sonatas and also wrote church, organ and chamber music including several duets for two organs. From 1753 he was organist (and a monk) at the Monastery of the Escorial, where he died.

SOMERVELL, Sir Arthur (1863–1937)

English composer and educationalist who was a pupil of Parry and Stanford. He became principal Inspector of Schools in Scotland and, later, in England. Apart from orchestral music and many educational publications and editions, he is remembered for his song cycles *Maud* and *The Shropshire Lad* as well as his five children's operas and church music (*The Passion of Christ* (1914) and the *Service in F*).

SOR (Sors), Fernando (1780–1839)

Spanish guitarist and composer who lived in Paris and London from 1808 and was largely responsible for the popularity of his instrument. His studies are still an essential part of a guitarist's training though his fluent galant style bears little inward relationship to the style of his idol, Mozart. Sor also wrote two ballets for the Paris Opéra and an opera when he was 19.

SORABJI, Kaikhosru (Leon Dudley) (1892–)
English composer and pianist, an eccentric of mixed Parsee and Spanish descent. He is largely self-taught but nevertheless an expert technician. His compositions are intentionally complex so as to be accessible only to those of similar skills and outlook. Works include three symphonies, five piano concertos, and some very elaborate piano and organ music which is now rarely heard.

SOUSA, John Philip (1854–1932)
Famous American composer of marches, his best known being *The Stars and Stripes Forever* and *The Washington Post*. He played as a violinist in variety theatres and from 1892 was conductor of the band of the US Marine Corps. Later his own band 'toured the world' from 1892 to 1911. He wrote many successful light operas, about 50 songs and some film music (including *Ben-Hur* and the *Last Days of Pompeii*).

SOWERBY, Leo (1895–1968)
American organist, pianist and composer who, after a period as a bandmaster during the 1st World War, won various composition awards. He toured as a concert pianist before becoming an organist and choirmaster in Chicago. He was also much in demand as a teacher.
His works include five symphonies, four concertos, much choral and chamber music and a popular organ suite (1933).

SPOHR, Ludwig (Louis) (1784–1859)
German violinist, composer and conductor who, in spite of precocity as a child, was at first largely self-taught. From 1802 he travelled with his teacher Franz Eck and met Clementi and Field. For several years he modelled his playing and compositions on those of Rode.
From 1805 his life was divided between concert tours, and playing in and conducting orchestras for which he wrote his 15 violin concertos and nine symphonies. His 11 operas include the famous *Jessonda* (1823). In his activities as an operatic conductor, he conducted two Wagner operas. He apparently had little sympathy for either *Fidelio* or Weber's works.
Spohr made many successful visits to England as a conductor, and his oratorios, especially *The Last Judgement*, almost set a fashion for this genre. He also introduced the baton into the Philharmonic concerts. His musical style has often been criticised as excessively chromatic; certainly the next generation of oratorio composers tended to emphasize this aspect of his style. Of more influence is his debt to Mozart.
Spohr's importance, however, is as a Romantic innovator. His opera *Faust* (1816) has been described as the first Romantic opera. Most of his symphonies are programme works. His works for violin and harp (his first wife was a harpist) created another Victorian fashion. Most important of all was the fact that he experimented widely with chamber music combinations. Besides 34 string quartets, he experimented with varying quintets, sextets, septets, and 'double string quartets' apart from the popular Octet and Nonet. Spohr also was one of the last of the French-style violinists, as opposed to the new and lighter style advocated by Paganini. His *Violin School* still retains its usefulness.

SPONTINI, Gasparo (1774–1851)
Italian operatic composer who, in *La Vestale* (1807), set the fashion for grand opera in Paris. He made his reputation with some church music and 11 operas in Italy before settling in Paris in 1803. Some of his earlier works had met with mixed reception. *La Vestale* and its successor, *Fernand Cortes* (1809), in spite of

opposition during rehearsal caused partly by Spontini's habit of continuous revision, were very successful. They won for the composer the interest of Napoleon, the Empress Josephine and King Frederick William III of Prussia. The last named had both operas performed in Berlin in 1814 and the composer moved there in 1819 as general director of music to the King.

Just before leaving Paris another grand opera *Olympie* was produced after several years of work. This had an unfavourable reception but was to achieve success in Berlin. His life in Berlin was stormy. He made enemies of Weber and the new Romantic nationalist party and used his position mainly to propagate his own works. His own fluent style of composing was lost, and, after the King's death in 1840, his own resignation became inevitable. Honours continued to fall on him but he wrote no more operas and retired to Italy in 1848.

SQUIRE, William Henry (1871–1963)
English cellist and composer. He wrote a cello concerto, many songs and two operettas but is remembered now only for some charming cello concert pieces.

STAINER, Sir John (1840–1901)
English organist, composer and scholar who, after a distinguished period at Magdalen College, Oxford, succeeded Goss in 1872 as organist at St. Paul's Cathedral. He retired in 1888 due to failing sight. Apart from working as a teacher, examiner and Inspector of Schools, he wrote the important study: *Dufay and his Contemporaries* (1898) and two excellent Novello primers on *Harmony* and the *Organ*.

His most important compositions are the cantata *The Daughter of Jairus* (1878) and the ever popular oratorio *The Crucifixion* (1887). He is still remembered for the *Sevenfold Amen*, several hymn tunes and the many simple anthems which met wide need until recent years. His cathedral music is rarely heard today.

STAMITZ, Johann (1717–1757)
Bohemian orchestral leader and composer who was associated with the newer style of orchestral music at Mannheim and who considerably influenced the Viennese school of composers. He was the first composer to use clarinets and horns in the orchestra and his orchestra was known for its discipline and observance of dynamics. In his 50 symphonies he generally used the Italian three-movement pattern with a final Minuet and Trio or Variations. He was noted for his 2nd subject contrast and developments in the first movement as well as his expressive and melodic slow movements. His 28 concertos include the first for clarinet and six for harpsichord and violin. His chamber music uses basso continuo in the trios and sonatas.

STANDFORD, Partic (b. 1939)
English composer who trained at the GSM with Rubbra, and later with Malipiero and Lutoslawski. His works have varied from the aleatoric *Notte* (1968) to Neo-Romantic symphonic works and concertos such as the *Cello Concerto* (1973). His major work so far has been the *Christus Requiem* (1972) which is marked by detailed craftmanship and mysticism rather than by stylistic integration.

STANFORD, Sir Charles Villiers (1852–1924)
Anglo-Irish composer and conductor. He made his reputation at Cambridge from 1870 although he also studied in Leipzig and Berlin (1874–76). His fluency as a composer and ability as a conductor made him the outstanding musician and teacher of his generation.

As an *émigré* Irishman, his nationalist sympathies invite comparison with Dvorák in the opera *Shamus O'Brien* (1896), the six *Irish Rhapsodies*, and such songs as *The*

Fairy Lough (1901). As an English musician in the tradition of Brahms, his seven symphonies, six concertos, eight string quartets and other chamber and piano music may, in the future, be rescued from their present oblivion.

His music for the Anglican church, however, retains its popularity today. The technical fluency of the services in B flat, G and C, introduced new standards into the organ-loft. Such works as the *Magnificat* in G and the three Latin motets are masterpieces by any standard.

Stanford's impact on his adopted country was largely as Professor of Music at Cambridge from 1887 and in his teaching at the RCM from 1883. Almost all of the next generation of English composers were taught either by him or by Parry. His wider influence spread through his provincial conducting activities and through choral works such as *Songs of the Sea* (1904) and *Songs of the Fleet* (1910), both written for the Leeds Festival. His many part-songs, such as the exquisite *Heraclitus*, have become staple fare in the Competitive Festival movement.

STANLEY, John (1713–1786)

English organist and composer who was blind from early childhood. He was a pupil of Maurice Greene and in 1734 was appointed one of the organists of the Temple Church in London. His works include six cantatas (1742), *Jephtha* (1757), several theatrical entertainments, eight flute solos, six concertos and three sets of organ voluntaries. He followed the tradition set by Handel in conducting oratorio performances and succeeded Boyce in 1779 as Master of the King's Band.

STEFFANI, Agostino (1654–1728)

Italian composer and, from 1696, diplomat in the German states. He was taken to Munich in 1667 where he studied with Kerll. He later came under the influence of Lully in Paris (1678–79). He had already published the successful 8-part psalms in 1674 and was appointed court organist the following year. Although he became a priest in 1680, he remained director of chamber music and published in 1683 sonatas da camera which have since been lost. Thereafter he wrote six operas for Munich and 10 more for Hanover.

During his diplomatic career he wrote three operas for Düsseldorf and his travels included a return visit to Italy. He was also president of the London Academy of Ancient Music. His later works include a famous 6-part *Stabat Mater* and many duets and vocal cantatas. His works had much influence on other North German composers, including Handel. The works are marked by fluent but often dissonant contrapuntal lines.

STEVENS, Bernard (1916–1982)

English composer who studied at Cambridge and the RCM. After war service (1940–46) during which he won a competition with his *Symphony of Liberation*, he became associated with the Workers Music Association. His other orchestral works have included two concertos and a Sinfonietta for strings. He has set two poems by the socialist poet, Randall Swingler for choir and various instruments.

STEVENS, Richard John Samuel (1757–1837)

London organist and composer of glees, the best known of which is *Ye Spotted Snakes*. He also wrote music for the stage.

STOCKHAUSEN, Karlheinz (b. 1928)

Important German avant-garde composer who became a competent player at an early age and supported himself financially first as a farm hand and later as a dance band pianist. He acquired a composing technique in his spare time. From 1947 to

1951 he studied in Cologne with Frank Martin and, alone, worked on analysing the music of Schönberg, Bartok and Webern. At the Darmstadt International Summer School in 1951 he came under the influence of Messiaen and Boulez. The immediate result was a preoccupation with Messiaen's total serialisation — i.e. not only of pitch but of duration and intensity. At this time he also began, with Boulez, to experiment with sound in the Musique Concrète studios of the Paris Radio. During this period he composed *Kontrapuncte* for 10 instruments, *Klavierstücke* Nos. 1-4, and several works that have since been withdrawn. *Kontrapuncte* is a type of 12-minute diminuendo, mathematically precise in its gradual elimination, but sensous in its tone colours.

Stockhausen and his wife moved from Paris in 1953 to the new electronic studios in Cologne where they have lived ever since. He soon became a well-known figure in international avant-garde circles and achieved prominence as a lecturer and writer. His formal thinking led, in 1960, to the concept of 'Moment-form' in *Contakte*. *Klavierstücke* Nos. 5-10 included attempts to use electronic effects on the keyboard. *Zeitmasse* (1956) and *Gruppen* (1957) dealt with metre/tempo and space/time continuum respectively. But soon, after the influence of the writings of Cage, the element of chance and the performer's whim reappeared in *Klavierstücke II* and *Momente* (1962). Concepts of space had already appeared in his best-known electronic work, *Gesang der Jünglinge* (1956) — a processed five-channel recording of a boy singing the Benedicite. The four 'regions' of *Hymnen* (1969) combine live performance with taped effects which fill the space around the audience. *Hymnen* contains the influence of 'pop existentialist philosophy... influenced by Eastern religion' (Stephen Walsh).

STOKER, Richard (b. 1938)

English composer who was a pupil of Lennox Berkeley at the RAM and, later, of Nadia Boulanger in Paris. His style is serially based but retains a tonal centre and his works, including two operas, have achieved importance in the chamber music media.

STORACE, Stephen (1763-1796)

English opera composer who was trained in Naples. After producing two of his Italian operas in Vienna, he returned to London to write 20 more stage works, most of which included favourite songs by composers such as Dittersdorf and Cherubini. *The Haunted Tower* (1789) remained in the repertoire for nearly 50 years.

His sister Anna, was the first 'Susanna' in Mozart's *Nozze di Figaro*.

STRADELLA, Alessandro (1642-1682)

Italian composer of six oratorios, five operas and 21 cantatas, which are marked by relatively long and defined arias with full string accompaniment and richly contrapuntal choruses.

He was murdered by assassins in an attempt to abduct a nobleman's mistress!

STRAUS, Oscar (1870-1954)

Renowned Austrian composer of operettas. He was a pupil of Max Bruch in Berlin and after holding various theatrical and cabaret positions made his reputation with *The Chocolate Soldier* (1908). He left Germany in 1927 for Paris and the USA. Among his works are a violin sonata, and other music for strings as well as shorter pieces for piano, violin and cello.

STRAUSS, Johann (1804-1849)

Father of the family which established the Viennese Waltz. After early musical promise and experience of performing in dance ensembles, he began to write his own

waltzes in 1826 and formed his own large orchestra in 1833. Apart from being responsible for court fêtes and dances from 1835, he toured extensively with his orchestra. His 251 separate publications include 152 waltzes, 24 galops, six cotillons, 32 quadrilles, 13 polkas and 18 marches. His best known piece is the *Radetzky March*. He tried, unsuccessfully, to discourage his legitimate sons from a career in music and spent most of his life with his mistress and illegitimate children, all of whom were quite unmusical — even the one called Johann.
His musical style owes much to the peasant dances of the area round Vienna and reflects the earlier military glories of the Hapsburgs.

STRAUSS, Johann (1825–1899)
Most brilliant of Johann's three sons who established an orchestra in 1844 to play his own and his father's waltzes. He combined the two orchestras when his father died five years later. The orchestra was taken over by his two brothers — Joseph (1827–70), who himself left many works, and Eduard (1835–1916) who wrote 318 dances, eventually disbanding the orchestra in 1902.
Johann (2) quickly became world-famous through such waltzes as *The Blue Danube* (1867) and *Wine, Women and Song* (1869). The Romantic richness and haunting musicality of *Tales from the Vienna Woods* earned the enthusiasm of Brahms, who became a close friend. Strauss' musical interests even included performances by his orchestra of Wagnerian extracts. Through him the relatively slight Viennese waltz became almost a symphonic art form, while his musical charm and effervescent tunefulness seem to represent the irresistible sophistication of Franz Joseph II's court.
As a composer of operettas he was less successful, but *Die Fledermaus* (1874) remains in the international repertoire as, to a lesser degree, does *The Gipsy Baron* (1885).

STRAUSS, Richard (1864–1949)
The 'Last German Romantic composer'. He was born of a musical family in Munich, and had several boyhood works published. When he left University in 1883 he became assistant conductor of the Meiningen Court Orchestra, for which von Bülow had already commissioned him to write a new work. Throughout his life his career as a conductor paralleled his composing activities. He held positions at the opera houses of Munich and Weimar, as well as with the Berlin Philharmonic Orchestra and Opera (1898–1918) and with the Vienna Opera (1919–24). Long before this, however, he became an international figure through his conducting at Bayreuth and London and at many other musical centres. He held no regular conducting or administrative post during the latter part of his life but continued to conduct many performances of his works. He also managed to continue his activities in Nazi Germany until a denazification court exonerated him from any charge of collaboration.
Strauss' early works moved from the classical background of the *String Quartet* Op. 2, through the Brahmsian period of his early songs to the Berlioz-Wagner-Liszt influence of the controversial tone poems. These latter contributed to his international reputation as a composer and include *Don Juan* (1888), *Tod und Verklärung* (1889), *Till Eulenspiegel* (1895), *Also sprach Zarathustra* (1896), *Don Quixote* (1897) and *Ein Heldenleben* (1898). All the tone poems are marked by orchestral virtuosity and what often seemed to his contemporaries to be bombastic and antimusical noise effects. Later musical criticism has drawn attention to the rich chamber music textures, the formal techniques and the origniality of invention.

In the new century, Strauss' musical emphasis moved from the tone poem to the opera. He wrote *Salomé* in 1905 and *Electra* in 1909, the latter on a libretto by Hofmannstal, who was to act as a catalyst for many of the composer's future operatic ideas. These two masterpieces were accused of having a perverse obsession with horror. The Strauss-Hofmannstal partnership turned next to the Viennese artificiality and neo-Mozartian sophistication of Strauss' greatest work, *Der Rosenkavalier* (1910). Strauss' 10 remaining operas did not maintain this standard but *Ariadne auf Naxos* (1912 and 1916), with its orchestral suite *Le Bourgeois Gentilhomme*, is still often heard.

This 18th century Neo-Classical influence extended to his later works but the Romantic textures and soaring vocal lines still retained their expansive character. Such later works include the 2nd Horn Concerto (1942), the *Oboe Concerto* (1946), the two *Sonatinas* for 16 wind-instruments (1944 and 1946) and the *Metamorphosen* for 23 solo strings (1946). His many songs culminated in the sublime richness of the *Four Last Songs* (1950).

STRAVINSKY, Igor (1882–1971)

Probably the greatest Russian composer of the 20th century whose international influence has been incalculable. He was born into a cultured and musical family in St. Petersburg but seems to have been a slow developer. He was influenced by operatic music, Tchaikovsky's ballets, Russian folk music and the music of the Orthodox Church. He acquired a sound piano technique and had some lessons in musical theory but it was not until his 20th year that he began to write descriptive piano pieces and to make some arrangements of the music of Glazunov and Rimsky-Korsakov. From 1903 he had regular lessons from Rimsky-Korsakov and had some of his own works performed. It was not until after the death of Rimsky-Korsakov in 1908 that he wrote his masterpiece — the ballet *The Firebird* (1910). Written for Diaghilev, it was a brilliant and personal result of Stravinsky's enthusiasm for the music of Tchaikovsky and Rimsky-Korsakov. As a result of this work he became internationally famous.

Le Sacre du Printemps (1913) is probably one of the most important single works of the 20th century. To the colour and taut rhythmic vitality of his earlier music was added the paganism of the subject. It contains continuous repetition and variation of motifs, superimposed chords and rhythms, and tonalities defined by repeated bass notes. This ballet together with the contemporary *Petrushka* (1911) pointed the direction for future composers and established Stravinsky as the leader of the avant-garde.

The immediate effect of the 1st World War was that Stravinsky wrote for smaller musical combinations. From this period comes *The Soldier's Tale* (1918) and *Les Noces* (1923) as well as such non-Russian works as *Ragtime* (1918) for piano. This led quite naturally, together with some of the adaptions for Diaghilev's ballets, into the Neo-Classical period of *Pulcinella* (1920) — a ballet with sets by Picasso and music based on Pergolesi. Stravinsky was also attracted at this time to the objective classical ideal as opposed to the subjective 'expressive' basis of Romanticism. The *Symphonies of Wind Instruments* (1921) and the wind *Octet* (1923) led to a whole Series of works which redeveloped the concepts of tonal centres and static sonorities. The latter also led to Stravinsky's concert appearances as conductor and pianist in his *Piano Concerto* (1924). His approach here has certainly influenced the generation of Boulez in its economy of gesture from the conductor during a performance. The 'Back to Bach' movement was apparent in the piano *Serenade* (1925) but his first great success in this style was the opera-oratorio *Oedipus Rex* (1927) and the statuesque and

popular *Symphony of Psalms* (1930) which followed a Tchaikovsky flirtation in *Le Baiser de la Fée* (1928).
Although Stravinsky became a French citizen in 1934, he became more and more involved in the American musical scene and considered himself an international artist. The *Dumbarton Oaks Concerto* (1938) for 16 wind instruments, and the *Symphony in C* (1940) were further fruits of Stravinsky's mature Neo-Classical period. They were followed by the *Mass* (1944) with double wind quintet, the *Symphony in Three Movements* (1946) and the *Ebony Concerto* (1946) for jazz band. The natural climax of this period was the opera, *The Rake's Progress* (1951), in which the Mozartian externals of secco recitative and aria are as separate sections, and Wagnerian music drama is completely avoided.
At the end of his life Stravinsky began to study the 'pure' music of Webern. In *In Memoriam Dylan Thomas* (1954) he uses a series of five notes only, while the *Canticum Sacrum* (1956) has 12 note movements as well as the block modality of his earlier style; it also includes retrograde procedures. From the time of the composition of *Threni* (1958) — an 'oratorio' with Latin text from Jeremiah — all his works are strictly serial and all brief and pointed in scale and idiom. Tonal implications abound and Stravinsky's style is still apparent. His musical vitality continued despite ill-health, and the varying pattern of his styles is at last seen to be integrated in his own musical vision and exploration.

SUK, Josef (1874–1935)
Czech composer and viola player, who was a pupil and son-in-law of Dvorák. His professional life was spent first as a member of the Bohemian String Quartet and then as teacher and rector (from 1930) of the Prague Conservatoire.
Suk wrote two symphonies and several descriptive works for orchestra, chorus, chamber combinations and piano. His style developed from Dvorák's Romantic folk idiom but later became contrapuntal and freer in metre, form and tonality. His later works also have programmes based on the Czech patriots of the 1st World War.

SULLIVAN, Sir Arthur (1842–1900)
Brilliant English composer, pianist and conductor who is today remembered for his collaboration with W.S. Gilbert in the series of Savoy operas commencing with *The Sorcerer* (1877) and ending with *The Grand Duke* (1896).
While a choirboy in the Chapel Royal an anthem of his was published. He later studied in Leipzig (1858–61) where he became enamoured of Schumann's music. In England he held various positions as organist and soon became well-known for his music to *The Tempest* (1866) and for the cantata *Kenilworth* (1864). The irony of 'Gilbert and Sullivan' is that neither took their work together very seriously and each of them had grandiose ambitions elsewhere. Unfortunately Sullivan's grand opera *Ivanhoe* (1891), his larger choral works and church music, the orchestral works and most of his songs are no longer performed today. Of his 56 hymn tunes only *Onward Christian Soldiers* is still used and only *The Yeoman of the Guard* (1888) has pretensions to serious drama.
Each of the 12 operettas has a stereotyped plot, sharply contrasted stage costumes and sets, very witty and topical lyrics, trite spoken dialogue and a conservative and slightly twisted sense of humour. A work like *Patience* (1881), with its treatment of the aesthetic movement, cannot avoid becoming dated.
Such is Sullivan's musical fluency and technique, his fresh originality and balanced style that the immortality of these works is still an accomplished fact. His musical style derives from Mozart and Donizetti but he uses Verdian parodies and academic counterpoint, though rarely

musical characterisation, to make his dramatic points. His personal 'small orchestral' sound is yet another tribute to his superb resourcefulness.
His best-known operettas include *H.M.S. Pinafore* (1878), *The Pirates of Penzance* (1879), *Iolanthe* (1882), *The Mikado* (1885) and *The Gondoliers* (1889).

SUMSION, Herbert (b. 1899)
English organist and composer of church music. He was a choirboy and later organist (from 1928) at Gloucester Cathedral. He was an articled pupil, and assistant, to Sir Herbert Brewer at Gloucester and then held posts in London and Philadelphia. His best-known works are the several sets of Evening Canticles in G and A which are marked by a fluent harmonic sense and melodic freshness.

SUPPE, Franz von (1819-1895)
Yugoslavian composer of operettas. He was of Belgian descent and studied in Italy and at the Vienna Conservatoire. Most of his life was spent in Vienna. He wrote church music, orchestral and chamber works as well as 211 stage works, of which 180 are farces and ballets. His 31 operettas are now remembered only by their overtures e.g. *Poet and Peasant* and *Light Cavalry* (1866).

SVENDSEN, Johan (1840-1911)
Norwegian composer who was an army bandsman at the age of 15 and later studied at the Leipzig Conservatoire (1863-67). He was active as a conductor in Leipzig, Norway and, from 1883, in Copenhagen. His several Norwegian Rhapsodies and arrangements of Scandinavian folksongs are still performed today. His two symphonies, two concertos, chamber music and shorter pieces are also occasionally heard.

SWEELINCK, Jan (1562-1621)
Dutch composer and organist. He succeeded his father, who was probably his teacher, as organist of the Old (Roman Catholic) Church in Amsterdam. He seems to have travelled only to nearby Flemish towns as part of his duties. His daily performances in the church were enormously popular and he attracted the friendship of the 'exiled' English virginalists John Bull and Peter Philips. Among his pupils was Scheidt, through whom he influenced later generations of German Baroque musicians.
His choral works were sufficiently popular to be found in 17th century manuscripts as far apart as Oxford, Sweden, Italy and Hungary. Most of them are settings of psalm verses in Renaissance styles but there are also about 40 secular chansons and *cantiones sacrae*, such as the well-known *Hodie*. Sweelinck's contrapuntal style makes use of major/minor tonality and there are striking homophonic passages as well as the expected madrigalian modality and polyphony.
It is, however, in his relatively few extant keyboard pieces that Sweelinck's historical importance lies. Their derivation from the style of the English virginalists is stressed by the inclusion of several sets of variations in the *Fitzwilliam Virginal Book*. The composition based on *Mein junges Leben* is, however, timeless in its almost Romantic beauty. Sweelinck seems to have been one of the first to write *chorale variations* while the fantasias and toccatas use both echo effects (in the six echo fancies) and occasional organ pedal passages. His treatment of fugue led quite naturally to the monothematic *Ricercare* and the later Baroque Fugue. The long-note themes are treated with augmentation and diminution and usually generate a whole series of counter subjects. He was succeeded at the *Oude Kerk* by his son and must be considered as the Father of the German Baroque.

SZYMANOWSKI, Karol (1882-1937)

Polish composer who spent his boyhood in the Ukraine. He played and improvised on the piano and before he was 20 had published nine piano preludes. He gradually learned to compose and was attracted to the music of Chopin throughout his life. He studied in Warsaw (1903-05) and then in Berlin until 1908, where he became immersed in the music of Wagner, Richard Strauss and Reger. In Russia he reacted against German Romanticism in favour of Russian Nationalism and the Impressionism of Debussy. By this time his first three symphonies (No. 3 was choral) had appeared. The influence of Ravel's musical exoticism and Stravinsky's Russian radicalism led to his rediscovery of the Polish national style. His piano music was played by Rubinstein and the Dionysian ecstasy of some of his songs was becoming internationally appreciated. Polish recognition eluded him, however, until 1926, when he became Director of the Warsaw Conservatoire. He retired two years later and began to receive honours for his music from various sources. His compositions during this mature period of his life include the opera *King Roger* (1926), choral settings of religious texts — *Stabat Mater* and *Veni Creator* (1929) — several Piano Mazurkas and Polish songs. He found his way to a truly 20th century Polish idiom without losing the international 'spirit of the age' and is the natural patron of Lutoslawski and Penderecki.

Szymanowski was partially lame from an early accident and suffered much from tuberculosis in his later years. He wrote extensively on musical and general topics. His three unpublished works have been lost or were destroyed.

T

TAILLEFERRE, Germaine (b. 1892)

French composer, trained at the Paris Conservatoire, who became a member of 'Les Six' in 1920. She later became a pupil of another member — Milhaud. Her musical style was polytonal, and marked by a certain freshness and vitality which brought her much international acclaim — as in her *Pastorale* for small orchestra (1920), String Quartet and Violin Sonata (1922). She also wrote a Piano Concerto (1924), a Harp Concentino, ballet scores and operas.

She emigrated to the USA in 1942 from which time she has written very little music — and her reputation as a composer has appeared to diminish.

TALLIS, Thomas (c. 1505–1585)

Great English composer and organist. After some earlier appointments, Tallis became organist at Waltham Abbey until such time as the Abbey was dissolved in 1540. After a few years at Canterbury in 1543 he became a Gentleman of the Chapel Royal, a position which he held until his death. Most of his music was written for the Latin rite but little can be ascribed with certainty to the Pre-Reformation period. Most of his motets were printed in *Cantiones Sacrae* (1575), a collection made by both Tallis and Byrd in accordance with the monopoly granted by the Queen in that year. In this publication a prefatory Latin poem refers to Tallis as 'an old man, worthy of honour'. His last years appear to have been spent at his home in Greenwich. The best-known of the motets in *Cantiones Sacrae* are *Salvator Mundi*, *In Jejunio et Fletu* and the easier O *Nato Lux*. Several motets such as O *Sacrum Convivium* were adapted to English words. Mention must also be made of the *Lamentations*. The wide variety of these works is only exceeded by the technical mastery of the legendary 40-part *Spem in Alium*, for five 8-part choirs — presumably spatially separated.

His secular and keyboard works are clearly less important than the sacred works for the English rite. These include such masterpieces as *If Ye Love Me* and O *Lord Give thy Holy Spirit*. The 'short' service in the Dorian mode proved to be a prototype for settings by many later composers, as did also the more elaborate 5-part *Te Deum*. Even more popular have been the settings of the Litany and Responses, while his eight hymn tunes have attracted attention from composers like Vaughan Williams in his *Fantasia on a Theme by Thomas Tallis*. *Tallis's Canon* is one of the more well-known hymn tunes.

TANEIEV, Alexander Sergeievich (1850–1918)

Russian composer who studied in Germany and with Rimsky-Korsakov. He wrote operas, three symphonies, three string quartets and many smaller-scale works. He was a distinguished civil servant in St. Petersburg and was noted for his collecting of Russian folk music.

TANEIEV, Sergius Ivanovich (1856–1915)

Russian composer and pianist and nephew of Alexander, above. After studying at the Moscow Conservatoire, he became a pupil of Tchaikovsky, whose B flat minor Piano Concerto he was often to play. He wrote an operatic trilogy, three symphonies, six string quartets and many other works, especially songs. He is remembered today for his piano arrangements of the music of Tchaikovsky and for his work as a teacher. His text-books on counterpoint represented an anti-Romantic tendency, and he used his influence very largely against the Nationalist aims of 'The Five'.

TARTINI, Giuseppe (1692–1770)
Italian violinist, composer and teacher. He composed the *Devil's Trill Sonata* while in the monastery of Assisi, and later became an orchestral leader in Padua and Vienna. His famous *School of Violin Playing* was partly based not only on theoretical writings and such acoustical discoveries as that of difference tones, but also on the use of thicker strings and lighter bow technique.
He is considered to be of the tradition of Corelli (although he was never his pupil) and his own pupils included such players as Nardini. Tartini's published compositions are almost entirely for strings: Sonatas à 5 and à 6 (1734 and 1745), solo sonatas, trio sonatas and concertos (*114* in manuscript); and the famous *50 Variations on a Gavotte by Corelli* which today is considered almost a handbook of 18th century bowing.

TATE, Phyllis (b. 1911)
English composer whose operetta *The Policeman's Serenade*, with words by A.P. Herbert, was produced while she was still a student at the RAM (1928–32). Most of her music of that period has been withdrawn, but instrumental works such as the *Saxaphone Concerto* (1944), the *String Quartet* (1952), various choral works, and two later operas, are marked by a polished technique and freshness of approach.

TAUSIG, Carl (1841–1871)
Polish-Bohemian pianist, and composer of virtuoso pieces for the piano. He was a pupil of Thalberg and also a favourite pupil of Liszt. He spent most of his life in Berlin and is best known for his many transcriptions, elaborations and for his *Daily Studies.*

TAVERNER, John (c. 1495–1545)
English composer and organist who worked successively at Tattershall Collegiate Church and Christ Church, Oxford. His eight masses, three magnificats and 28 Latin motets were probably all written before 1530. In 1528 he was imprisoned for his heretical religious opinions and although released by Cardinal Wolsey, he was replaced at Oxford in 1530. In later years he 'repented him very muche that he had made Songes to Popish Ditties in the time of his blindness' (Foxe) and became a paid agent of Thomas Cromwell in the suppression of the monasteries.
Taverner's technical mastery in such works as the masses *The Western Wynde* and *Sine Nomine* represents the final peak of English Pre-Reformation music. They are noted for their refinement of the elaboration of Fayrfax and the long vocal lines that belonged to the future. Several of his Latin works were adapted to English texts for Day's *Certaine Notes* (1560).

TCHAIKOVSKY, Peter Ilich (1840–1893)
Prominent Russian Romantic composer. He showed early keyboard facility although he received no systematic teaching or general musical experience. There were early signs of his neurotic disposition which was to plague his later life. Although he had received some piano lessons in St. Petersburg in 1850, it was not until he was 23, and had been a lawyer's clerk for several years that he became a professional musician. By this time he was a pupil of Anton Rubinstein at the Conservatoire and trying to earn a living by spasmodic teaching. His compositions were consistently rejected by the public in St. Petersburg.
He was appointed to a teaching post at the Moscow Conservatoire in 1866 under Anton Rubinstein's brother, Nicholas, and very soon his works were being performed by Nicholas. These included the 1st Symphony (1868) and the Overture

Romeo and Juliet (1870). Throughout his life Tchaikovsky was unusually facile and almost equally self-critical so that he destroyed or decried much of his own work. At this time there followed in quick succession at least four operas (which failed), three string quartets (of which only the 1st has retained its popularity), two more symphonies, the fantasy *The Tempest* (1893) and the well-known 1st Piano Concerto (1875).
Tchaikovsky had already had a breakdown in health in his early days in Moscow and persistent attacks of nervous disability continued to affect him. He met such contemporaries as Tolstoy, Berlioz, Liszt and Wagner and his friendship with the Rubinsteins was often strained. Even his first ballet, *Swan Lake* (1877), was, at first, a failure. His marriage did not work out and, as a result, he attempted to commit suicide, after which his health again collapsed. He was partially saved by his astonishing relationship with Nadejda von Meck, nine years his senior. She freed Tchaikovsky from financial worries until 1890 but stipulated that they should never meet. His many letters to her are both intimate and musically revealing.
Many successful works followed his meeting with Mme. von Meck: the 4th Symphony (1878), the opera *Eugene Onegin* (1879), the *Italian Capriccio* and the string *Serenade* (1880). His fame began to spread abroad. The first performance of the *Violin Concerto* was in New York in 1879 and he sufficiently overcame his shyness to conduct his works in most European capitals. He visited America in 1891.
To his last period belong the 5th Symphony (1888), the Fantasy-Overture *Hamlet* (1888), the two ballets, *The Sleeping Beauty* (1890) and *Casse Noisette* (1892), the opera *The Queen of Spades* (1890) and finally the almost autobiographical *Pathetic* Symphony (1893) which he conducted in St. Petersburg just before his death.
Both during his life and since, Tchaikovsky has been criticised by intellectual musicians for his frank emotionalism and uneven formal control. The Nationalists ('The Five') found him meretricious and lacking in Russian identity. Although he recognised their genius (with the exception of the music of Rimsky-Korsakov), he found their music of an amateur nature. Besides the gloomy self-absorption of the symphonies, his works show the colour and vitality of life and he even found his Mozartian ideal in the balance of 'classical' Russian ballet. His fantastic box office success since his death has generally outclassed the success of the music of both Brahms and Wagner. We are perhaps now ready for a revival of his many songs and piano pieces.

TCHEREPNIN,
Alexander (b. 1899)
Russian composer, the son of Nicolas below, who has been resident in the USA since 1949. He is a naturalised citizen and has taught at Chicago University. He has travelled widely as a pianist and had much influence on Chinese and Japanese musicians between 1934 and 1937. His works include three operas, 13 ballets, four symphonies, five piano concertos and some chamber and choral music. His prolific and Prokofiev-like style is heard in some rather slight works for more unusual instruments: the *Harmonica Concerto* (1956), two sonatinas for saxaphone and timpani, and an *Andante* for tuba and piano.

TCHEREPNIN,
Nicolas (1873–1945)
Russian composer who was a pupil of Rimsky-Korsakov and conductor of the Diaghilev Ballet in Paris (1909–14). He completed Mussorgsky's opera *The Fair at Sorochintsy*, and several of his own operas and ballets were produced by Diaghilev.

His music is broadly in the style of 'The Five', but is not uninfluenced by Impressionism. He lived in Paris with his son from 1921 until his death in 1945.

TELEMANN, Georg Philipp (1681–1766)
Eminent German composer and friend of J.S. Bach. The authorities in Leipzig would have preferred the appointment of Telemann to J.S. Bach in 1722 as successor to Kuhnau in their city. Most of Telemann's long life from 1721 was spent in Hamburg. He was an unusually prolific composer and in 1704 was engaged to supply a composition every fortnight for St. Thomas', Leipzig. By then he had already written several operas for the theatre (while a law student at Leipzig University). His other early appointments include a position at Eisenach, where he became godfather to C.P.E. Bach.
Handel knew him well and said that Telemann could write an 8-part motet as easily as other people could write a letter. His 50 or so operas were less influential in his day than his realistic and Italianate church music. This includes 44 Passions, 12 complete sets of services for the whole of the Church Year, many popular oratorios, church cantatas and other works.
His instrumental music has been rediscovered in the 20th century. It includes 600 overtures in the French style, the published violin sonatas and trio sonatas for two violins and continuo, the concertos and *Tafelmusik*. Most recently attention has been directed to the many flute and recorder works as well as the six suites for violin, flute or oboe and continuo (1716).

THALBERG, Sigismond (1812–1871)
Pianist and composer who was probably of Austrian origin. He was a pupil of Hummel and Kalkbrenner and a rival to Liszt. His compositions, with the exception of two successful operas, a piano tutor and a concerto, consist mostly of virtuosic pieces. He is credited with the invention of the type of pianistic texture in which the melody is divided between the hands, with treble arpeggios and bass, thus giving a 'three hand' effect.

THIMAN, Eric (1900–1975)
English composer, organist and teacher. Although he composed light orchestral music, he is best known for his many easy anthems, part-songs and organ music. It is in his church music that he seems to express the English Nonconformist tradition. Almost of equal importance are the 'theoretical' textbooks he has written for music students.

THOMAS, Ambroise (1811–1896)
French composer of 16 opéras-comiques including the once famous *Mignon* (1866). He had a most distinguished career at the Paris Conservatoire and between 1839 and 1846 made several unsuccessful attempts at writing ballet music and more serious works for the Paris Opéra. He was eventually rewarded by the success of the opera *Hamlet* (1868) which led to his appointment to succeed Auber as Director of the Paris Conservatoire in 1871. His once popular part songs and choral works are seldom performed today although the Overture to *Raymond* (1851) is still occasionally heard.

THOMAS, Arthur Goring (1850–1892)
English operatic composer who studied under Sullivan at the RAM, and also in Paris. Of the operas commissioned by Carl Rosa, *Esmeralda* (1883) and *Nadeshda* (1885) were both popular in French and German translations. His many songs are no longer heard.
His early death was due to mental illness.

THOMAS, John (1826–1913)
Welsh harpist, teacher, conductor and composer. He wrote extensively for his

instrument, including two harp concertos. He was a well-known judge at various Eisteddfods for which he wrote several cantatas. Earlier in his life he was a leading orchestral player and during this time two operas, a symphony, several overtures and quartets of his were performed. During the 1850's he toured internationally as a concert artist and in 1872 was appointed harpist to Queen Victoria. He published a large collection of Welsh folk melodies in 1862.

THOMPSON, Randall (b. 1899)
American composer who has held various academic and administrative posts including the Professorship of Music at Harvard University from 1948. His choral works have been possibly his most successful compositions e.g. *Americana* (1932), and *The Testament of Freedom* (1943) to words by Thomas Jefferson. His orchestral works include three symphonies and *Jazz Poem* (1928) with solo piano. His incidental music for *The Straw Hat* (1926) is still often heard.

THOMSON, Virgil (b. 1896)
American composer who, after a precocious musical childhood in Kansas and at Harvard after the 1st World War, studied with Nadia Boulanger (1921–28). During this period he was also performing and conducting in Boston and New York. He then became associated with Gertrude Stein in Paris in the opera *Four Saints in Three Acts.* After a concert of his own works in Paris in 1928 he returned to the USA but despite the success of several pieces on Broadway, returned to Paris again for most of the period between 1934 and 1940. These years were largely occupied with the composition of music for the ballet, incidental music for Orson Welles' Shakespearian productions as well as film and radio scores.
With the invasion of France in the 2nd World War he became chief music critic of the New York *Herald Tribune* for 14 eventful years and still continues to write on a freelance basis. His early attraction to the musical textures and ethos of Erik Satie has brought 'daylight' into his music. However, the hymnody, marches and Gertrude Stein's language in the opera *The Mother of Us All* (1947) stress its American provenance. His orchestral works include two symphonies, a cello concerto (1949) and a concerto for flute, strings and percussion (1954). There are also many songs and choral works (including a Requiem in 1960), three string quartets, four piano sonatas as well as works for band, unaccompanied flute (*Sonata*, 1943) and violin (*Seven Portraits*, 1928).

TIPPETT, Sir Michael (b. 1905)
English composer who after study at the RCM with Charles Wood, spent several years teaching and in rural music making. At the age of 25 he returned to the RCM to study counterpoint with R.O. Morris. Almost all of his earlier music was withdrawn at this time. There followed another period of practical work with amateurs. This led to his appointment as musical director of Morley College (1940–51). Like his friend Benjamin Britten he was a conscientious objector during the 2nd World War and was, for a time, imprisoned for his refusal to do noncombatant war work. His involvement with the issues of Nazism was expressed in the oratorio *A Child of Our Time* (first performed in 1944). This work at last brought his name before a wider public. This was partly due to the topicality of the subject but mainly to the originality of his style that was by now clearly emerging.
After the War he soon achieved recognition as a major composer. His 1st Symphony (1947) was followed by his opera *The Midsummer Marriage* (first performed in 1955) and such works as *Fantasia Concertante on a Theme of Corelli* (1953) for strings, and the *Piano Concerto* (1955).

Several of his earlier works were at last published, namely, the three string quartets (1934–46), the *Concerto for Double String Orchestra* (1939) as well as motets, cantatas and song-cycles. Succeeding works confirmed his standing as a composer — the operas *King Priam* (1962) and *The Knot Garden* (1970), the 3rd Symphony (1972), *The Vision of St. Augustine* (1965) for baritone, chorus and orchestra, the *Concerto for Orchestra* (1963) and three Piano sonatas. In 1976 he wrote his fourth opera, *The Ice Break* which is based on contemporary problems of communication. The 4th Symphony was also written in 1976. During his slow musical development, Tippett absorbed many influences from Beethoven to Purcell and from the negro spirituals of *A Child of Our Time* to Jungian psycho-analysis. His musical textures are often very complex but held together by lyrical freshness and finely wrought detail. Almost all his large-scale libretti, even the free adaption of Blake in the vocal finale of his 3rd Symphony, are his own work, although neither these nor some of his other literary productions are totally free from the obscurantism that has marred some of his music.

TITELOUZE, Jean (1563–1633)
French organist and composer who was organist of Rouen Cathedral from 1588. His music is based on Renaissance vocal polyphony although his only extant vocal works are two masses. His organ music is found in *Hymnes de l'Eglise* (1623), a didactic collection based on his famous improvisations on plainsong themes. The *Magnificat* (1626) contains 'alternatim' versets on a smaller scale.
Titelouze became a canon of Rouen in 1610.

TOMKINS, Thomas (1572–1656)
English church and madrigal composer and the most famous member of a large musical family of the 16th and 17th centuries. He was organist of Worcester Cathedral from about 1596 to 1646, the time when the choral establishment was disbanded under the Commonwealth. From 1621 he was one of the organists of the Chapel Royal. He continued to compose until the end of his long life and was a contemporary of Weelkes and Wilbye. His published compositions such as *Songs or Madrigals* (1622), which contains madrigals like *Oyez! Has Any Found a Lad?*, and the English 'anthems' such as the magnificent *When David Heard* are broadly in the style of Weelkes and Wilbye.
Most of his church music was published posthumously in *Musica Deo Sacra* (1668). It includes five services and 95 anthems, many of which are in solo 'verse' form although the 12-part *O Praise the Lord*, like *When David Heard*, is a full anthem.
Tomkins also wrote virginal music (some of which is included in the *Fitzwilliam Virginal Book*) and music for viols in the Jacobean style. He was a pupil of Byrd and contributed to *The Triumphes of Oriana* (1602).

TORELLI, Giuseppe (1658–1709)
Italian violinist and composer who was one of the major figures in the early history of the concerto. Although Torelli was a contemporary of Corelli, he presents a far more individual and progressive attitude to the *concerto grosso*. Torelli also leans far more towards the solo concerto, and is perhaps more of a melodist than his contemporary. He was one of the first to use the *ritornello* principle, and his music was influential and widely known in his lifetime. Eight volumes of sonatas and concertos were published between 1686 and 1709.

TOSELLI, Enrico (1883–1926)
Italian pianist and composer who is remembered for his popular *Serenata* and for his elopement in 1907 with the Crown

Princess of Saxony. She wrote the libretto for his operetta *La Principessa Bizarra*. He also wrote songs, chamber and piano music and a symphonic poem (*Fuoco*).

TOSTI, Sir Paolo (1846–1916)
Popular Neapolitan song writer, who became singing teacher to the future Queen of Italy and to the English Royal Family (1880). His songs use Italian, French and English words and his phenomenal success on his yearly visits to London from 1875 led to his knighthood in 1908.
His first success was *Non m'ama più* (1869) and his drawing-room songs, *Forever, Goodbye* and *Mother* have been recently revived.

TOURNEMIRE, Charles (1870–1939)
French organist and composer. He studied at and was later professor of chamber music at the Paris Conservatoire. He was also a pupil of d'Indy. As a player he toured widely in France and abroad and succeeded Pierné (and indirectly Franck) at St. Clothilde (1898) in Paris.
One of his two operas was produced at the Opéra (1924) and he also wrote eight symphonies, several symphonic poems, chamber and choral works. He is best remembered for *L'Orgue Mystique*, an organ collection for the liturgical year of 255 pieces.

TOURS, Berthold (1838–1897)
English organist and violinist of Dutch origins. He studied in Brussels and Leipzig and moved to London in 1861 as an orchestral violinist. He was soon also active as an organist and adviser to Novello, for whom he wrote a popular *Primer of the Violin*.
His many compositions include popular church music (especially hymns), choral and piano pieces.

TOVEY, Sir Donald (1875–1940)
Brilliant English pianist, scholar and composer who is remembered for his *Essays in Musical Analysis*. These were originally programme notes for the concerts which he conducted as Reid Professor at Edinburgh University. Before his appointment to Edinburgh in 1914, he had an outstanding academic and performing career which included memorised performances of such works as Bach's *Goldberg Variations* and of his own works. His music stemmed from the Viennese classics and included an opera, a symphony (1913), a piano concerto (1903) and a cello concerto for Casals (1935), and much chamber and piano music.

TRAVERS, John (1703–1758)
English organist and composer who became organist of the Chapel Royal in 1737. He published a complete book of metrical psalms (c. 1750) and the popular *Eighteen Canzonets. 12 Voluntaries for the Organ and Harpsichord* were published after his death. Among his many church works the rather vapid *Service in F* is still occasionally heard. The tuneful *Ascribe unto the Lord* is a repertoire work in most cathedrals today.

TRIMBLE, Joan (b. 1915)
Irish pianist and composer best known for her two-piano performances with her sister Valerie, and for her arrangements for this medium. She studied at Trinity College, Dublin, and with Howells at the RCM. Compositions for two pianos include a Sonatina (1940) and some descriptive pieces.

TUDWAY, Thomas (c. 1650–1726)
English organist, composer and editor. He was a chorister under Blow at the Chapel Royal and most of his life from about 1670 was organist of King's College, Cambridge. He was, however, temporarily suspended in 1706 for his remarks about Queen Anne and her ministers. From 1714

to 1720 he made a collection of cathedral music at the request of Lord Harley. His service, orchestral *Te Deum* and 18 anthems are known today.

TURINA, Joaquin (1882-1949)
Spanish pianist and composer. He studied in his birthplace Seville, in Madrid, and later with d'Indy in Paris. He did not return to Spain for nine years during which time he and his compatriot Falla were involved with the Parisian circle of Debussy, Ravel and Dukas. Following his return to his own country in 1914, he was important as a Spanish nationalist composer, and as a pianist and occasional conductor in the Romantic tradition. His works include two operas, several orchestral works including works such as *Danzas Fantasticas* (1920), and many piano pieces with descriptive titles e.g. *Jardines de Andalusia* (1924). He was very successful as a chamber music composer, the two piano trios being especially popular, and was a prolific song writer.

TURLE, James (1802-1882)
English organist and composer who was organist at Westminster Abbey from 1831. Although he wrote much church music and produced several secular publications of more general interest, he is remembered nowadays almost exclusively for his popular Anglican chants.

TURNER, William (1651-1740)
English composer who at the Restoration was one of 'Captain Cooke's' first choirboys at the Chapel Royal. From 1669 he sang counter tenor in the choirs of both St. Paul's Cathedral and Westminster Abbey. Apart from much church music, he is known to have written an *Ode for St. Cecilia's Day* (1685) a *Birthday Ode* (1698) and songs for various London stage performances.

V

VARÈSE, Edgard (1883–1965)

Born in Paris and became a pupil of Widor, Roussel and d'Indy. He emigrated to the USA in 1915 and became the leading avant-garde composer in that country. In Paris, Berlin and New York he conducted orchestras and choirs to perform new music, including his own *Offrandes* (1921) and *Intégrales* (1931).

From the beginning he was influenced by African drum music, medievalism and 'bruitisme' — the Futurists' 'art of noises' in space. Technically, he used tone-clusters and repeated violent rhythms, and began to anticipate future electronic effects. *Intégrales* uses 41 percussion instruments and *Déserts* (1954) is for an ensemble with a pre-recorded stereophonic tape. *Poème Electronique* (1958) was 'distributed' through a pavilion at the Brussels Exhibition.

VAUGHAN WILLIAMS, Ralph (1872–1958)

Leading English composer, who studied with Parry, Stanford and Charles Wood in London and Cambridge and abroad with Max Bruch and Ravel. During his years of study he acquired much practical experience of working with amateurs which was subsequently extended through his long connection with the Leith Hill Festival. Even more important was his early musical involvement with Holst and English folk song. In 1906 he edited *The English Hymnal* and his melodic invention was to be shaped permanently by some of the traditional tunes he used. From his early Wagnerian enthusiasm he moved towards the freedom from German influences of English music and to the rediscovery of England's national heritage of Elizabethan music and even of Puritan hymnody.

Major works in a traditional but highly personal style began to appear: *Fantasia on a Theme by Tallis* (1910) with its magical string evocation of medievalism, *A Sea Symphony* (1910) based on Whitman, *A London Symphony* (1914) with its Elgarian associations, and *Fantasia on Christmas Carols* (1912).

After war service, Vaughan Williams seems to have been drawn towards pantheism, as in the *Pastoral Symphony* (1922), to mysticism in *Flos Campi* (1925) and to English polyphony in the unaccompanied *Mass in G Minor* (1923). His religious beliefs led him to write the highly original *Te Deum in G* (1928), the nonliturgical *Benedicite* (1929) and the oratorio *Dona Nobis Pacem* (1936). At the same time, the fascination of the writings of Bunyan found expression firstly in a 'pastoral episode' for the operatic stage (1922) and much later in the full-scale opera, *The Pilgrim's Progress* (1951). The opera *Sir John in Love* (1929) explored Elizabethan England, and the ballet *Job* (1931) showed an agnostic's awareness of the most profound religious instincts.

His 4th Symphony (1935) seemed to mark a more European awareness of the approaching World War in its harsh linear clashes. By this time Vaughan Williams was said to be speaking for humanity as well as setting out to appeal to the ear with such popular pieces as the *Fantasia on Greensleeves* (from *Sir John in Love*), his film music of the 1940's and hymn tunes such as *Come Down O Love Divine* and *For All the Saints.*

The 5th Symphony (1943) seems to return to the spirituality and hope of Bunyan, while the 7th (1953) uses his film music for *Scott of the Antarctic*. Even in his eighties his Verdian fluency continued with Symphonies 8 and 9. His many songs were written throughout his life and exuberance

even showed in his last years with the *Brass Band Variations* of 1957.
In one sense Vaughan Williams' very virtue and universality militated against England coming to terms with the continental 'modernism' of Stravinsky and Schönberg. He was considered to be a towering national figure coming between Elgar and Britten.

VAUTOR, Thomas (fl. 1619)
One of the last English madrigal composers whose publication of 1619 includes the popular *Sweet Suffolk Owl – Apt for Vyols and Voices*. He was BMus of Lincoln College, Oxford and spent most of his life in Leicestershire.

VECCHI, Orazio (1550–1605)
Italian madrigal composer whose suite of madrigals *L'Amfiparnasso* in three acts was presumably meant to accompany the spoken dialogue of the *commedia dell'arte*. It was very popular during its time. A cleric and choirmaster of Modena Cathedral from 1596, some of his church music has survived.

VERACINI, Antonio (fl. 1692–1696)
Italian violinist and composer whose trio and solo sonatas with continuo contributed to the development of the Italian style of string writing.

VERACINI, Francesca (1690–1750)
Nephew and pupil of Antonio above and Florentine violinist and composer whose performances impressed Tartini. He visited Venice, London, Dresden and Prague. Several of his operas were performed in London and 24 of his sonatas were published in 1721 and 1744. There also exist concertos, sonatas and symphonies in manuscript.

VERDELOT, Philippe (fl. 1530–1549)
Flemish composer who was a singer at St. Mark's, Venice and choirmaster in Florence. Some of his 100 madrigals were published in 1533, 1537 and 1541 and some motets and a mass are also extant.

VERDI, Giuseppe (1813–1901)
Great Italian operatic composer, who was rejected as a student at the Milan Conservatoire when he was 19. He later returned to Milan in 1838 with his first wife and, in the following year, achieved some success with his first opera at La Scala. He had learned his trade mostly by writing brass band marches, concertos, serenades and church music for his home town and clearly showed much early ability, although under these circumstances he could not be other than a slow musical developer.
During the next year his two children and then also his wife died, and his second opera — a comedy — was a failure. But he at last became established as a composer through the brilliant success of *Nabucco* (1842). From that time Verdi wrote a series of successful operas and from this early period several have joined the permanent operatic repertoire: *Ernani* (1844), *Macbeth* (1847) and *Luisa Miller* (1849). His popularity was perhaps due as much to the blatant patriotism of some of the marches and choruses as it was to the endless flow of 'barrel organ' tunes. At all events he was counted the composer of the Risorgimento against the unpopular Austrian occupation of Italy. From 1860 to 1865 he served as an elected deputy to the First National Parliament. Even his name was a watchword: *V*iva *E*mmanuele *R*e *D'I*talia (Long live Emmanuel, King of Italy).
Verdi's already-impressive operatic technique soon led him in newer directions in such works as the melodramatic *Rigoletto* (1851), the tuneful *Il Trovatore* (1853), and the moving *La Traviata* (1853). His fame soon became international. *La Forza del Destino* (1862) was produced in St. Petersburg and *Don Carlos* (1867) was,

apart from several revision works, his second opera for the Parisian stage. Meyerbeer's influence in *Don Carlos* was carried further in the grand opera style of the famous *Aida* (1871) written for the opening of the Suez Canal at Cairo.
Verdi's last period is naturally marked by the *Requiem* (1874) which is so utterly original and overpowering that contemporaries were slow to appreciate its greatness. Even more significant was the arrival of Arrigo Boito at the farm which was now Verdi's home in his own home town. Boito had been the librettist and composer of the successful opera *Mefistofele* (1868) and now urged Verdi to renew his interest in the works of Shakespeare. He was the only first-rate librettist with whom Verdi ever collaborated. The results of this collaboration were the two masterpieces of Verdi's old age: *Otello* (1887) and *Falstaff* (1893). Even in his 85th year he wrote his *Four Sacred Pieces* in which his technique and vitality seem quite unimpaired. He heard his first Wagner opera only just before writing *Aida*, and was resilient enough in his originality to forge his own solution to the operatic problem. The human voice remained supreme to him but he learned to use the orchestra in as subtle a way as his great German rival, Wagner. His operatic structures were to move easily from the separate numbers of *Nabucco* to the fluid continuity of *Falstaff*. Even his contrapuntal skill was dramatically integrated into the stage realism of his lyrical music.

VIADANA, Lodovico Grossi (c. 1564–1645)
Italian composer of madrigals and church music who, in his *Concerti Ecclesiastici* (Venice, 1602) is considered to be the first composer to use a basso continuo (unfigured). In these works he combined 1, 2, 3 and 4 voices with an instrumental bass. He was born near Mantua where he was maestro di cappella from 1590 to 1609. His later years were spent as a Franciscan.

VICTORIA, Tomas Luis de (c. 1548–1611)
Spanish composer of church music who, with Lassus and Palestrina, is considered to be one of the greatest representatives of the Catholic High Renaissance. He went to Rome in 1565 and was probably taught by Palestrina, whom he succeeded at the Collegium Romanum in 1571. He held various musical posts, including for five years that of choirmaster at St. Philip Neri's famous Oratory after he was ordained in 1575. His return to Spain does not seem to have been until 1596, when, as chaplain to the sister of Philip II, he became choirmaster of a convent in Madrid until his death. Most of his 20 masses, 44 motets, 34 hymns, etc. were published in Rome (1572–92). His most famous work is the *Office for the Dead*. Victoria's style is marked by a serene spirituality, seen in such popular motets as *O Vos Omnes*, *O Quam Gloriosum* or *O Magnum Mystericum*. His larger-scaled works, such as the 8-part *Salve Regina* mass, show an easy command of polyphonic resources in no way inferior to that of his older rivals.

VIERNE, Louis (1870–1937)
French organist and composer who was a pupil of Franck and Widor at the Paris Conservatoire and from 1900 organist at Notre Dame. He was well-known as a touring recitalist in most European countries and particularly renowned for his five organ symphonies and the short Impressionist pieces of his *24 Pièces en Style Libre* and *24 Pièces de Fantasie*. Vierne also composed an orchestral symphony, a string quartet and other chamber music.

VIEUXTEMPS, Henri (1820–1881)
Belgian violinist and composer who moved to Paris as a pupil of de Bériot while still a child, and began his many European tours at the age of thirteen. Apart from many concert pieces for the violin, he composed

six concertos which are still in the student repertoire today.

VILLA-LOBOS, Heitor (1887–1959)
Brazilian composer and educationalist. He showed early musical talents but was for some time discouraged at home and played with street bands. At 18 he made the first of several tours to different parts of Brazil, listening to folk music and composing. In spite of several attempts at more conventional study in Rio de Janeiro, he was essentially self-taught and earned his living as a player in various instrumental groups. Later, as a member of the Rio de Janeiro symphony and opera orchestras, he became familiar with the Italian opera repertoire, including the operas of Puccini, the Russian Romantic composers and the music of Richard Strauss. In 1917 he played with Stravinsky and in 1918 met Milhaud who was, at that time, a French diplomat in Brazil.
By this time Villa-Lobos had written several operas and ballets, four symphonies and numerous orchestral and piano works. These works were mostly based on Afro-Brazilian patterns, although he neither collected nor quoted actual folk melodies. In 1921 he was introduced to French Impressionism by the pianist Arthur Rubinstein and during a year in Paris (1923–24) met Ravel. Soon after his return to Brazil, he became active as a conductor and was the centre of controversy over his exotic and complex *Amazonas*. Vocal music such as *Chansons Typiques Brasiliennes* made him popular and the early *Choros* began to appear. These are instrumental pieces, often for unusual combinations, and based on Brazilian idioms. He was able to return to Paris (1927–30) where he conducted some of his works, revived the spirit of 'Les Six' in the First *Suite Suggestive* and made his acquaintance with Neo-Classicism. The immediate effect of the latter on him was to compose the first two of his series of *Bachianas Brasileiras*, on his return to Brazil. These pieces are a reworking of Bach's technique using Brazilian musical material. During the 1930's Villa-Lobos was Director of Musical Education first in Rio and then throughout the whole of Brazil. He wrote educational music of all kinds as well as works such as the four suites for chorus and orchestra — *Descobrimento do Brazil* (1937). He conducted large choruses and massed-band concerts as well as introducing to Brazil works like Bach's B minor Mass. During the early 1940's he returned to 'mainstream' compositions like the string quartets, Nos. 5–8, the five piano concertos and the later concertos for guitar (1951), harp (1953) and harmonica (1955). In 1944 Villa-Lobos made his first visit to the USA — the first of many such visits. His later years were divided between work in Brazil, Paris and the USA. Honours were bestowed on him. (1957 was 'Villa-Lobos Year' in Brazil.)
Besides being Brazil's only great composer, Villa-Lobos set international standards through the inventive and innovatory style of his many compositions. More important still is the uniformly-high standard he reached in his many works. The *Choros* and *Bachianas Brasileiras* in particular are now regarded as standard repertoire, and compositions such as the *Saudades da Juventude* Suite (1940) are still striking in their impact.

VIOTTI, Jean Baptiste (1755–1824)
Italian violinist and composer who was a pupil of Pugnani. He was the accompanist of Marie Antoinette and later directed the Opéra in Paris (1819–22). He was in London with Haydn for the Salomon Concerts in the 1790's. He is remembered for his unusually modern 29 violin concertos but also wrote 21 string quartets, 21 string trios, 51 violin duets, 18 violin sonatas (with bass) and nine piano sonatas.

VITALI, Filippo (b.c. 1600)
Florentine choirmaster and tenor in the Papal Chapel who composed *L'Avetusa* (1620), which was one of the early monodic operas intermedi. He also wrote madrigals and church music.

VITALI,
Giovanni Battista (c. 1644–1692)
Italian viol-player, violinist and composer. He held various church and court appointments in Bologna and Modena and was a prolific composer of string music, dances (correnti, allemandes, etc.) for two violins and bass. His sonatas for 2, 3, 4, and 5 instruments with bass were probably influenced by Purcell. He also wrote stage and church music.

VITALI,
Tommaso Antonio (c. 1665–c. 1720)
Composer, the son of Giovanni above, who held similar appointments to his father. He is remembered for a popular *Ciaccona* for violin solo and figured bass, but also published sonatas and concertos for two and three-stringed instruments and continuo (1693 and 1701).

VIVALDI, Antonio (c. 1675–1741)
Italian violinist and composer who was nicknamed 'The red priest' after the colour of his hair. He was employed, while still a child, as a violinist at St. Mark's, Venice under Legrenzi and seems to have lapsed from his priesthood soon after ordination in 1703. From 1703 to 1740 he was associated, as violinist, teacher and director, with La Pièta — an orphanage for girls which was in effect a musical academy in Venice. Only at the end of his time there did his absences and the scandal of his life lead to his dismissal. He was buried in a pauper's grave in Vienna. His reputation as a violinist was equal to that of Corelli and he was, for his time, an unusually prolific composer. He wrote some 400 concertos — 48 for bassoon, 25 for cello, 60 for ripieni (sinfonias), concertos for most other instruments including mandolins and several hundred for one or more violins. These were often arranged by J.S. Bach for keyboard and certainly formed the basis of Bach's own concertos. Vivaldi's concerto for four violins is as familiar in Bach's adaptation for four claviers as it is in its original form. The *Four Seasons* are the prototypes of the later solo concerto. He also wrote sonatas for solo violin (1709) and trio sonatas (1705).
From 1713 Vivaldi was active as an operatic composer. 46 such works have survived although the composer claimed to have written a hundred. In the 1720's he travelled extensively and played before the Emperor and the Pope. He composed three large-scale oratorios and much sacred music including the popular *Gloria.* Much of his music has been revived in recent years and of his artistic achievements there has never been any doubt.

VOGLER, Georg Joseph (Abt Vogler) (1749–1814)
German composer and teacher of Weber and Meyerbeer. He was ordained in Rome in 1773 and held various Papal honours. He was an active operatic composer in South Germany on his return from Rome and also wrote several cantatas, church and chamber music as well as several concertos. He wrote extensively on theoretical and acoustical subjects and is the subject of a famous poem by Browning.

VULPIUS, Melchior (c. 1560–1615)
German composer of church music, both in the contrapuntal style of *Cantiones Sacrae* (1602) for 6, 7 and 8 voices and in the simpler style of *Kirchengesänge und geistliche Lieder* (1604). He composed several chorale melodies which became part of the Lutheran tradition and familiar to us through Bach's harmonisations of such chorales as *Jesu Leiden* or *Christus der ist mein Leben.* He was Cantor in Weimar from 1602.

WAGNER, Richard (1813-1883)
German operatic composer and man of letters. He had early contact with the theatre and the writings of Homer, Shakespeare and Goethe. Apart from learning to play the piano, he was a self-taught composer. His motivation seems to have been to provide incidental music to an early tragedy he had written, the inspiration for which came from Beethoven's music to Goethe's *Egmont*. Gradually he became more and more involved in music and throughout his life wrote many pamphlets and was always his own librettist. During an unsatisfactory period at Leipzig University, he changed from copying out Beethoven's scores to having lessons with one of Bach's successors at St. Thomas'. The immediate result was the composition of a symphony and the offer of a position as chorus master. His first complete opera, *Die Feen*, soon followed.

In 1834 Wagner became a theatrical orchestral conductor and married his first wife — an actress — Minna. His second opera *Das Liebesverbot* was based on Shakespeare's *Measure for Measure*. At his next post in Riga he worked on *Rienzi* which was his first work to reach the opera house. His life assumed the pattern of stormy personal and professional relationships together with feckless financial habits that were to continue throughout his life. *Rienzi* was performed in Dresden in 1842 and was followed in 1843 by *The Flying Dutchman* and by Wagner's appointment as Director to the Royal Theatre in Dresden. In *The Flying Dutchman* the influence of Meyerbeer apparent in *Rienzi* had been superseded by the influence of Weber. *The Flying Dutchman* is generally considered to be the first of his 'canonic' works. His time in Saxony was marked by the completion of *Tannhaüser* (Dresden, 1845) and *Lohengrin* and the emergence of Wagner as a major conductor of Beethoven's works. Before *Lohengrin* could be staged Wagner became involved with the revolutionary activities of 1849 and was banished from Saxony.

For the next 10 years he lived in Switzerland and was largely dependent on Liszt's productions in Weimar for the staging of his operas. He had already done much work on his major project — *Der Ring des Nibelungen* — and what had started as a single opera became an enormous cycle of four, in a new aesthetic approach to the problem of opera and drama. After writing several pamphlets he completed the libretto of the whole cycle and the music of *The Rhinegold*, *The Valkyrie* and the first two acts of *Siegfried* (1857). He was then interrupted by a combination of Schopenhauer's philosophy and a love affair with Mathilde Wesendonk. The immediate result was the setting of five of the latter's poems, followed by the composition of his great tragedy — *Tristan and Isolde* (1859). The genial and patriotic *Mastersingers* was soon started in Paris but only completed on his return to Germany. By this time it had become clear to Wagner that his mature operatic style was impracticable under contemporary theatrical conditions. The Vienna Court Opera had withdrawn *Tristan* as 'unperformable' after 77 rehearsals. The only hope seemed to be a special theatre with almost unlimited funds, and it is a measure of Wagner's personality that this was achieved following the accession of King Ludwig II of Bavaria (1864). *Tristan* was at last performed in Munich (1865) and *The Mastersingers* in 1868. Wagner then returned to writing *The Ring*. *Siegfried* was completed and the *Twilight of the Gods* planned.

On the death of his estranged wife Minna in 1870, Wagner married Liszt's daughter Cosima. She was the former wife of van Bülow, who had conducted the premiere of *Tristan*. The Festival Theatre at Bayreuth was opened with a production of the completed *Ring* in 1876 although the first two operas had been performed earlier before King Ludwig in 1869 and 1870. Wagner's final work, *Parsifal* was based on Christian spirituality and a kind of elevated asceticism.

The new theatre at Bayreuth made possible the projection of the sung text over the continuous rich orchestral texture whilst the short alliterative medieval lines of Wagner's verse helped the singers to be understood. The musical structure of these long works was unified by an extension of the Berlioz-Liszt system of *leitmotif* and by an unprecedented ability to think on an enormous musical scale. Gone were the trivialities of the Italian opera houses. The *Music Drama*, with the new theatre's absence of boxes and its invisible conductor and orchestra, was more like a religious ceremony. The extra-large orchestra with its 'Wagner tubas' was to result in a new experience for the operagoer. No future composer could ignore Wagner — only 'work through him' or react against him.

WALDTEUFEL, Emil (1837–1915)

Alsatian pianist and composer, who was the French parallel to the Viennese Strauss. His best known piece is the *Skater's Waltz*.

WALLACE, William Vincent (1812–1865)

Irish operatic composer whose best-known work is *Maritana* (London, 1845). Wallace was a colourful person who spent some time as a settler in Australia, and was a good enough violinist to be called the 'Australian Paganini'. He is even said to have fished for whales in New Zealand and Van Diemen's Land before touring Chile. *Maritana* is still performed by amateur companies although such operas as *Lurline* (1860) are now forgotten.

WALMISLEY, Thomas Attwood (1814–1856)

English organist and composer who is today remembered almost entirely for his Evening Service in D minor. He was well-known in his day as Professor of Music at Cambridge, organist of St. John's and Trinity Colleges, and as a distinguished mathematician and poet. Apart from other service settings, anthems and chants, he wrote several odes for University installations.

WALTHER, Johann Gottfried (1684–1748)

German organist, composer and lexicographer. He was friendly with J.S. Bach at Weimar and his organ choral variations and preludes and fugues are still played. His musical dictionary has been a source book to later compilers.

WALTON, Sir William (1902–1983)

English composer, who after a rather precocious period at Christ Church, Oxford as a choirboy and undergraduate, was 'adopted' by the Sitwell family. He made his name with *Façade* (1922) which was originally written for speaker and instruments and was in the brilliant style of 'Les Six'. Another aspect of his personality had been shown in some earlier chamber music performed at the Saltzburg ISCM Festival in 1923. This was soon confirmed in his mature *Viola Concerto* (1929) with its malicious humour and lyrical melancholy, expressed with crisp and virtuosic technique. His reputation was further enhanced by the oratorio, *Balshazzar's Feast* (1931) and the powerful 1st Symphony (1935) which was only paralleled by Vaughan Williams' 4th Symphony the same year. The influence of Elgar began to

appear, as in the march *Crown Imperial* (1937), and in some of the film music from the 2nd World War, e.g. *Henry V*. This Elgarian influence again appeared in *Orb and Sceptre* and the *Coronation Te Deum* of 1953.
By this time Walton was living in Italy with his Argentinian wife and was only seen in public conducting his own works in London and the USA. Always a fastidious and slow composer (the 1st Symphony originally appeared without a final movement), Walton continued the flow of expertly-wrought scores. It sometimes seemed, however, that the fire shown in the earlier works was now less strong — the Violin Concerto (1939), a Cello Concerto (1957), the 2nd Symphony (1960). In 1954 Walton's first opera, *Troilus and Cressida*, appeared, which emphasized the composer's Italian lyricism. It appears to belong to the period of Strauss and Puccini with perhaps the 'Romanticism' of Hindemith. It is certainly far removed from the style of Stravinsky or Schönberg. Walton wrote as a professional for the enjoyment of his audience.

WARD, John (d.c. 1640)
English composer of madrigals, church and string music. His madrigals, which were published in 1613, are still relatively unknown. The string music is largely in manuscript although the two Evening Services are now part of the cathedral repertoire.

WARLOCK, Peter
See *Heseltine*.

WEBBE, Samuel (1740–1816)
Remembered as a composer of 300 glees and catches, he was also prominent as an English Roman Catholic composer of masses and motets, as well as several popular hymn tunes including *Melcombe* sung to *New Every Morning is the Love*. He also wrote a harpsichord concerto and *Divertissements* for wind band.

WEBBE, Samuel (1770–1834)
The son of the above and also the composer of many glees. He wrote motets, solo songs, and a book on figured bass.

WEBER, Carl Maria von (1786–1826)
The first operatic composer in the Romantic Nationalist tradition. He was related to Mozart by marriage and came from a musical and theatrical family. He was a good pianist and his father tried to launch him as an infant prodigy. His first (unperformed) opera dates from his thirteenth year and his first published work (six *Fughettas* for piano) appeared while he was a choirboy under Michael Haydn at Salzburg. He had some lessons from Abt Vogler and, although two further operas were unsuccessful in performance, he proved to be an excellent operatic conductor and administrator.
Most of Weber's life was spent in more-or-less unsuccessful attempts at operatic recognition in Breslau, Stuggart, Mannheim, Prague, Dresden and Berlin. His romantic opera *Silvana* (1810) appeared in Frankfurt and the one-act oriental Singspiel *Abu Hassan* (1811) in Munich. The most obvious result of his many tours was the continuous flow of instrumental works and his anticipation of Wagner's attempts at the reformation of various opera houses. Weber's two early symphonies were followed by two piano concertos (1810 and 1812), two concertos for clarinet, and one for bassoon (all 1811), and a series of piano concert pieces, often with programmatic sub-titles. The four piano sonatas were written between 1812 and 1822, and perhaps his most famous instrumental works, *The Invitation to the Dance* (1819) and the *Concertstück* (1821), bear witness to both his pianistic virtuosity and his Romantic approach to programme music. During most of this period he anticipated

Schumann and Wagner as a music critic and was active in providing incidental music to 10 plays, of which *Preciosa* (1821) is still heard today. He also wrote church music, cantatas, and many songs, often with guitar accompaniment, which are now neglected.

The last five years of Weber's life were marked by his three greatest operas of which *Der Freischütz* (Berlin, 1821), although it still uses the spoken dialogue of *singspiel*, is the most integrated work. Here his Romantic exaggeration and nationalist scene painting are tied in his highly original melodic style. The other two operas were not so fortunate. *Euryanthe* (Vienna, 1823) is a grand opera and the first German musical tragedy. It contains much fine music but its lack of success was due to a weak libretto and to Weber's lack of symphonic construction. Already ill with consumption, he prepared *Oberon* for the London stage where, in the tradition of Purcell, spoken drama was mixed with musical supernatural effects in a kind of Shakespearian phantasmagoria. Fine music was again not enough, and he died before he could rework the opera for the German opera house.

WEBERN, Anton (1883–1945)

Together with Schönberg and Berg, an influential member of the '2nd Viennese School' of composers. After studying piano and musicology at the Vienna Conservatoire, he became a pupil, with Berg, of Schönberg (1904–10). Webern also became a conductor at various small theatres, on the Austrian radio, and, later, of an excellent 'workers chorus'.

Although his attitude to tonality and structure changed with the passage of time, his musical personality was already apparent in his Op. 1 — the *Passacaglia for Orchestra* (1908). In this work, variation form, close intervals like minor 2nds and 3rds, contrapuntal elaboration (especially unusual canons) and strikingly-original orchestral balances are already characteristic. Webern soon followed Schönberg in abandoning tonality in the song-cycles of Op. 3 and 4 (1909), in favour of the angular vocal lines of expressionism. The *Five Movements for String Quartet* also abandon development in favour of the gnomic brevity that was the mark of all his later works.

Most of Webern's works from 1912 to 1925 are song cycles with unusual instrumental combinations. They culminated in the *Five Canons Op. 16* (1924) for voice, clarinet and bass clarinet. From Op. 18 he adopted Schönberg's serial technique in an ever-more-refined and generally consistently-rigorous style. The complexity of polyphonic texture of the earlier works is gradually superseded by transparency and a deceptive simplicity. He begins again to use classical structures such as rondo and one becomes increasingly aware of the many rests in the score. His concept of *Klangenfarben melodie* involves a wide ranging melodic line passed from one instrument to another.

The characteristic works of this mature style are perhaps the two-movement *Symphony* (1928) for clarinet, bass clarinet, two horns, harp and strings (without double-bass), the *Concerto for Nine Instruments* (1934) and the *Variations for Orchestra* (1940). Practically all these works were ignored during Webern's lifetime but have been very influential in shaping a new generation of composers. The series of vocal works continued to the end of his life and at least one — the 'undoctrinaire' *Das Augenlicht* (1935) — was warmly received in England in 1939.

Just as his excellence as a conductor never caught the popular imagination, so Webern's compositions seem fated, despite the refined simplicity of their lyrical classical textures.

WEELKES, Thomas (d. 1623)

English organist and composer. His madrigals of three to six voices were published in

1597 and further collections appeared in 1598, 1600 and 1608. His most famous madrigals are *O Care, Thou Wilt Despatch Me*, and *As Vesta Was from Latmos Hill Descending*, and which was his contribution to *The Triumphes of Oriana*.
When he took his degree at Oxford in 1602 he was described as having had '16 years study and practice of music' and he is known to have moved from Winchester College to Chichester Cathedral soon afterwards. By 1608 he had become a Gentleman of the Chapel Royal.
If he was almost the equal of Morley as a madrigalist, his church music approached the perfection and variety of Byrd. His 10 settings of the Anglican canticles are unique in their scope, but all have had their missing parts reconstructed. His 50 or so anthems are more often heard. *Gloria in Excelsis*, *Hosanna* and *When David Heard* are typical of the grandeur and poignancy of his style.

WEILL, Kurt
(1900–1950)
German theatrical composer who was resident in the USA from 1935. His early training as an operatic coach and with Humperdinck and Busoni led to early success in popular opera in the Berlin of the 1920's. His reputation grew from his collaboration with Brecht in *Mahogonny* (1927). This satire on American prosperity was followed by a modern 'Beggar's Opera' — *The Threepenny Opera* which is based on the harshness, jazziness and haunting decadence of the Berlin underworld. Succeeding works in a similar vein were mixed with ballet, instrumental and choral pieces. The Nazis had even less time for this cultural decadence than for the Jewish Weill. After some attempts at popular opera in Paris and London, he became associated with the theatres of Broadway and achieved success in such songs as *September Song*. He also wrote the folk opera *Down in the Valley* (1948) for Indiana University.

WEINBERGER, Jaromír (1896–1967)
Czech composer who studied with Reger in Germany and was active as a conductor and teacher in various musical centres until he settled permanently in Florida in 1939. Although he wrote prolifically in various media he is remembered almost exclusively for the opera *Schwanda, the Bagpiper* (Prague, 1927) which is based on a folk tale imbued with national colour. The *Polka* and *Fugue* from this opera are still popular concert items today.

WELDON, John (1676–1736)
English organist and composer who was a pupil of Purcell and organist successively of New College, Oxford and the Chapel Royal. He wrote a musical setting of a masque by Congreve and contributed items to several London plays. He also contributed church music to Boyce's, and Arnold's *Cathedral Music*.

WELLESZ, Egon (1885–1974)
Viennese musicologist and composer. He was lecturer in Byzantine music at Oxford University from 1939. As a composer he was a pupil of Schönberg and the conductor, Bruno Walter. He first made his name as a composer with four operas and four ballets (1921–31) which are largely on Greek subjects. In England he composed prolifically in the broad Viennese tradition of Mahler, rather than in the style of Schönberg. His works include nine symphonies, nine string quartets, several masses and motets and other choral and chamber works.

WERT, Giaches de (1535–1596)
Flemish composer who lived in Italy. Primarily a madrigal composer, Wert was an important forerunner of the later chromatic and dissonant style of Monteverdi. 16 volumes of his madrigals were published between 1558 and 1608. Well-known and respected in his day, Palestrina described him as a 'virtuoso raro'.

WESLEY, Samuel (1766–1837)
The son of Charles Wesley the hymn writer, and nephew of John the founder of Methodism. He became a convert to the Roman Catholic Church in 1784. He was an infant prodigy as a musician and a famous organist and conductor who was largely responsible for the introduction of J.S. Bach's music to England. As a composer he is remembered for his Latin motets in the polyphonic style, especially *In Exitu Israel*, as well as some charming organ voluntaries. He also wrote oratorios (one at 8 years of age), glees, symphonies, overtures and organ concertos, many songs and piano pieces.

WESLEY, Samuel Sebastian (1810–1876)
Son of Samuel above and an Anglican cathedral organist and composer. After some experience as a theatrical conductor and church organist in London, he became organist successively at Hereford and Exeter cathedrals, Leeds Parish Church and Winchester and Gloucester cathedrals. Apart from some minor works, his output as a composer was almost entirely for the church. Most of his anthems are in the nature of cantatas — such as *Blessed be the God and Father*, *Ascribe unto the Lord* and *The Wilderness*. Most of these are remarkable for the Romantic tone colours of the organ part as well as the spacious and often chromatic compositional style. This expansive style is also found in the *Great Service in E*. Wesley was perhaps even more successful in the 'full' style of the unaccompanied *Cast Me Not Away*.
Several organ works by Wesley are still often heard, notably the *Choral Song and Fugue* which owes something to the fugal style of Mozart.

WHITE (Whyte), Robert (c. 1530–1574)
English church music composer who held musical appointments successively at Ely and Chester cathedrals and Westminster Abbey. His compositions consist of 20 Latin motets (not all of which are complete) and 6–12 English anthems (depending on authenticity) which are the more popular, especially his two settings of O *Praise God*. Viol and lute music also exists — and various arrangements.

WHITLOCK, Percy (1903–1946)
English organist and composer. He held several church appointments and wrote church music. His reputation grew from his many recitals and compositions. His works include a symphony for the organ and orchestra, an organ sonata and several popular groups of organ pieces: *Five Pieces*, *Four Improvisations* and the *Plymouth Suite*.

WHYTHORNE, Thomas (1528–c.1590)
Amateur English musician who published in 1571 some excellent songs in 3–5 parts, These were made popular by Philip Heseltine. The best known is *Whythorne's Shadow* which was used by Moeran. He also published 52 duets for beginners to sing or play (1590).

WIDOR, Charles-Marie (1844–1937)
French organist and composer who was a pupil of Lemmens, organist at St. Sulpice and professor at the Paris Conservatoire. He taught Schweitzer and collaborated with him in an edition of Bach's organ works. He was also active as a critic, writer and conductor.
His three operas, stage works, orchestral, chamber and piano music, are now largely forgotten, but his large-scale symphonies for organ are still performed, especially the famous Toccata from the 5th Symphony. His *Mass* for two choirs and two organs has recently been successfully revived.

WIENIAWSKI, Henryk (1835–1880)
Polish violinist who trained at the Paris

Conservatoire and toured extensively with his brother, Joseph, who was a distinguished piano pupil of Liszt. He later taught at the Conservatoire at St. Petersburg and Brussels. He is remembered for his 2nd Violin Concerto (1878) and the popular *Légende*. Of his total output of 30 violin pieces several have been lost, and the remainder seem little more than a vehicle for his phenomenal technique (which was vouched for by Joachim).

WILBYE, John (1574–1638)
English madrigalian composer who was resident musician in the household of Hengrave Hall in Essex from 1593 until his retirement to Colchester in 1628. His two sets of madrigals were published in 1598 and 1609 but he also contributed to *The Triumphes of Oriana* and Leighton's 1614 publication.
Of Wilbye's superb compositions, the best known are the 3-part *Weep O Mine Eyes*, the 4-part *Adieu, Sweet Amaryllis* the 5-part *Sweet Honey-sucking Bees* and the 6-part *Draw on Sweet Night*.

WILLAERT, Adriaan (1490–1562)
Flemish composer, who after travel to France, Italy and Hungary, became maestro di capella of St. Mark's, Venice from 1527. Among his many pupils at the singing school he founded at Venice were Zarlino and Cypriano di Rore.
His many compositions include five masses (1536), three sets of motets (1539–45), two sets of madrigals (1546 and 1563), psalms (1550 and 1555), hymns (1542) and instrumental *Canzonas* (1545), *Fantasias* and *Ricercare* (1559). Not only do these works expand the traditions of Josquin but they also exploit the spatial separation of the two galleries in St. Mark's, each with its own organ and choir. Almost all of these compositions were famous throughout Europe and were only superseded by the works of the Gabrielis.

WILLAN, Healey (1880–1968)
English organist and composer who worked in Canada from 1913, and taught at Toronto University. He was active as a choral conductor and as a plainsong scholar in the Anglo-Catholic tradition.
From 1936 he composed several large-scale works — two symphonies, a piano concerto, two operas and various choral works. His reputation rests upon his earlier organ music: two preludes and fugues and the well known *Introduction, Passacaglia and Fugue* (1916).

WILLIAMS, Alberto (1862–1952)
Argentinian educator, conductor and composer, who was trained at the Paris Conservatoire. His compositions include nine symphonies, three orchestral suites, much chamber and piano music as well as several choral settings of his own poems.

WILLIAMS,
Charles Lee (1853–1935)
English organist and church music composer. The last of his appointments was as organist of Gloucester Cathedral (1882–98) where he five times conducted the Three Choirs Festival. He also wrote several sacred cantatas for the Festivals. His many easy anthems and services were once very popular.

WILLIAMS, Grace (1906–1977)
Welsh composer and teacher who studied with Vaughan Williams and Gordon Jacob, and taught in London (1931–46). Her concert overture *Hen Walia* (1930) makes use of Welsh folk songs, as does also much of her later music, which is still occasionally heard. Much of her work consists of songs and descriptive orchestral works such as *Owen Glendower* (1943), and evocative string pieces such as *The Dark Island* (1950).

WILLIAMSON, Malcolm (b. 1931)
Master of the Queen's Music.

Australian composer, pianist and organist who studied in Sydney with Eugene Goossens and with Elizabeth Lutyens in London. He earned his living first of all as an Anglican church organist and jazz pianist and occasionally the latter influence shows in his compositions. His early organ works, e.g. *Vision of Christ Phoenix* (1962) owe much to the style of Messiaen. He is a convert to the Roman Catholic faith.
He has written a series of operas including *Our Man in Havana* (1963) and *The Violins of St. Jacques* (1966). Several other operas like *The Happy Prince* (1971) have been designed as children's operas based on religious themes and aim to break down the division between audience and performers.
Two *Symphonies* (1956 and 1969) and other orchestral and chamber works have been well received although works like the lengthy *Organ Symphony* (1971) still await full recognition.

WILSON, John (c. 1595–1674)
English lutenist, violinist, singer and composer. He was a King's Musician in 1635, Professor of Music at Oxford in 1656 and a Gentleman of the Chapel Royal from 1662.
His first-known composition is a masque for Grays Inn (for Twelfth Night) in 1613. He published settings of several of Shakespeare's works and probably acted in some of his plays. His *Psalterium Carolinum* for three voices and accompaniment appeared in 1657. These were metrical 'devotions of his Sacred Majesty in his ... sufferings'. Several of his other songs were published by Playford.

WILSON, Thomas (b. 1927)
Born in the USA, now a prominent composer in Scotland. His works include two operas, three symphonies, four string quartets and the other important chamber and choral works such as *Canti Notturni* (1972) and *Cancion* (1979).

WINTERS, Geoffrey (b. 1928)
English composer who studied at the RAM with Priaulx Rainier, Alan Bush and Howard Ferguson. He has been active for 25 years in various aspects of education. Apart from his extensive musical output for young people, he has written two symphonies (1973 and 1976), two string quartets and two viola sonatas.

WIREN, Dag (b. 1905)
Swedish composer and critic who was trained in Stockholm and Paris. He became known through his *Serenade for Strings* (1937). Much of his music is for films and plays but of two radio operas (1940 and 1941), one is inspired by Winston Churchill's words — 'blood, sweat and tears'.
He has written four symphonies, three string quartets, as well as other orchestral music, piano pieces and songs. He was once hailed by Cecil Gray, the English critic, as a significant composer 'of the future' (1924).

WISE, Michael (c. 1648–1687)
English composer of church music who was one of the 'first generation' choirboys of 'Captain Cooke' in the Chapel Royal at the time of the Restoration in 1660. He later became organist of Salisbury Cathedral (1668) before returning to the Chapel Royal in 1675. He seems to have been disgraced by a satirical song, *The Wilshire Ballad*, which led to his suspension in 1680. He was killed by a night watchman in a brawl.
Several of his anthems, including *Prepare Ye the Way*, were printed by Boyce. His *Evening Service in F* was printed by Rimbault. Both of these are still in the cathedral repertoire today. Some of his secular songs also became popular in the 18th century.

WOLF, Hugo (1860–1903)
Composer of Lieder. He came from mixed

ancestry from what is now Yugoslavia. After a difficult childhood he went to the Vienna Conservatoire at the age of 15 but left after two years when he fell foul of authority.
The following years saw him in a variety of musical and teaching posts and as a critic. He was convinced his compositions were deliberately ignored, and one of his many imagined enemies was Brahms.
In 1887 several of his songs were at last accepted for publication and the *Italian Serenade*, Wolf's only mature instrumental work, was completed. Almost immediately his remarkable early songs were followed by the major collections: 31 settings of various poets (1877–97), the *Mörike-Lieder* of 53 songs (1888), the *Eichendorff-Lieder* of 20 songs (1880–88), the *Goethe-Lieder* of 51 songs (1888–89), the *Spanish Songbook* of 44 songs (1889–90) and the *Italian Songbook* of 46 songs (1890–96). His only complete opera, *Der Corregidor* (1895) has been universally praised for its music but rarely performed owing to difficulties in staging. His final years were marred by tragic insanity and paralysis, although well before this time his songs had been accepted eagerly by an enthusiastic public, and he was hailed 'the Wagner of Song'.
Wolf's strong point is his psychological insight into the words of the poets whose texts he used and this insight is often expressed instrumentally as it is in the music of Wagner. The fusion of voice and piano seems in a direct link with Schumann, and it invariably grows naturally from the lyricism of the poem. Rarely does one feel Brahmsian musicality added to the verses. The harmonic texture owes much to Wagnerian chromaticism, but Wolf's writing seems almost Italian in its uninhibited flow.

WOLF-FERRARI, Ermanno (1876–1948)

Italian operatic composer of half-German descent who, overcoming parental opposition, was finally allowed to study with the German organist, Rheinberger, in Munich. Of his 13 operas the best known are *Susanna's Secret* (1909) and *The Jewels of the Madonna* (1911). He also wrote oratorios, orchestral and chamber music. Wolf-Ferrari's style owes much to Mozart in its apparent charm and simplicity, although his technique is in no way Neo-Classical. His style seems to share 18th century wit and outlook with a Romantic texture.

WOOD, Charles (1866–1926)

Anglo-Irish composer and teacher. He was a pupil of Stanford, whom he followed as Professor of music at Cambridge. He wrote extensively for choir and orchestra but is now remembered almost entirely for his church music. His many canticle settings (about 20) and such anthems as O *Thou the Central Orb* and *Expectans Expectavi* are still popular in the cathedral repertoire. Following his earlier Romantic style, he moved to the ascetic modalism of his *Service in the Phrygian Mode* and to the strangely objective *St. Mark Passion.*

WOOD, Haydn (1882–1959)

English composer and violinist who as a player impressed both Joachim and Sarante. He studied with Stanford. He wrote prolifically in a light-orchestral style: nine rhapsodies, eight overtures and 15 suites, as well as more ambitious concertos. He is remembered for his seven marches for military band and such popular songs as *Roses of Picardy.*

WOOD, Thomas (1892–1950)

English composer, writer, and teacher who was trained at Oxford and the RCM. His interest in the sea is evident in several compositions for chorus and orchestra. He also wrote many unison and part songs, and works for military band.

WOODWARD, George Ratcliffe (1848–1934)
Anglican clergyman and hymnologist who was responsible for many carol arrangements in the *Cowley Carol Book* (1901 and 1919).

WOODWARD, Herbert Hall (1847–1909)
Anglican clergyman who published much popular church music including a *Service in E flat.*

WOODWARD, Richard (1744–1777)
Irish organist in Dublin who published *Songs, Canons and Catches* (1767), and *Cathedral Music* (1771). The latter work includes some Anglican chants still in use today.

WORDSWORTH, William (b. 1908)
English composer and descendant of the poet's brother. He was a pupil of Sir Donald Tovey in Edinburgh and now lives in Scotland. His compositions include seven symphonies, three concertos, five string quartets, chamber music and songs.

WRIGHT, Denis (1895–1968)
English brass band composer and conductor, who is better known for his many arrangements and for his work as an adjudicator, teacher and writer on band scoring.

Y

YON, Pietro Alessandro (1886–1943)
Italian organist and composer who, moving to New York in 1907, became organist of St. Patrick's Cathedral in 1926. He studied successively in Milan, Turin and Rome and was, for a time, sub-organist at the Vatican. Apart from several masses and motets and some piano pieces and songs, his compositions are solely for the organ. Two sonatas and several concert pieces are still heard today.

YOULL, Henry (fl. c. 1608)
English composer known only today for his very attractive collection of *24 Canzonets for Three Voices* published in 1608. These include ballets such as *In the Merry Month of May*. He also wrote music for *Cynthia's Revels* by Ben Jonson (1600).

YSAŸE, Eugène (1858–1931)
Belgian violinist, conductor and composer, who was a pupil of both Wieniawski and Vieuxtemps and the dedicatee of the Franck *Violin Sonata*. After teaching and conducting in Brussels, and touring widely, he became conductor of the Cincinnati Symphony Orchestra. He was associated with a fiery style of playing and seemingly exaggerated rubato. He composed many violin concertos, six sonatas for unaccompanied violin, and many smaller concert pieces with orchestral or piano accompaniment.

Z

ZACHAU, Friedrich Wilhelm (1663–1712)
German organist, composer, and teacher of Handel in Halle. His published works consist of Preludes, Fugues and Chorale Preludes for organ, and some cantatas are still in manuscript.

ZARLINO, Gioseffe (1517–1590)
Italian scholar, theorist and composer. He was a Franciscan and was ordained before becoming a pupil of Willaert whom he succeeded in 1565 as maestro di capella at St. Mark's, Venice. He was a typical Renaissance polymath — a Hebrew scholar and philosopher, mathematician and scientist. He was noted for his rationalisation of harmony and his advocacy of tuning the lute by equal temperament. His compositions are mostly lost but include a 4-part mass, two motets, three *Lectiones pro Mortuis* and the 21 published 6-part *Modulationes* (1566).

ZEMLINSKY, Alexander von (1872–1942)
Viennese conductor and composer, who moved to Prague in 1911 and to Berlin in 1927. He returned to Vienna in 1932, finally emigrating to New York in 1938. As an operatic and choral conductor and teacher, he had much influence on the younger generation of Austrian composers. He taught Schönberg (and became his brother-in-law). He composed six operas and three symphonies as well as several choral works.

ZUMSTEEG, Johann Rudolf (1760–1802)
German conductor and composer, who was a friend of Schiller and remembered as the pioneer in ballad-setting. These works were very popular and had much influence on the writings of Schubert. His 'romantic' operas, *Ossian* and *Klopstock* were based on Shakespeare and were very forward-looking.